IMAGES
of America

CLEMMONS

I0806286

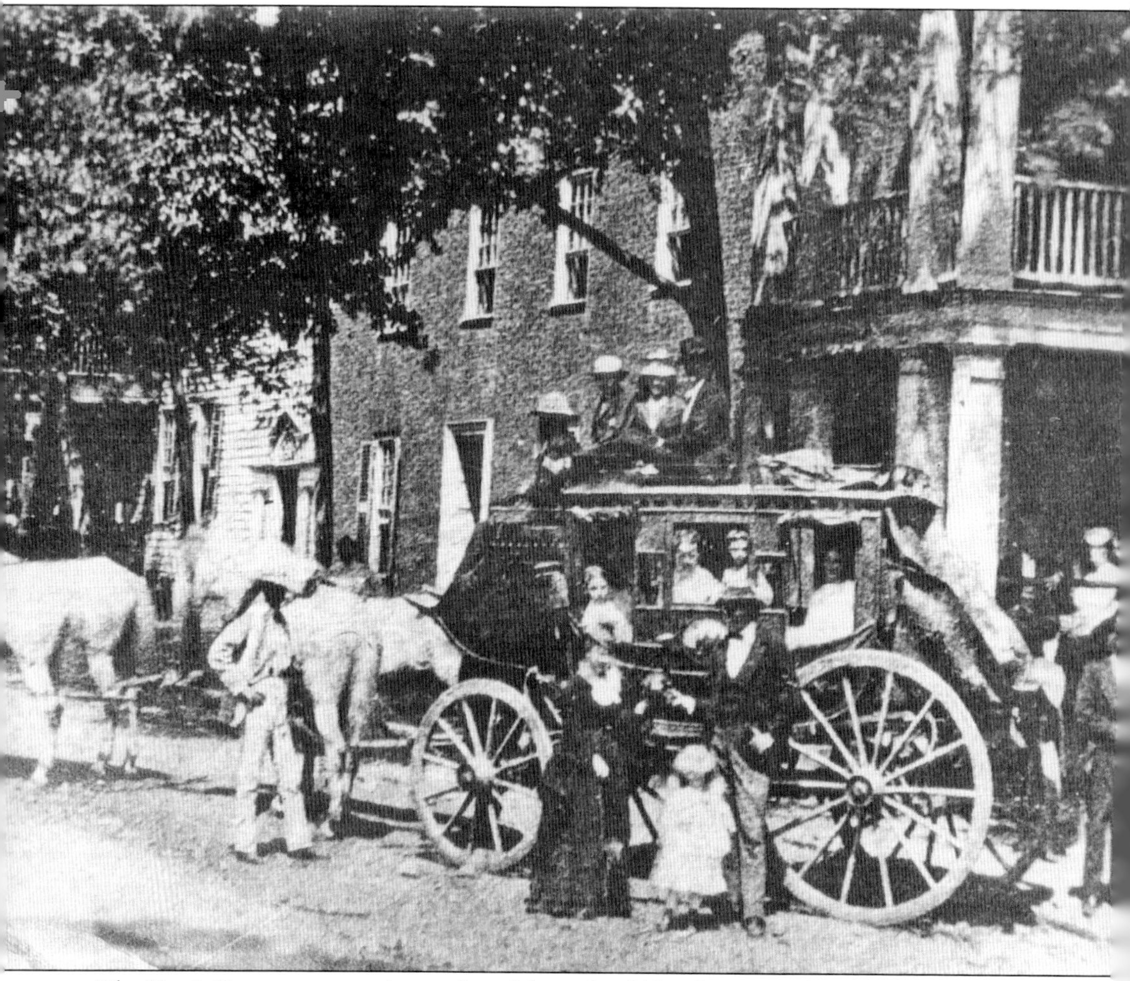

The *Hattie Butner* stagecoach, purchased from the Abbot-Downing Company in Concord, New Hampshire, stands in front of the Second Eagle Hotel in Asheville in this 1872 photograph. One of the major stagecoach lines that E.T. Clemmons ran was between Asheville and the area that became Winston-Salem. (Courtesy Forsyth County Public Library.)

On the Cover: The old C.E. Strupe store supplied general merchandise, coffins, and Star brand shoes to residents of Clemmons and the surrounding area in the late 1800s and early 1900s. The brick building was constructed by Carlos Strupe around 1875 and was known simply as the Strupe store. By 1910, when this photograph was taken, it had transferred ownership to R.S. Ferebee and was known as the Clemmons Supply Store. The covered wagon in the photograph is most likely from Davie County. Wagon trains visited the store frequently and it had a water well for animals at the rear of the property. The building also at various times operated or housed a hat shop, a tavern, a tannery, and a sawmill. In 1889, the local Moravian congregation held its first service on the second floor of the building. The store, which no longer stands, was at the northwest corner of the intersection of Highway 158 and Lewisville-Clemmons Road. (Courtesy Cookie Snyder Photography.)

IMAGES
of America

CLEMMONS

Kevin White in association with the
Clemmons Historical Society

ARCADIA
PUBLISHING

ISBN 978-0-7385-9276-3

Published by Arcadia Publishing
Charleston, South Carolina

Printed in the United States of America

Library of Congress Control Number: 2012932291

For all general information, please contact Arcadia Publishing:
Telephone 843-853-2070
Fax 843-853-0044
E-mail sales@arcadiapublishing.com
For customer service and orders:
Toll-Free 1-888-313-2665

Visit us on the Internet at www.arcadiapublishing.com

I would like to dedicate this book to my parents, who early on instilled a sense of appreciation for all things history.

Contents

ACKNOWLEDGMENTS

Without help and assistance from the following people and organizations, this book would not have been possible. Every effort was made to locate material for this book, and to those that responded or were willing to assist, I am grateful. I am much indebted to the Clemmons Historical Society; in particular, president Janet Banzhof, vice president David H. Hauser, and director Tom Branen, who were instrumental in helping to bring much of the resource material together. I am also indebted to Michael Bricker for some directional conversations very early on in this project. I would also like to thank Cookie Snyder and Pam Corum, of Snyder Photography, and the administrative staff at Tanglewood Park for the vast amount of material they graciously allowed me to include in this book.

I would also be remiss if I did not thank Ann Sheek, Gardner Gidley, Jerry Johnson, Mike Parks, Caspar Howard, Joanna Lyall, Ed Brewer, the *Clemmons Courier*, Anne Grant Photography, Carl Monson, Clemmons United Methodist Church, Louise Berrier, Fraternity Church of the Brethren, Frank Morgan, Barbara Mahannah, Genevieve Lesher, Becky Tesh, Clemmons First Baptist Church, Todd Hinson, Warner's Chapel Church of Christ, James and Ruby Rucker, Capernaum Church of Christ, Alyson Shulz Photography, Sammy Conrad, Hill Hunter, Martha Linker, Bill Hunter III, Richard Starbuck, Moravian Archives (Winston-Salem), Estelle Hill, Centenary United Methodist Church, Clemmons Public Library, Forsyth County Public Library, Molly Rawls, Michele Doyle, Old Salem Museums and Gardens, Jerry Brooks, the Clemmons Fire Department, Bud Spaugh, and the editorial staff at Arcadia Publishing for providing their assistance in assembling the material for this book. Every effort has been made to recognize each individual that has assisted with this book; if anyone was overlooked, it was an unfortunate oversight.

I would also like to thank my wife, Keena, and our children, Taylar, Ethan, and Brody, for their support and encouragement during this project and for putting up with me running off at odd times to go scan photographs.

INTRODUCTION

The area that became known as Clemmons, North Carolina, had its beginnings in 1757 when William Johnson purchased 640 acres of mostly uninhabited land that had been held by William Linville, Lord Granville's agent for the North Carolina colony. The area that Johnson purchased and settled is now Tanglewood Park. A monument in the park designates the approximate site where Johnson built his house and fort to protect himself and his family from attacks from Native Americans during the French and Indian Wars, which were occurring at the time.

Mount Pleasant Methodist Church, known as the "Old Church," is also located within the Tanglewood property, and its cemetery holds the remains of Johnson and some of his family. The church was named for Mount Pleasant, the highest point on the property, built in 1809. Although services are only held on special occasions, the church still stands and is the oldest surviving Methodist church in Forsyth County.

About 1802, a farmer named Peter Clemmons moved to the area. In 1805, he built a 15-room home that still stands along the road that eventually became Clemmons Road and later Highway 158. Clemmons had moved to the Guilford County area in 1777 from Delaware. He also built and operated a store and grain mill and opened his home up to travelers coming and going through the area. This sparse community became known as Clemmonstown around 1816, making it one of the oldest established communities in the Triad area. Clemmonstown became Clemmonsville around 1826 and sometime after was simply named Clemmons. It officially incorporated as the Village of Clemmons in 1986.

Clemmons is notable for several reasons. Probably the most widely familiar attraction is Tanglewood Park. William Neal Reynolds, of the Reynolds Tobacco family, purchased land from the descendants of William Johnson in 1921. After Reynolds's death in 1951, the park was bequeathed in his will to Forsyth County for use as a public park. The park now encompasses more than 1,400 acres of land and offers visitors amenities such as horseback riding, a community swimming pool, tennis, hiking, fishing, parks and recreational facilities, camping, a manor home for more formal activities, biking trails, and two 18-hole golf courses.

From the 1970s through the 1990s, the Championship Golf Course at Tanglewood was a stop on the Professional Golf Association (PGA) and PGA Senior tours. The park is also the home of the Tanglewood Festival of Lights each Christmas season, one of the largest outdoor lighting displays in the southeastern United States. The park also hosts other activities throughout the year, such as 5K races, community events, and the occasional steeplechase.

Idol's Dam is another standout in the history of Clemmons. Originally built as a hydroelectric generating station plant on the Yadkin River in 1898, it operated for many years and eventually came under the ownership of the Duke Power Company before ceasing to operate. The dam is significant and important to local history, as it was the first hydroelectric generating station of its size in North Carolina to use the long-distance transmission of power. It provided alternating current (AC) power over a distance of 13 miles to various textile mills and other industries. The plant ultimately helped what would become the town of Winston-Salem develop as a major industrial and manufacturing center in North Carolina. The plant also powered Winston-Salem's trolleys. Thomas Edison was a financial backer of the plant and one of its most famous visitors.

Clemmons also played a role in North Carolina's stagecoach industry in the mid-1800s. Edwin Theodore "E.T." Clemmons, a great-grandson of village founder Peter Clemmons, started several large stagecoach lines that ran throughout the state from the 1840s to the 1870s. As the railroads began taking their toll on the stagecoach industry and Clemmons saw his business decline, he began to operate predominantly where there was limited rail. The last and largest of Clemmons's stagecoaches was the *Hattie Butner*, named for his wife. Upon E.T. Clemmons's death in 1896, the *Hattie Butner* was retired. In 1937, it was transferred to the Wachovia Historical Society, where it was put on display before being donated in 1993 to the Village of Clemmons, where it is now on public display at the Village Hall.

In addition to his stagecoach legacy, Clemmons provided funding for the building of Clemmons Moravian Church and School in his will. The property was to contain a church, school, and parsonage. Additionally, purchased land was to be subdivided and sold to Moravian families for $1 per lot. Children of these families could attend the school for free. The first building was completed in the fall of 1901. The school has gone through several phases and eventually became part of the Forsyth County School System. Although the original Moravian school buildings no longer exist, the church is still in operation today and is a cornerstone of the Moravian community in Clemmons.

The history of Clemmons also includes other notable people, families, and homes that have played some role in its past. The father of modern Methodism in the United States, Bishop Francis Asbury, made several stops in the Clemmons area in the late 1700s as he tirelessly devoted his life to spread Methodism in the frontier settlements of the new nation. Asbury met at George McKnight's house in Clemmons several times between 1787 and 1791, hosting the Annual Methodist Episcopal Church Conference there at least three times.

The Moravian Church also has deep roots in Forsyth County, and some of those roots can be traced to Clemmons. The Old Order German Baptist Church was founded in North Carolina in 1775 in the Muddy Creek area, just east of Clemmons. Clemmons is also the home of the oldest African American Church of Christ congregation, which was established as Capernaum Church of Christ in 1904. The oldest African American church is the Hickory Grove African Methodist Episcopal Zion Church on Harper Road, which was organized in 1878. Clemmons was and still is home to many descendants of its original and early settlers.

What began as a small area of a few farms and a crossroads is now a desirable community that has grown to cover approximately 12 miles.

One

THE CLEMMONS FAMILY AND THE *HATTIE BUTNER*

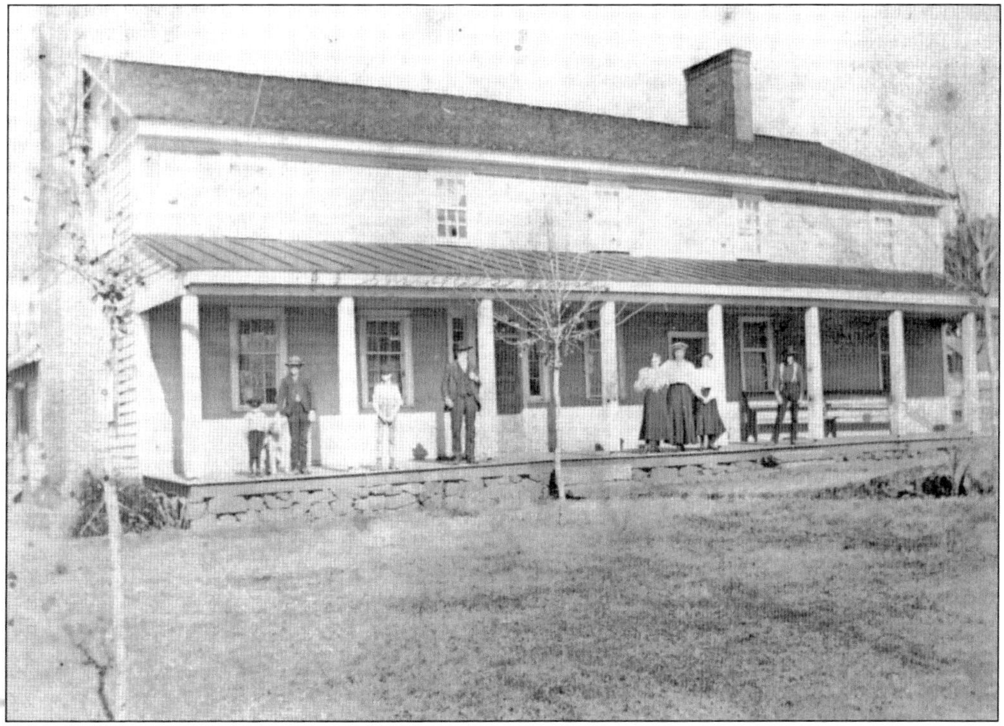

The 1805 Peter Clemmons Home, seen here in the mid-1800s, is one of the oldest remaining frame structures in Clemmons. Peter Clemmons moved to the area about 1802 from Delaware and purchased more than 1,400 acres of land, founding the small town that would eventually bear his name. Although other settlers lived in the area, Clemmons was the first to develop it into a community. This home has been occupied by the Clemmons, Fries, Sprinkle, and Ogburn families throughout its existence and still stands along Highway 158 in Clemmons just west of the United Methodist Church. The house was also used by Clemmons's great-grandson E.T. Clemmons, as a stop on his successful stagecoach line between Salem and Asheville. (Courtesy Clemmons Historical Society.)

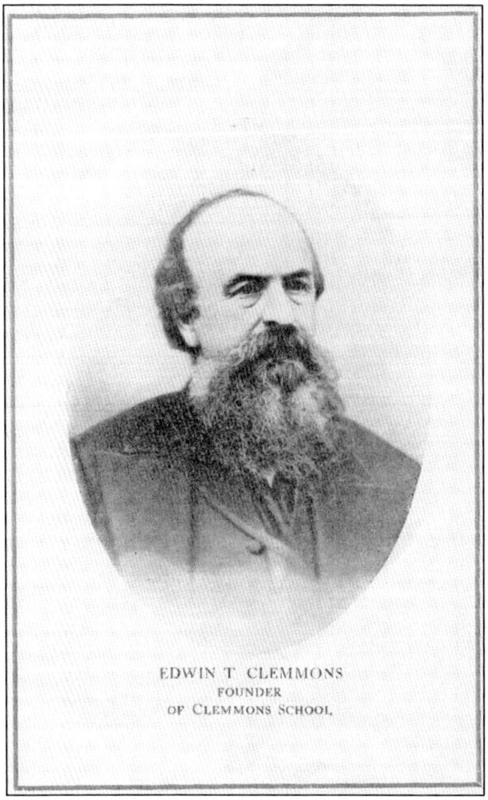

Edwin Theodore Clemmons, seen here around 1870, was the great-grandson of Peter Clemmons and built a prosperous stagecoach line through North Carolina in the latter half of the 19th century. (Collection of the Wachovia Historical Society; courtesy Old Salem Museums and Gardens.)

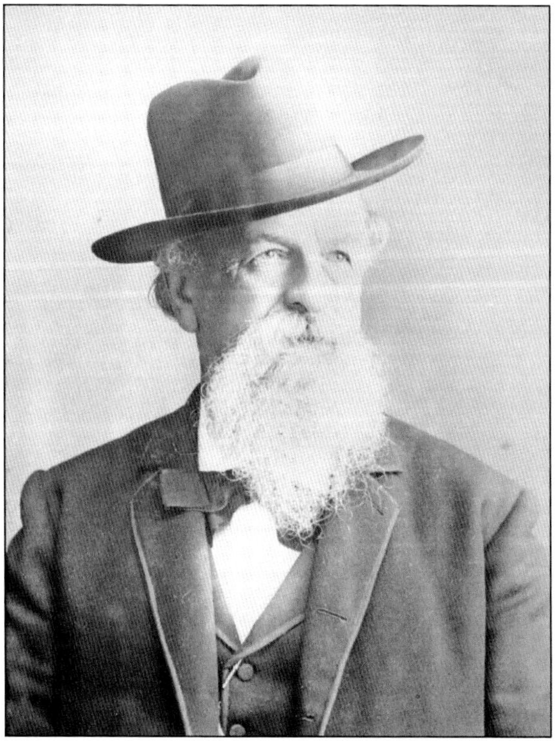

This photographic portrait of Edwin Theodore Clemmons was made around 1890 by the Applegate Studio of Philadelphia. He was born in Clemmons in 1826 and died in Salem on December 20, 1896. (Collection of the Wachovia Historical Society; courtesy Old Salem Museums and Gardens.)

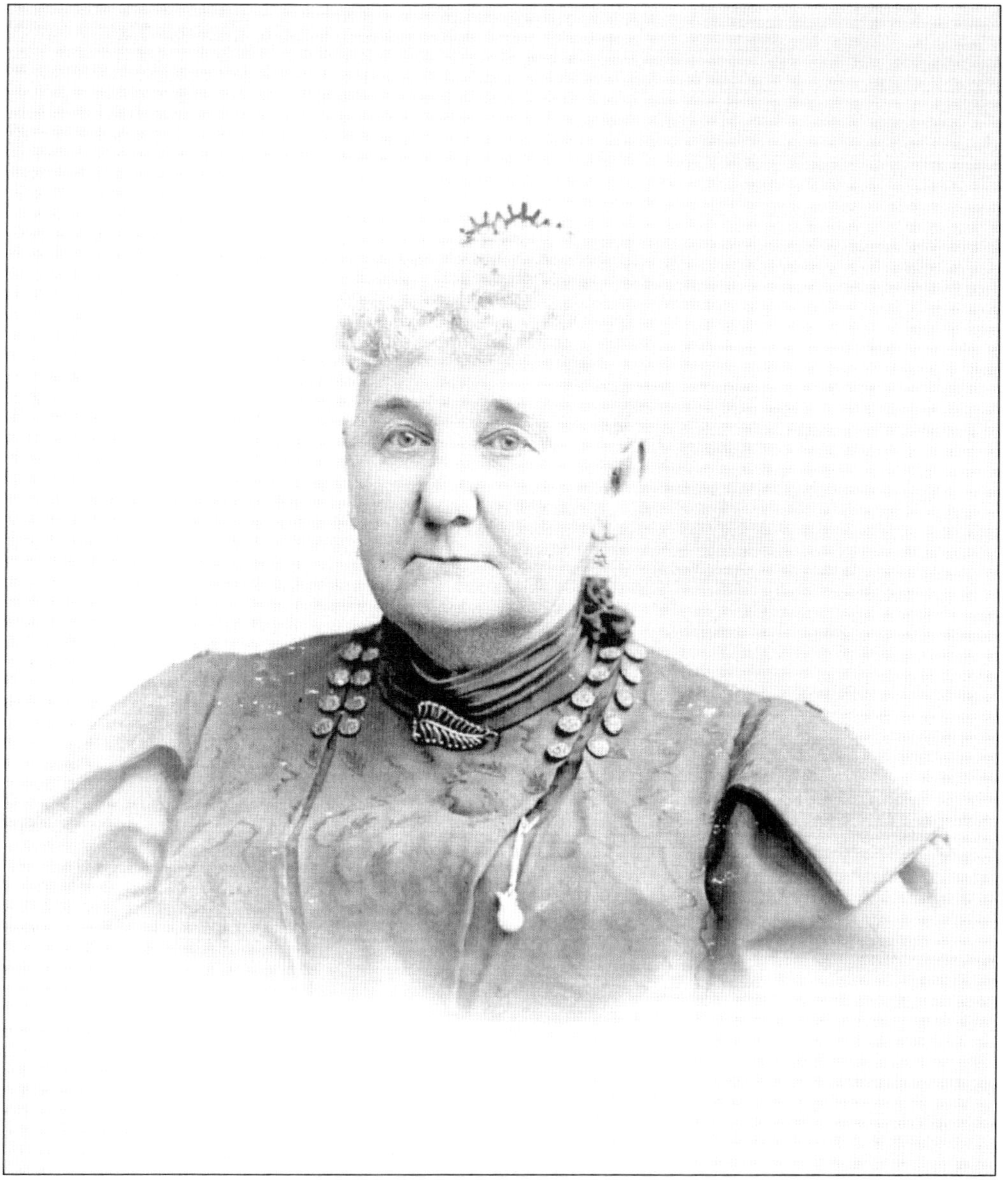

Hattie Butner Clemmons, the wife of E.T. Clemmons, is seen here around 1890 in a photographic portrait by the Applegate Studio of Philadelphia. E.T. Clemmons's last major stagecoach purchase was named the *Hattie Butner* after her. Hattie Butner outlived Edwin to see the construction of the Clemmons Moravian Church and School, which was funded by her late husband's will. Hattie Butner Clemmons died in 1910. (Collection of the Wachovia Historical Society; courtesy Old Salem Museums and Gardens.)

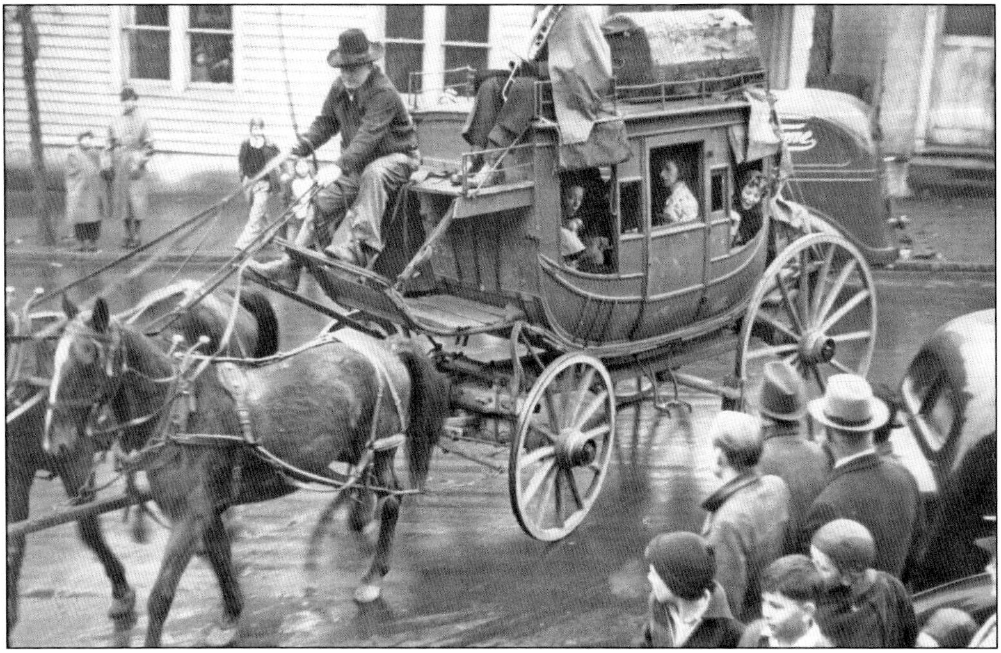

Above, the *Hattie Butner* stagecoach is delivered to the Hall of History at the Wachovia Historical Society of North Carolina in December 1937. Ed Anderson is driving the coach on what looks like a chilly North Carolina winter day. In 1993, the Wachovia Historical Society officially donated the *Hattie Butner* to the Village of Clemmons, where it is now on exhibit at the Village Hall on Highway 158. There are only approximately 12 of this type of stagecoach left in the entire United States and the *Hattie Butner* is considered to be the best-conditioned example. The stagecoach still has its original paint and is conserved by the Clemmons Historical Society. (Above, courtesy Moravian Archives, Winston-Salem, NC; below, courtesy David H. Hauser.)

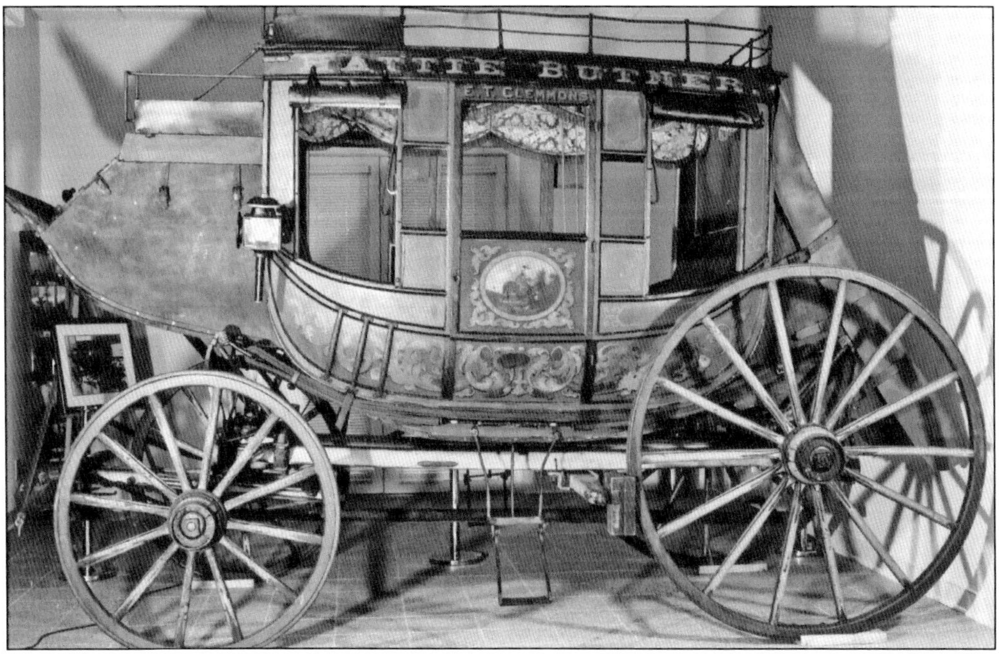

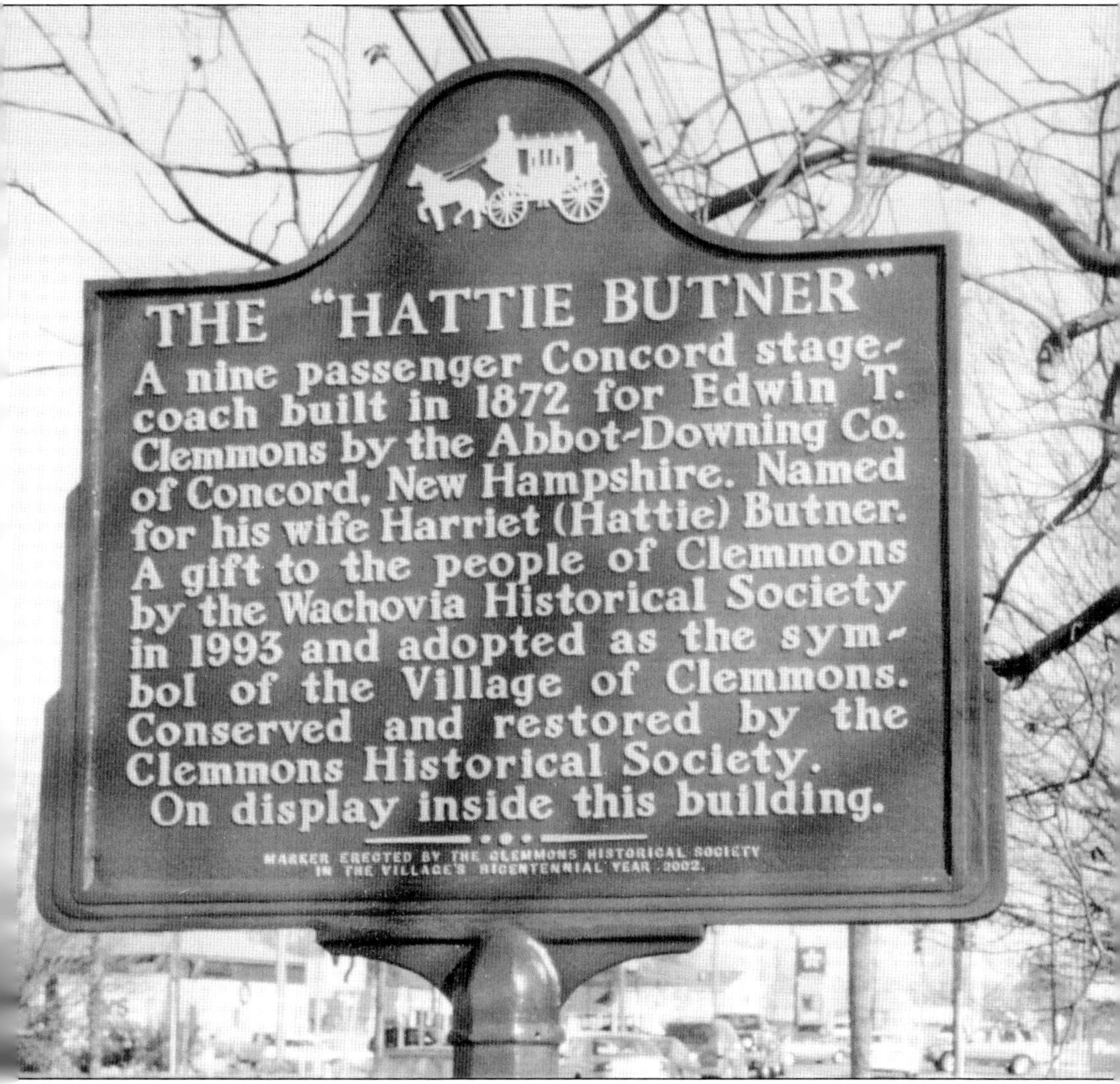

This historical marker on the *Hattie Butner* stagecoach was erected by the Clemmons Historical Society in 2002 in honor of the bicentennial of Clemmons. The sign stands in front of the Village Hall on Highway 158. (Courtesy Clemmons Historical Society.)

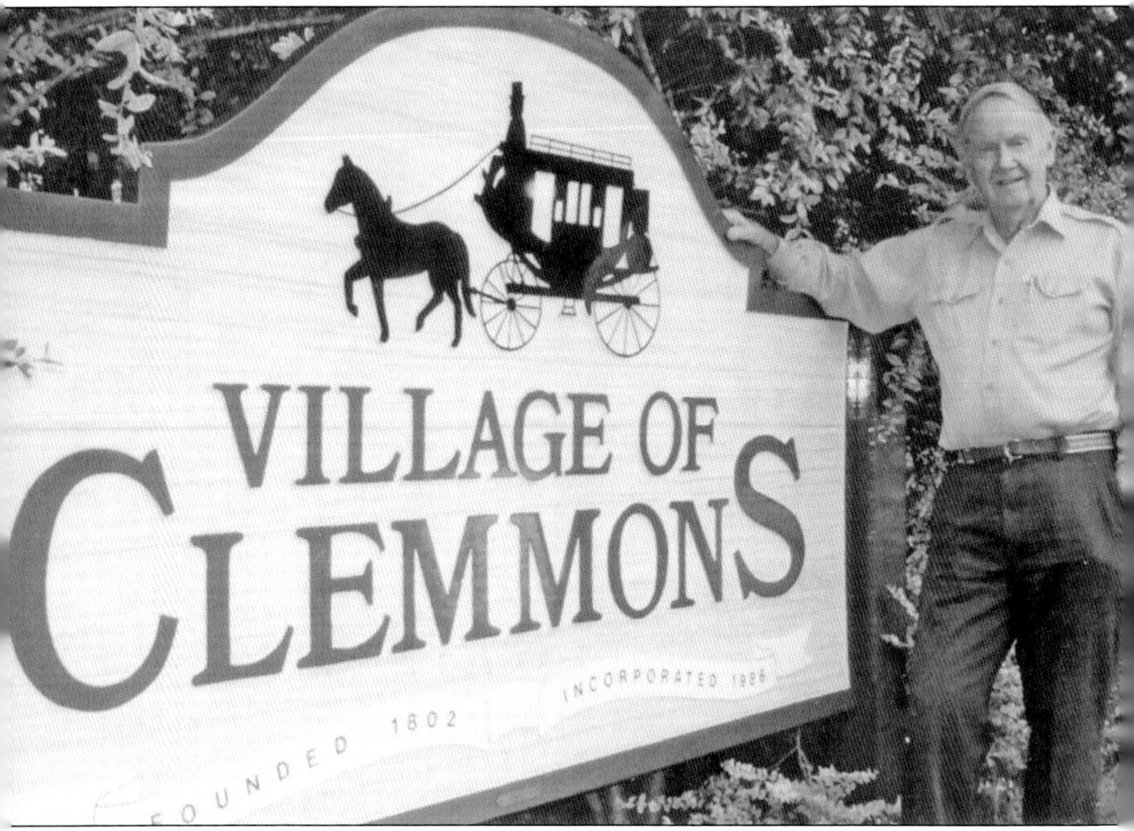

The Village of Clemmons logo and sign were created by J.W. "Bill" Edwards at the request of the first village council. Edwards was a professional illustrator for Western Electric Company and is now a local artist. Since the early growth of the village was influenced by the Concord coaches of E.T. Clemmons, Edwards thought it was appropriate for the design to include a horse-driven stagecoach with the words "Village of Clemmons" beneath. (Courtesy David H. Hauser.)

Two

People

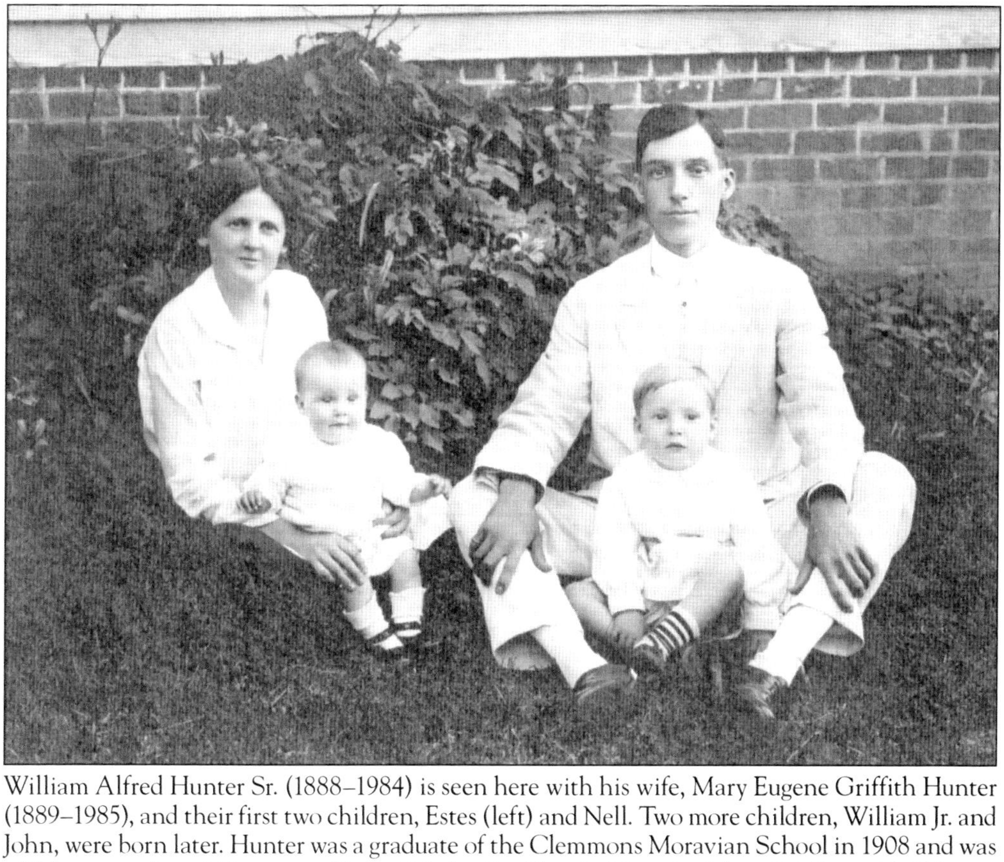

William Alfred Hunter Sr. (1888–1984) is seen here with his wife, Mary Eugene Griffith Hunter (1889–1985), and their first two children, Estes (left) and Nell. Two more children, William Jr. and John, were born later. Hunter was a graduate of the Clemmons Moravian School in 1908 and was a lifelong member of Clemmons United Methodist Church. He retired from R.J. Reynolds Tobacco in 1957 as the superintendent of Plant No. 11 after 42 years of service. Hunter was very active in the Clemmons community, and his various accomplishments include establishing Clemmons's first Boy Scout troop—Troop 24, which later became Troop 736—serving as president of the Clemmons School Parent Teacher Association, and being a charter member of both the Clemmons Civic Club and the Clemmons Fire Department. He led efforts to pave Lewisville-Clemmons Road, helped obtain phone service for Clemmons, served on the Clemmons Street Lighting Committee, and helped raise money to get Northwestern Bank to come to Clemmons. He also became the first chairman of Northwestern Bank's board of directors. (Courtesy W.A. Hunter III.)

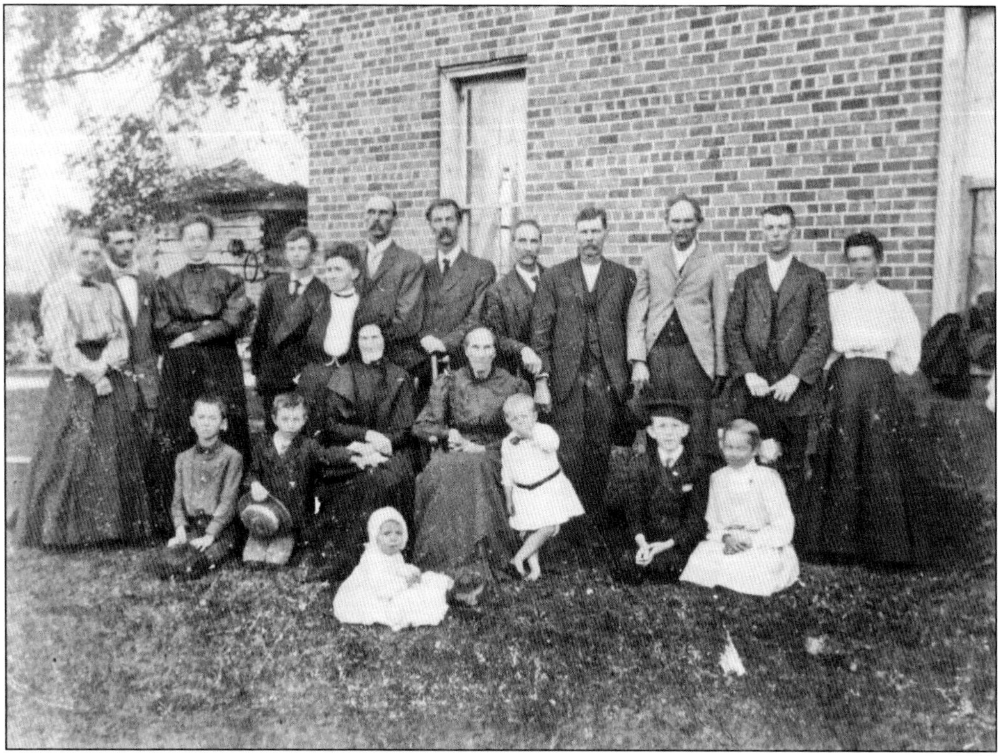

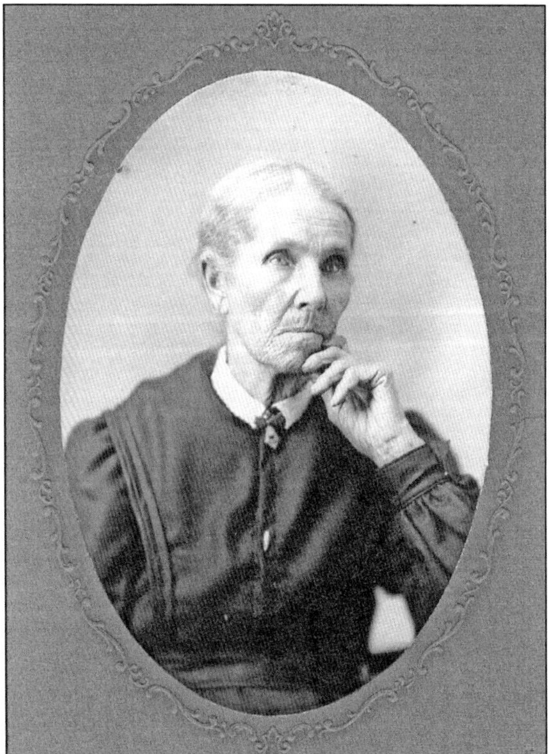

In 1909, the Cook family reunion was held at the home of Nancy Rebecca Jarvis Cook In the image above, she is seated in the center surrounded by her family. The portrait of her on the left was taken in 1905. The Cook and Jarvis families have deep roots in Clemmons, and many members of the families still live in the area. Nancy Cook was born in 1823 and married Jacob Cook in 1841. Jacob died from an accident in 1859 at the age of 45, leaving Nancy a widow with nine children to raise. Their children all lived and died in the Clemmons area, with some of her sons serving in Confederate Army during the Civil War. When the Muddy Creek Baptist Church decided to move to Clemmons, she donated land across the street from her home to the church. That land is now the site of the First Baptist Church of Clemmons. Nancy also taught Sunday school at the new church for a number of years and was loved by the children. (Both, courtesy Cookie Snyder Photography.)

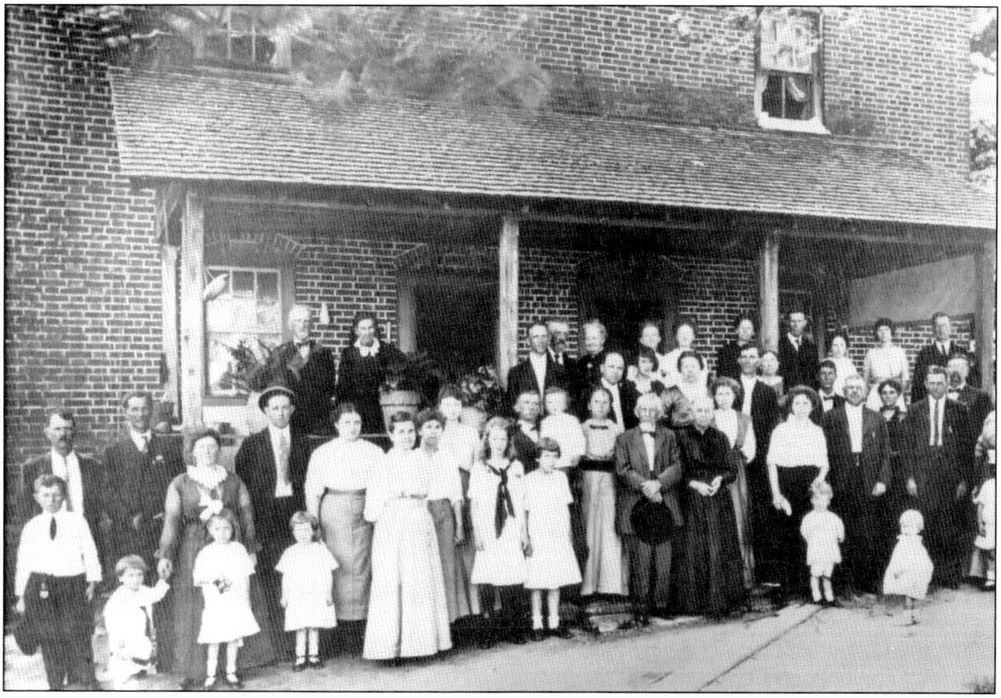

Above, the Wommack and Cook families gather for a photograph in front of the Phillip Hanes house around 1910. (Courtesy Cookie Snyder Photography.)

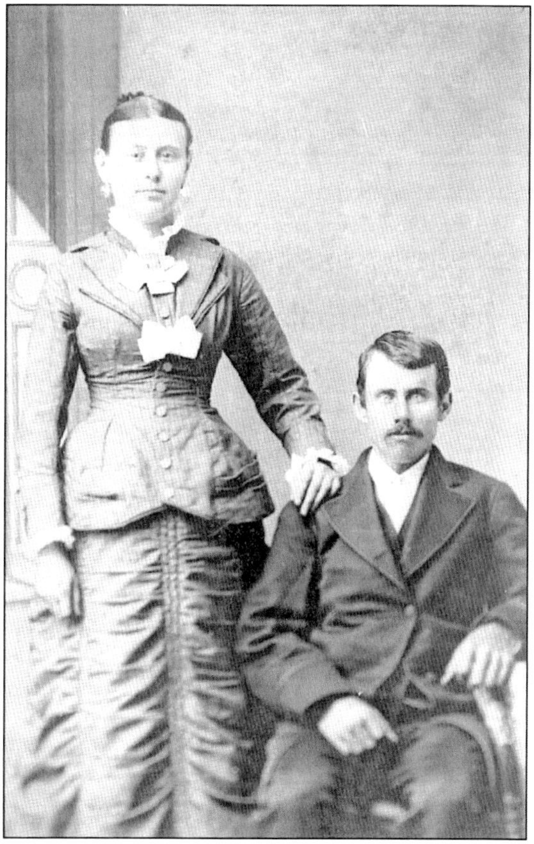

Henry Johnson (1856–1942) and his wife, Elizabeth Sides Johnson, pose for a c. 1880 photograph. Johnson was a descendant of William Johnson and was the first licensed breeder of Guernsey cattle in North Carolina. Guernsey dairy cows originated on the British Channel Island of Guernsey and are renowned for their rich milk. Johnson, a resident of the Clemmons area, ran his dairy farm in Winston-Salem off what is now Jonestown Road. (Courtesy Jerry Johnson).

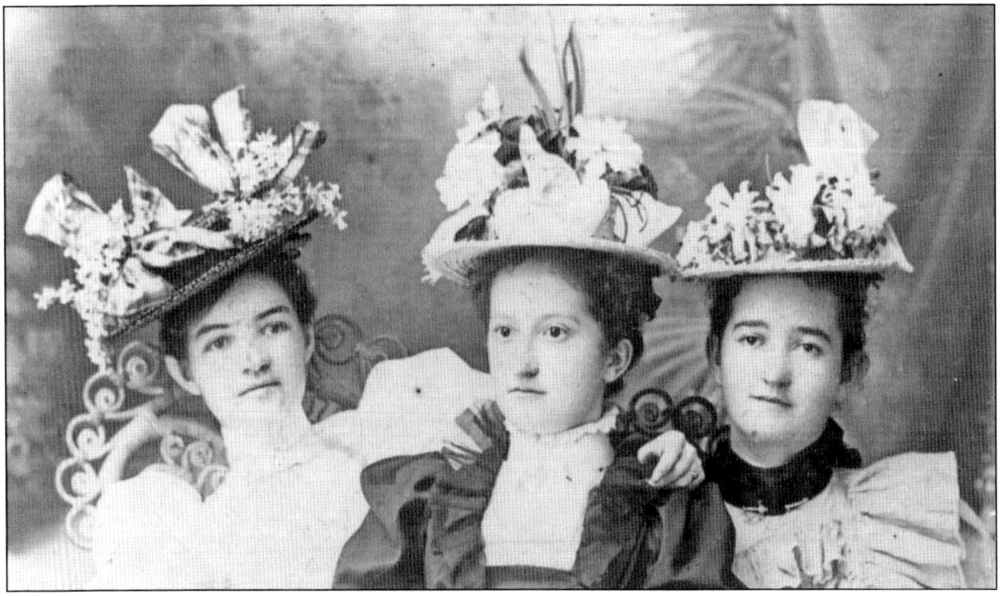

These three women posed with fancy hats for this late-1800s photograph. The woman in the center is Bettie Cooper Strupe, the wife of Ed Strupe, who owned the Strupe store. (Courtesy Cookie Snyder Photography.)

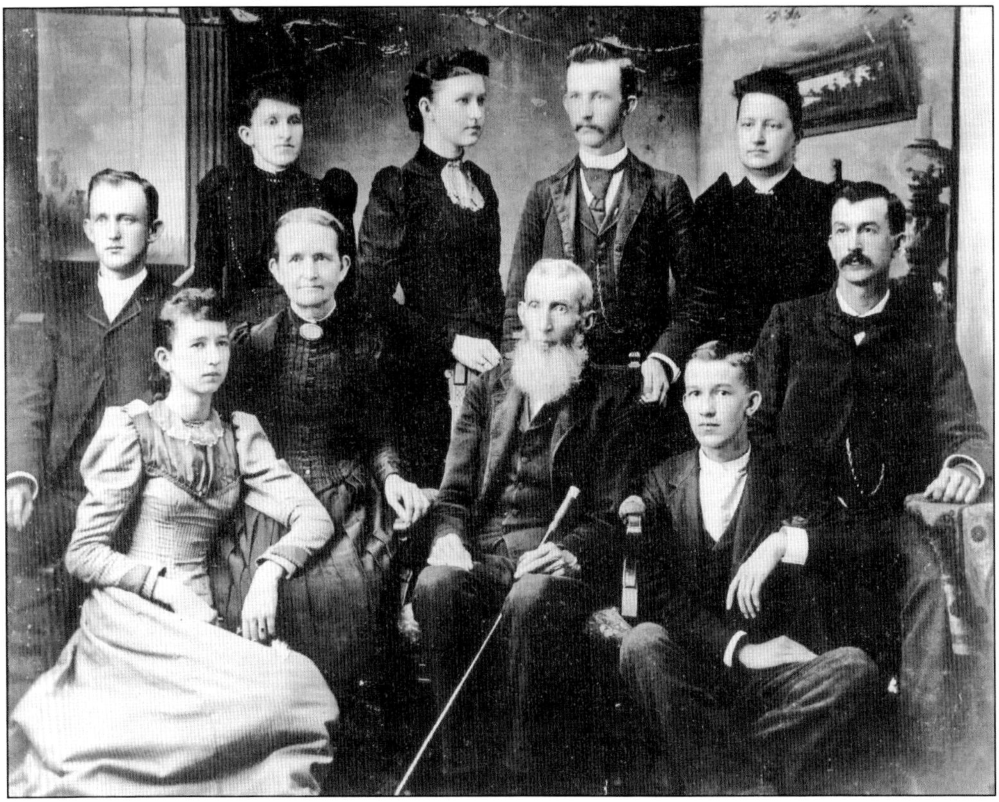

The Cooper family poses for a portrait in the summer of 1892. The Cooper family has been a part of the Clemmons area since its founding. (Courtesy Cookie Snyder Photography.)

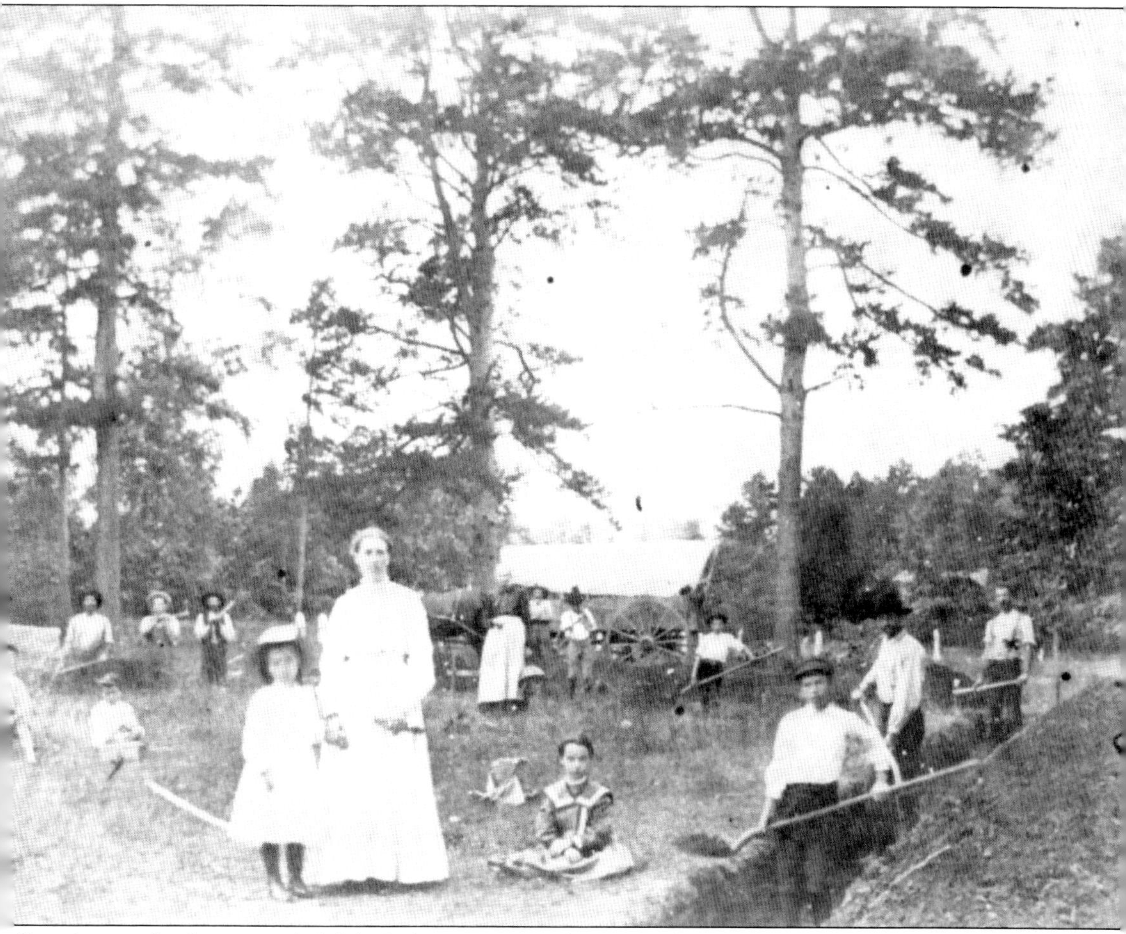

Standing in the foreground, Adelia Rebecca Cooper (1859–1921) was the wife of Frank Cook and the daughter-in-law of longtime Clemmons resident Nancy Cook. She is seen here participating in the laying of the foundation for the first brick building of the Clemmons First Baptist Church in 1905. Note the covered wagon in the background. (Courtesy Clemmons First Baptist Church.)

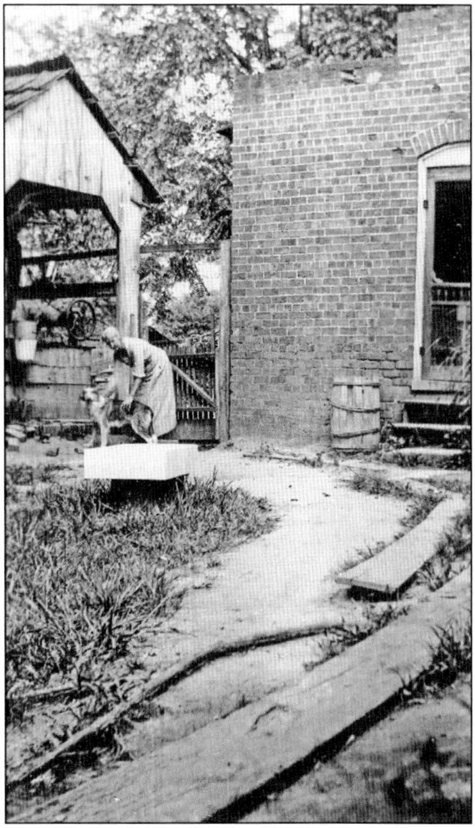

Lena Cooper (1877–1960) plays with Jimps the dog by the water well in this c. 1905 photograph taken behind the Strupe store. Cooper was a lifelong resident of Clemmons. (Courtesy Cookie Snyder Photography.)

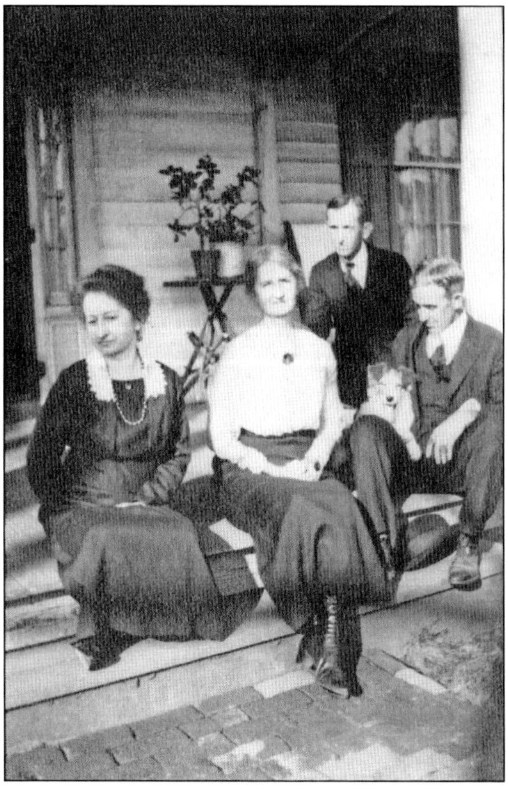

The Strupe and Cooper families relax on the front porch of a house adjacent to the Strupe store about 1907. From left to right are Carrie Strupe, Lena Cooper, Carl Strupe, and George Cooper. Jimps the dog seems to be having a good time as well. (Courtesy Cookie Snyder Photography.)

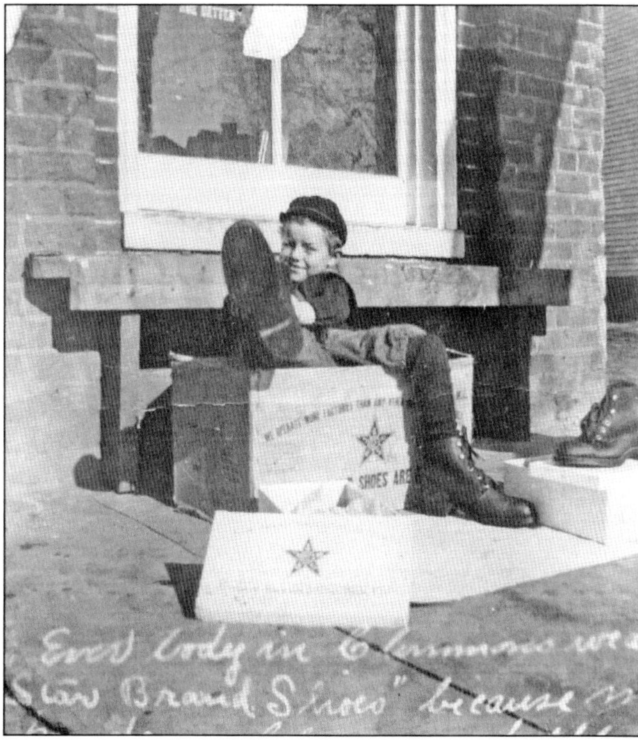

Tom Cook tries on a pair of Star brand shoes in front of the Strupe store around 1910. Star was a popular brand of shoe in the early 1900s. (Courtesy Cookie Snyder Photography.)

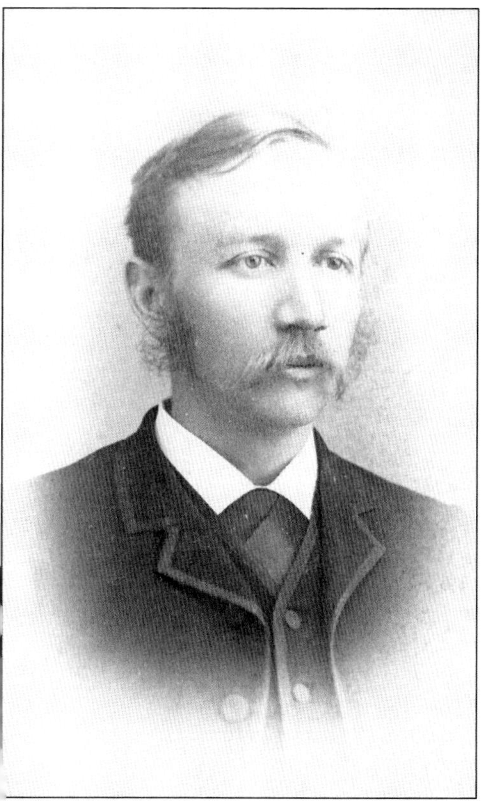

Henry E. Fries (1857–1949) of Salem founded the Fries Manufacturing and Power Company in 1898 to harness the hydroelectric capabilities of the Yadkin River. Construction began at the old Idol's Ferry just south of Clemmons, and the plant became known as Idol's Hydroelectric Station. The dam built for the hydroelectric station was 482 feet long, and its reservoir covered about 35 acres. The flow of the dam generated more than 2,000 horsepower. Fries Manufacturing and Power Company was the first to transmit electrical power over a long distance: 13.25 miles to Fries's Arista textile mill. (Courtesy Moravian Archives, Winston-Salem, NC.)

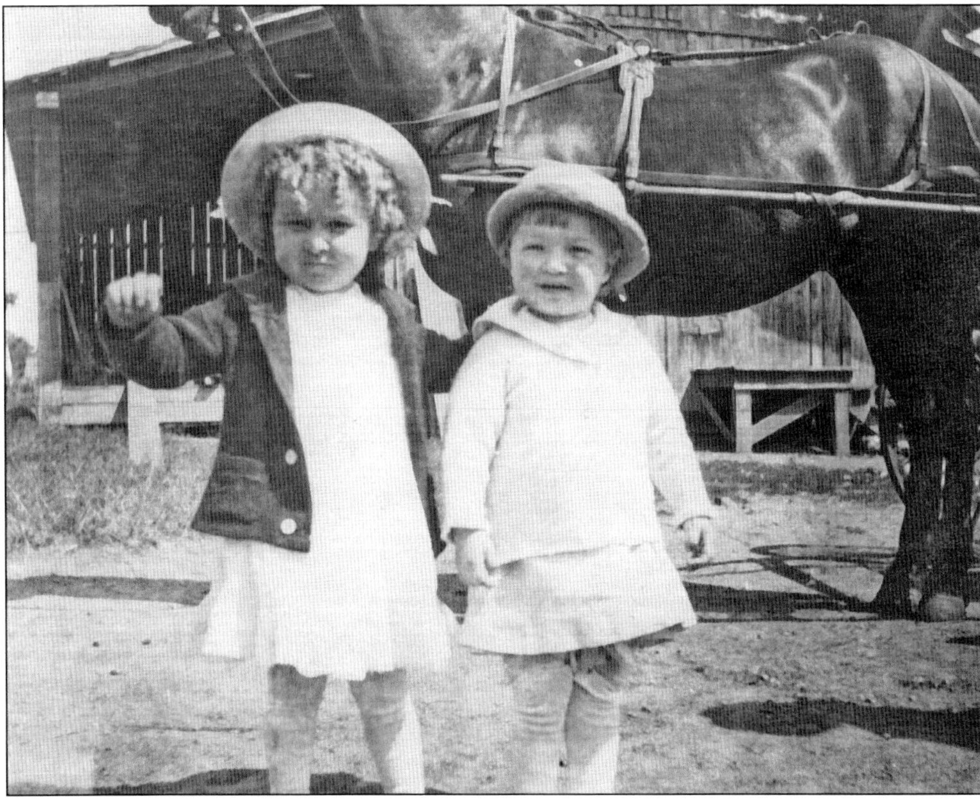

Sarah Cooper and Cooper "Bumper" Cook are seen here in front of Cook's granary and cannery building near the intersection of what is now Highway 158 and the Lewisville-Clemmons Road around 1915. (Courtesy Cookie Snyder Photography.)

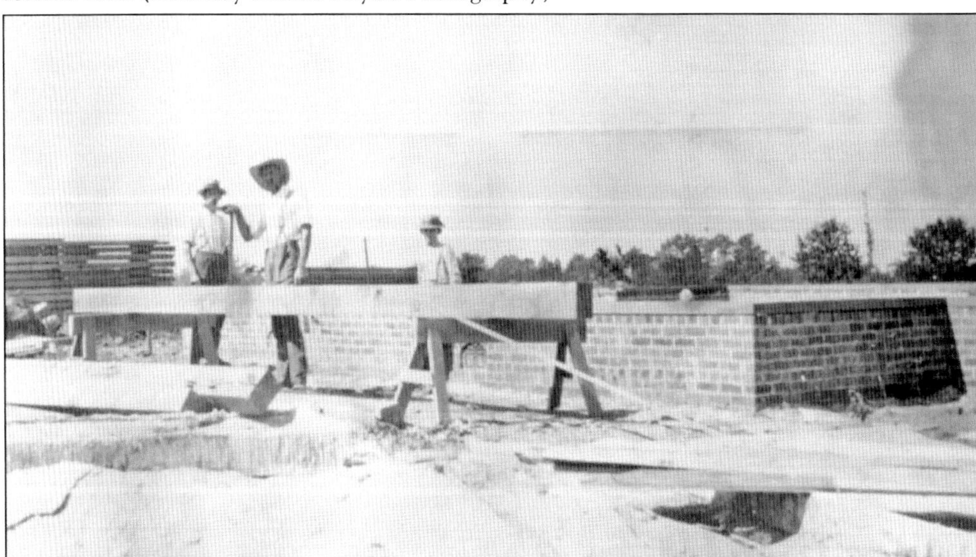

Frank Cook, Charles Cooper, and Will Hall pause for this photograph as they build the first parsonage at Clemmons First Baptist Church in 1918. The parsonage is no longer standing. (Courtesy Clemmons First Baptist Church.)

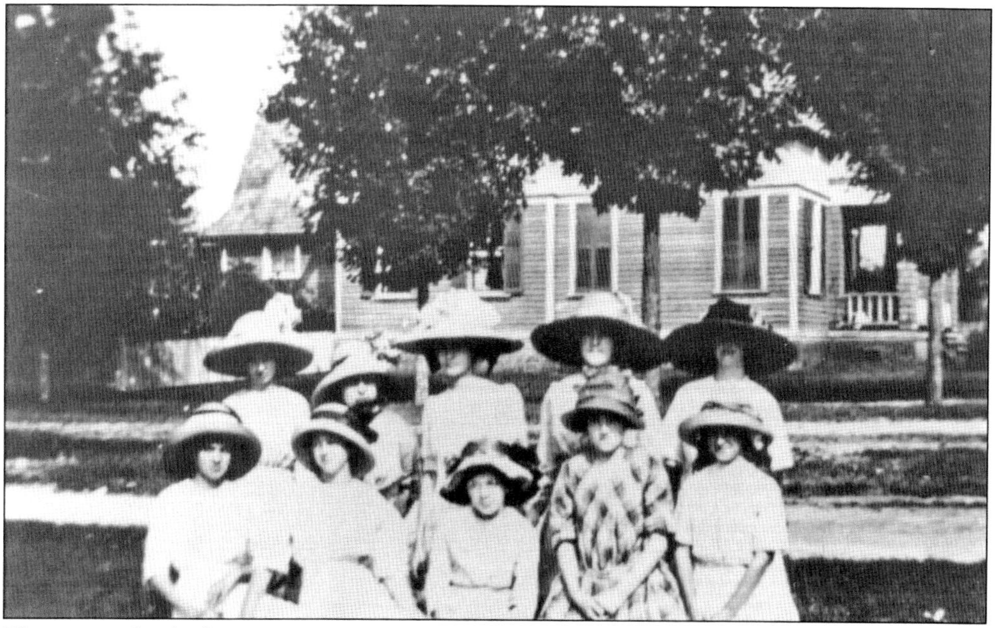

The group of girls above poses in front of the parsonage at Clemmons Moravian Church around 1920. (Courtesy Pam Corum, Snyder Photography.)

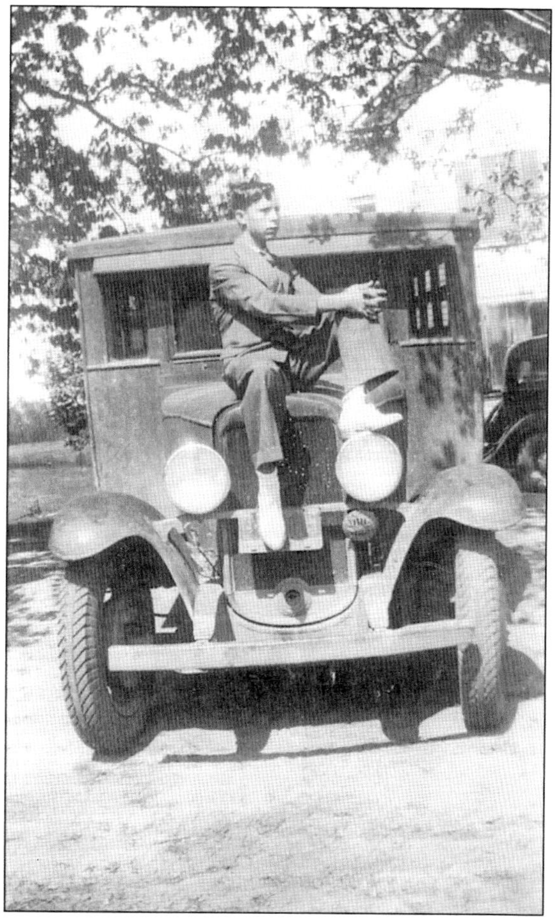

Lifelong Clemmons resident Jim Harper (1920–2010) is seen here in 1936, posing on top of the hood of the school bus that he drove in the Clemmons area. (Courtesy Neal Harper.)

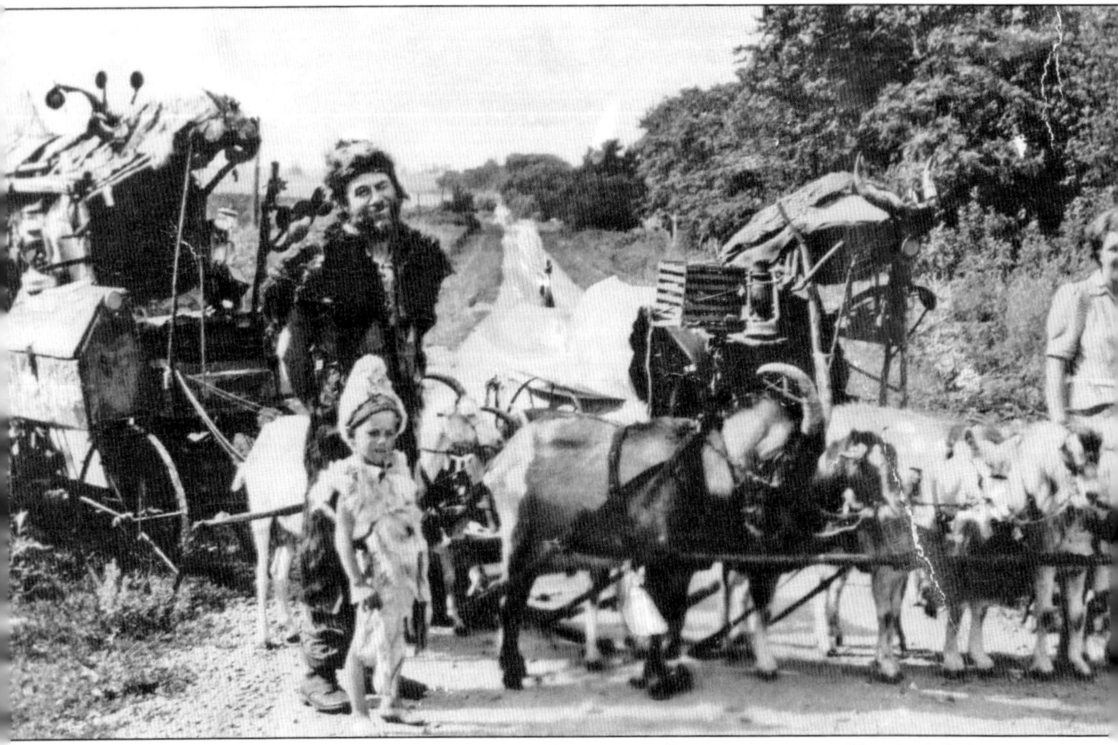

The goat train passed through the area in the 1950s. The train's owner, Charles McCartney, was from Georgia. After a work-related injury with the Works Progress Administration (WPA) during the Great Depression, McCartney had a spiritual awakening and decided to travel the United States on his goat train preaching repentance for sinners. It was said that one could trace his path by following the signs he left posted on trees promoting his religious views. When he was in Georgia, author Flannery O'Connor noticed him and remarked about him in her personal letters. The train made several stops in Clemmons, at the artesian well, in the old triangle of Highway 158 and Lasater Road. (Courtesy Mike Parks.)

James Peter Sprinkle, one of the owners of the Stagecoach house after the Clemmons family, poses for the camera in the backyard of the house in 1940. Sprinkle was a descendant of Peter Sprinkle (Sprenckel), who immigrated to the United States in the early 1700s. James Sprinkle's great-grandfather George moved to the Yadkin area around 1780. He was born in 1866 and lived in Clemmons until his death in 1955. (Courtesy Cookie Snyder Photography.)

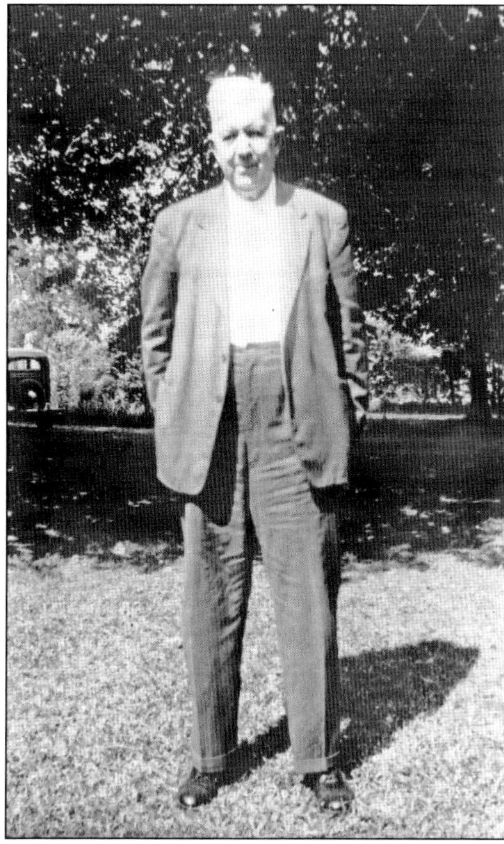

A group of young people from Clemmons gather to peel apples in the c. 1940 photograph below. It is possible that this photograph was made in the canning factory located in the basement of the Clemmons School gymnasium, which operated during World War II. (Courtesy Fraternity Church of the Brethren.)

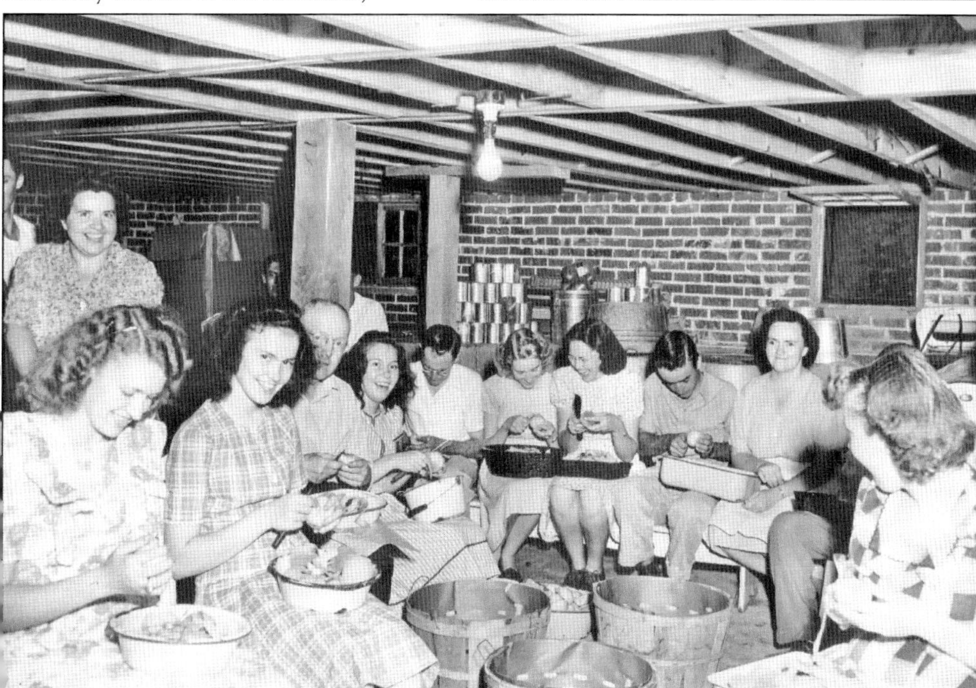

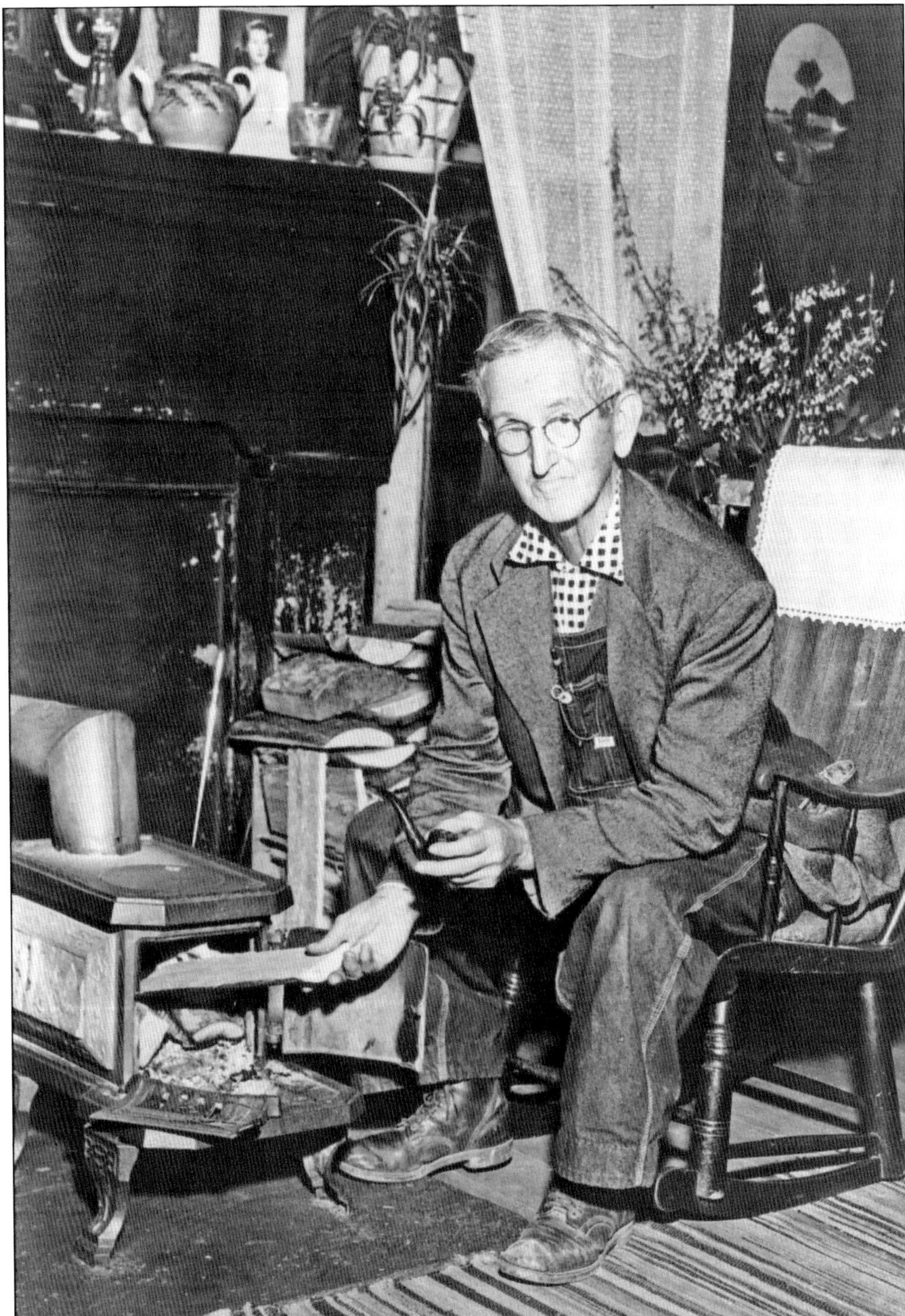

Carl Strupe, the grandson of early settler Carlos Strupe, relaxes in his home next to the store his family operated in about 1955. (Courtesy Cookie Snyder Photography.)

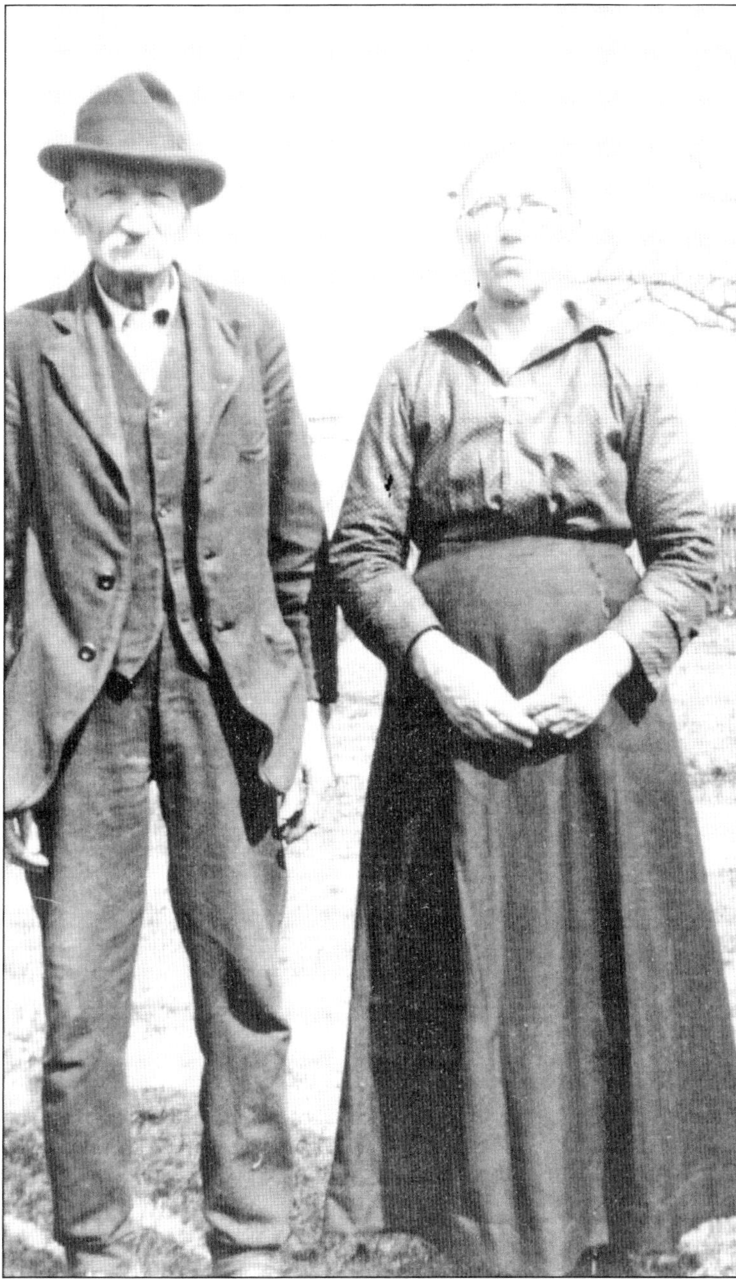

George W. Phelps (1859–1937) and Laura Jane Ellis Phelps (1863–1956) were lifelong residents of the Clemmons area and were both members of the Clemmons First Baptist Church when the original congregation moved to Clemmons from the Muddy Creek area. Late in life, Laura, as the oldest member of the church, attended several ceremonies marking achievements in the church history, such as building expansions and new building construction. In 1947, she gave the first offering for a new cement drive and walkway. George, Laura, and their six children were primarily farmers, and at one time, they owned one of the largest apple orchards in North Carolina. As the story goes, the land the orchard was on was traded for a wagon and a mule. (Courtesy Jo Ann (Phelps) Wilhelm.)

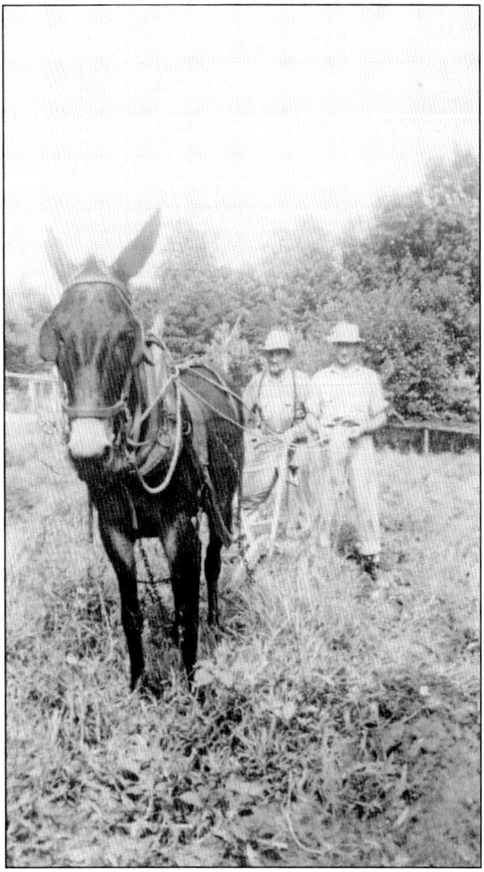

Dallas Odell Johnson (right) and sharecropper Powhatan David Simpson cultivate a farm on Hope Church Road in the 1940s. Johnson was a direct descendant of William Johnson, who settled in what became Tanglewood Park in the mid-1700s. (Courtesy Jerry Johnson.)

Below, Dallas Johnson and his sons Mark (middle) and Jerry drill a water well on their farm on Hope Church Road in the 1950s. The Johnson family, descendants of the original Johnsons that moved to the area in the 1750s, is still in the area. (Courtesy Jerry Johnson.)

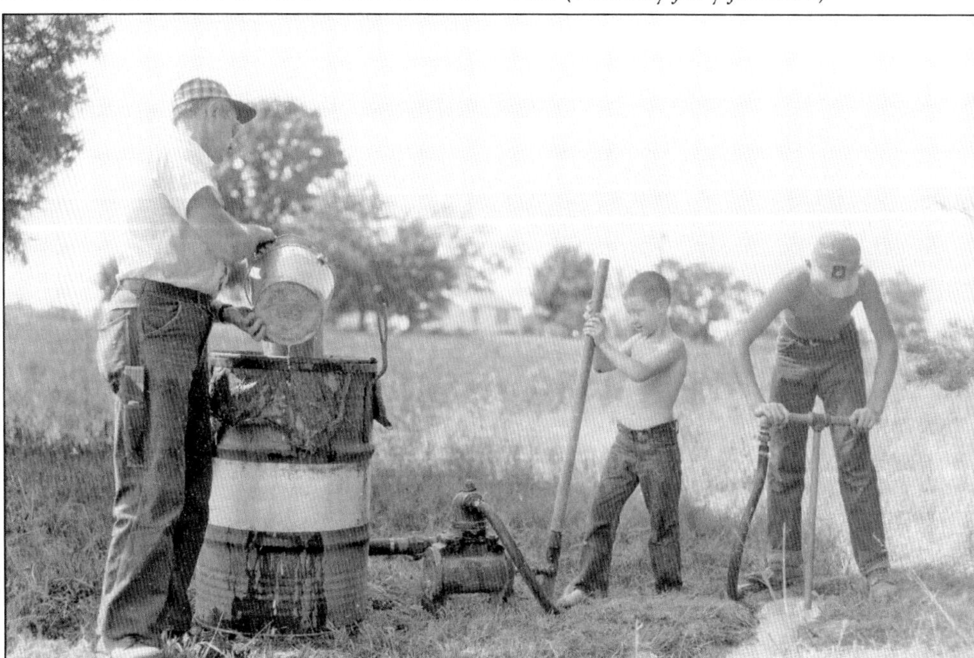

Dodd Linker Sr. (1910–2003), a native of Salisbury, graduated from the University of North Carolina at Chapel Hill with a master's degree in mathematics. He came to Clemmons School as a teacher of mathematics and foreign languages and an athletic coach from 1932 to 1943. He joined the Ernst & Ernst accounting firm as a CPA after passing the exam on his first try and eventually retired as the vice president of Wachovia Bank in 1969. He was also a charter member and past president of the Clemmons Civic Club, served as treasurer for the Clemmons Hosiery Mill and Clemmons Enterprises, and was chairman of the Clemmons School Committee for two terms. He was also a member of Clemmons Moravian Church and was a past chairman and member of the church's board of trustees. (Courtesy Martha Linker.)

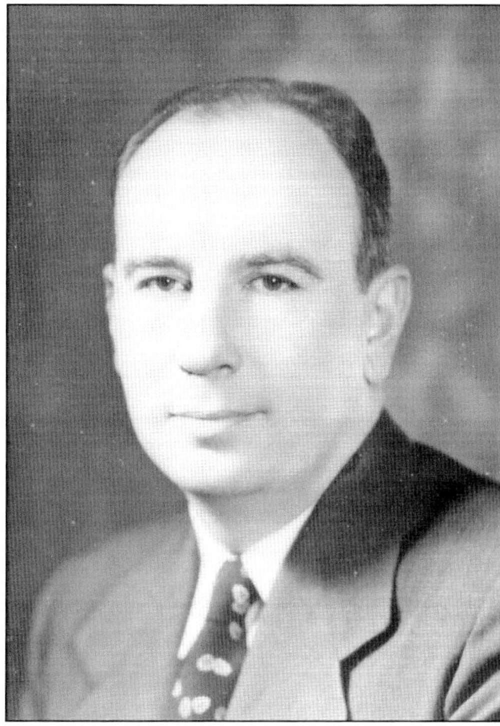

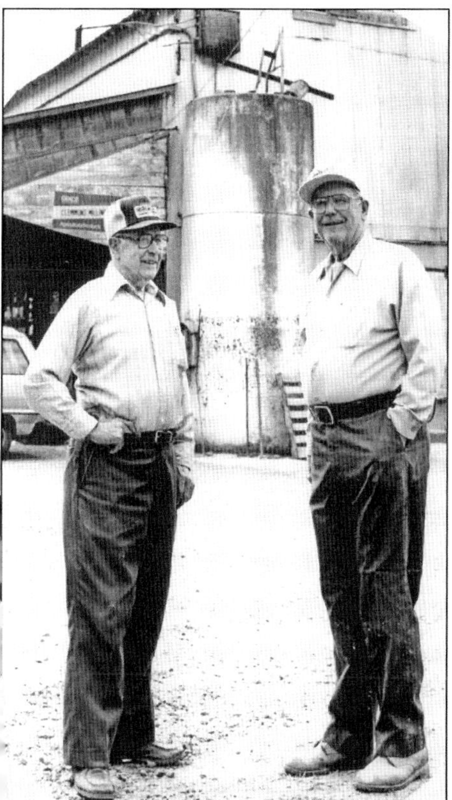

Brothers Dennis (left) and Robert Plato Brewer are seen here in the 1970s. Their family operated the Clemmons Milling Company from 1921 until it was sold in 1988. Here, they are probably discussing business and farming in front of the mill. (Courtesy the *Clemmons Courier*.)

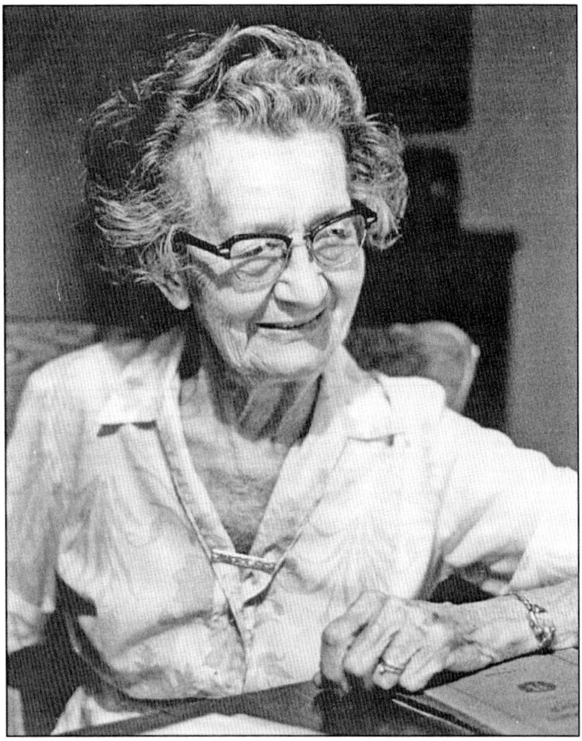

Fannie Sprinkle Ogburn (1889–1985) lived in the Peter Clemmons stagecoach house after her father, J.P. Sprinkle, a lumberman, purchased the home and 400 acres in 1903. She graduated from Clemmons Moravian School in 1906, obtained a teachers certificate, and taught school in Forsyth County and in Clemmons. She married Henly Ogburn, one of Forsyth County's first game wardens, in 1917. She stopped teaching in 1918 to take care of her aging parents while her husband worked at Hanes Knitting. They raised two sons, Henly Ogburn Jr. and James Ogburn. (Photograph by George Futch, courtesy the *Clemmons Courier*.)

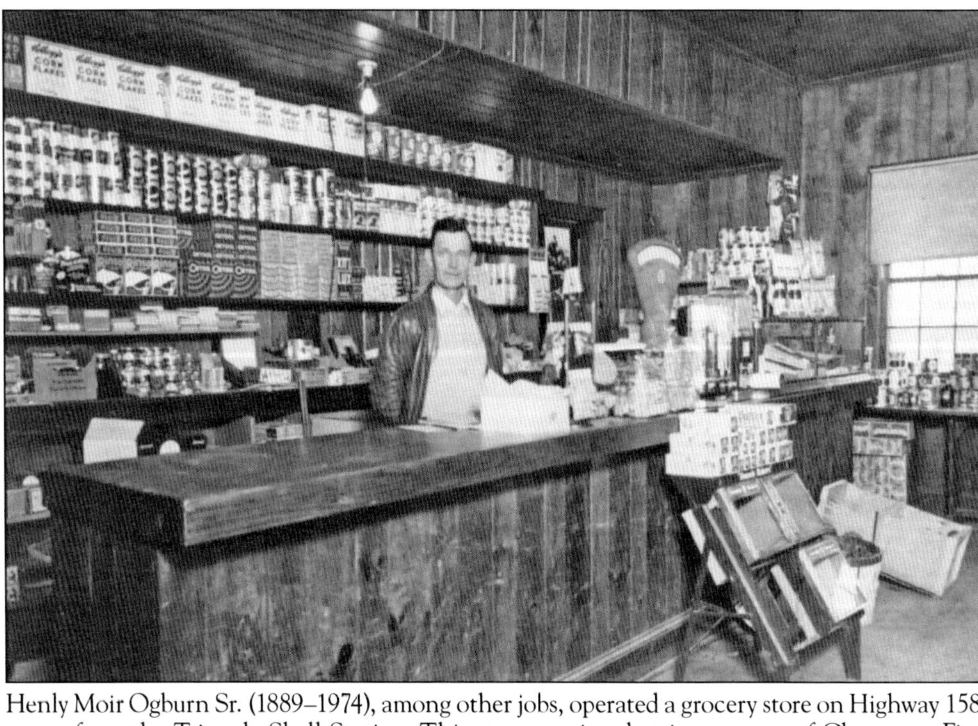

Henly Moir Ogburn Sr. (1889–1974), among other jobs, operated a grocery store on Highway 158, across from the Triangle Shell Station. This store was in what is now part of Clemmons First Baptist Church's parking lot. This photograph is from 1942, and it appears Kellogg's Corn Flakes were as popular then as they are today. (Courtesy Cookie Snyder Photography.)

In 1932, John Frank Holder Jr. (1891–1971) was hired to help install the irrigation system at Robert Lassiter's 1,200-acre Forest Hills Farm. After that, he helped build the rock dam for the millpond on Blanket Bottom Creek, where Lassiter was building a water-powered gristmill like one he had seen in England. Eventually, Holder was hired to run the mill, which he did until 1945. Holder also managed the other parts of the estate. (Courtesy David H. Hauser.)

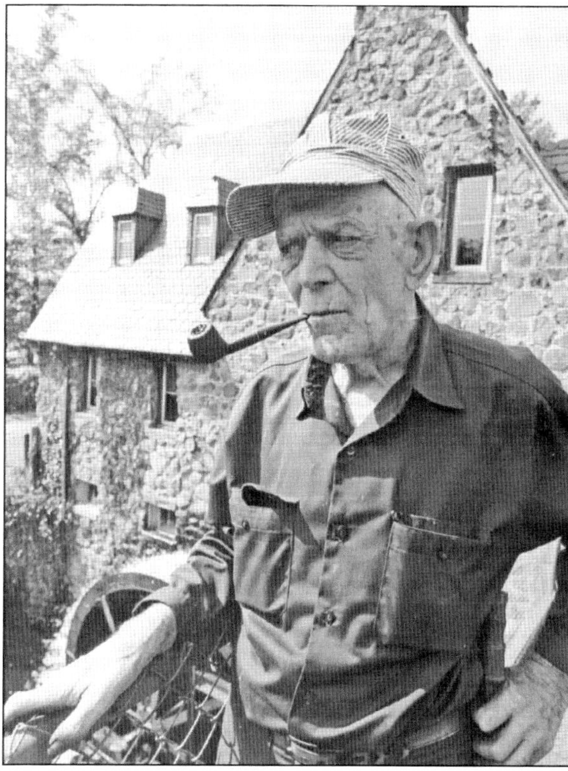

Below, Janie Hall Hege celebrates her 95th birthday with the Brownies of Clemmons Moravian Church, Troop 180, in February 1975. Hege's father operated Hall's Ferry on the Yadkin River, where Highway 158 crosses over into Davie County. (Courtesy David H. Hauser.)

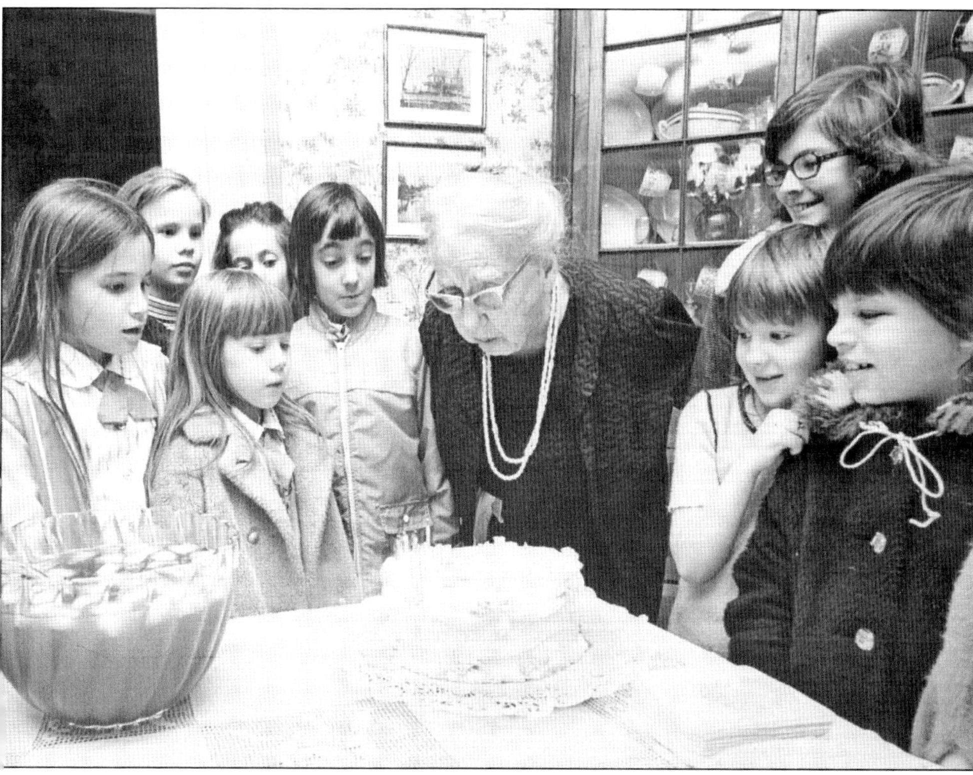

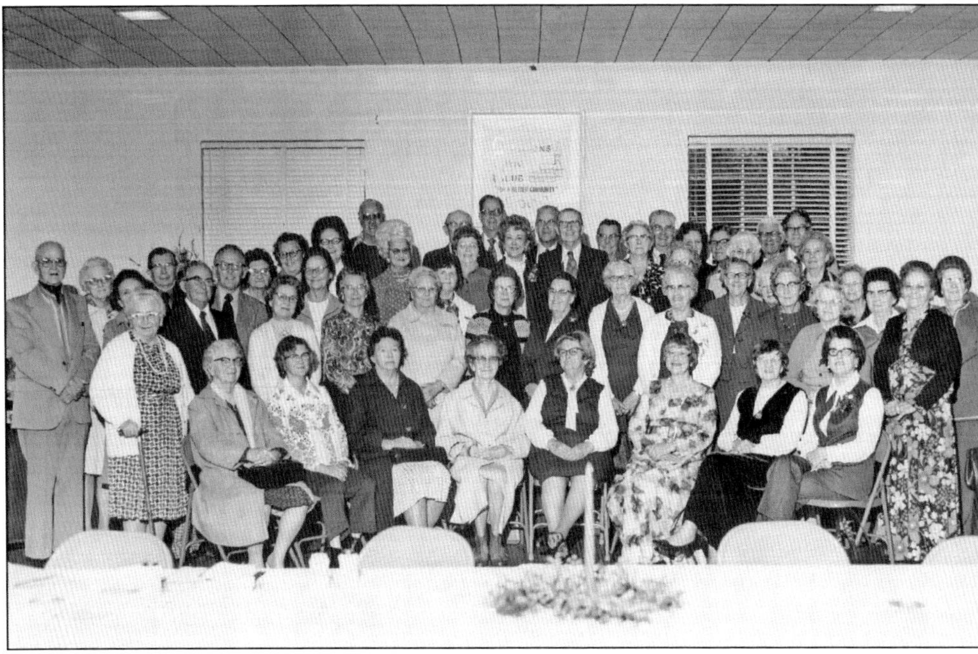

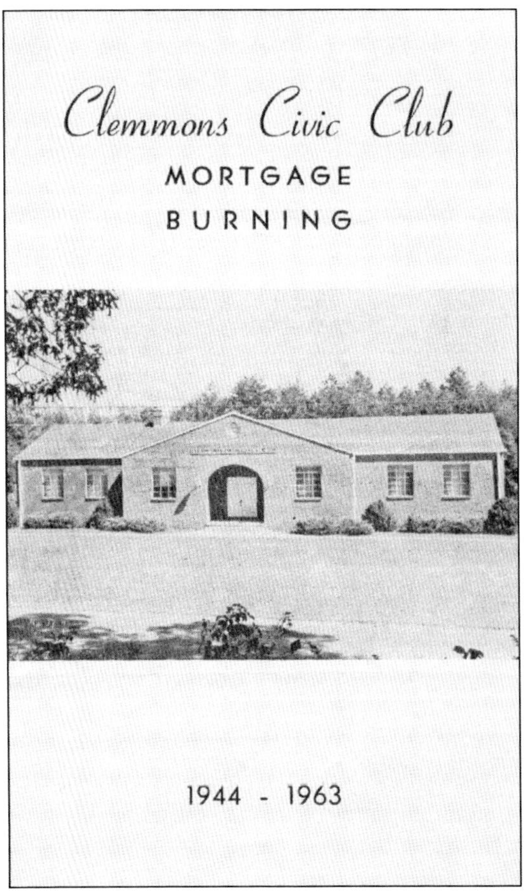

Above, a group of Clemmons senior citizens gathered at the Clemmons Civic Club on Middlebrook Drive in the late 1970s. The Civic Club was organized in 1944 by 17 charter members, mostly local businessmen and leaders. A nonpartisan and nonreligious club, its goals were simply to make the Clemmons community a better place to live. The paving of Lewisville-Clemmons Road, early telephone service, the establishment of the fire department, and the building the Clemmons School athletic field were all accomplishments made by the Civic Club. The land for the building was acquired from the J.F. Brower family, and in 1963, the club was able to "burn the mortgage." The charter members were Fred Bingham, Carlos T. Cooper, G. Linnett Potts, Dennis E. Brewer, James Estes Hunter, Theodore Rondthaler, Dr. J.C. Casstevens Sr., W. Alfred Hunter Sr., Ray E. Snyder, J. Dodd Linker, David F. Stilwell, Robert F. Cook, J. Thomas Cook Sr., Vernon R. Woodford, George T. Moody, W. Jarvis Cook, and Glenn I. Williamson. (Above, courtesy David H. Hauser; left, courtesy Clemmons Public Library.)

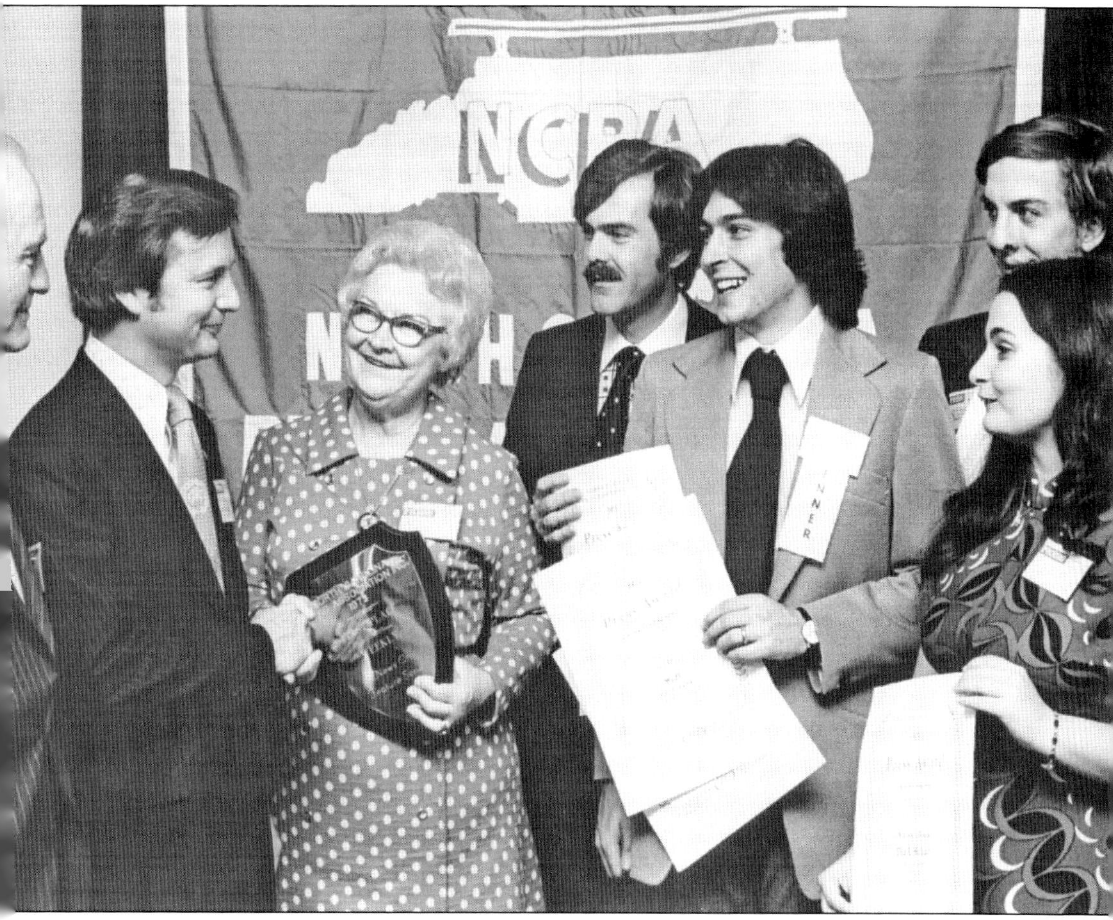

The *Clemmons Courier*, southwest Forsyth County's weekly newspaper, was honored by the North Carolina Press Association (NCPA) in Chapel Hill in 1973. NCPA president Sam Ragan and North Carolina lieutenant governor Jim Hunt presented the awards to editor Myrtle Tomlinson, associate editor David H. Hauser, news editor Frank Tursi, former news editor Nita (Hilliard) Smith, and cartoonist David Hoyle for their journalistic achievements. Tomlinson started the newspaper on December 1, 1960. Dwight Sparks became editor in 1985 and continues in that capacity today. (Photograph by Gordon Tomlinson, courtesy David H. Hauser.)

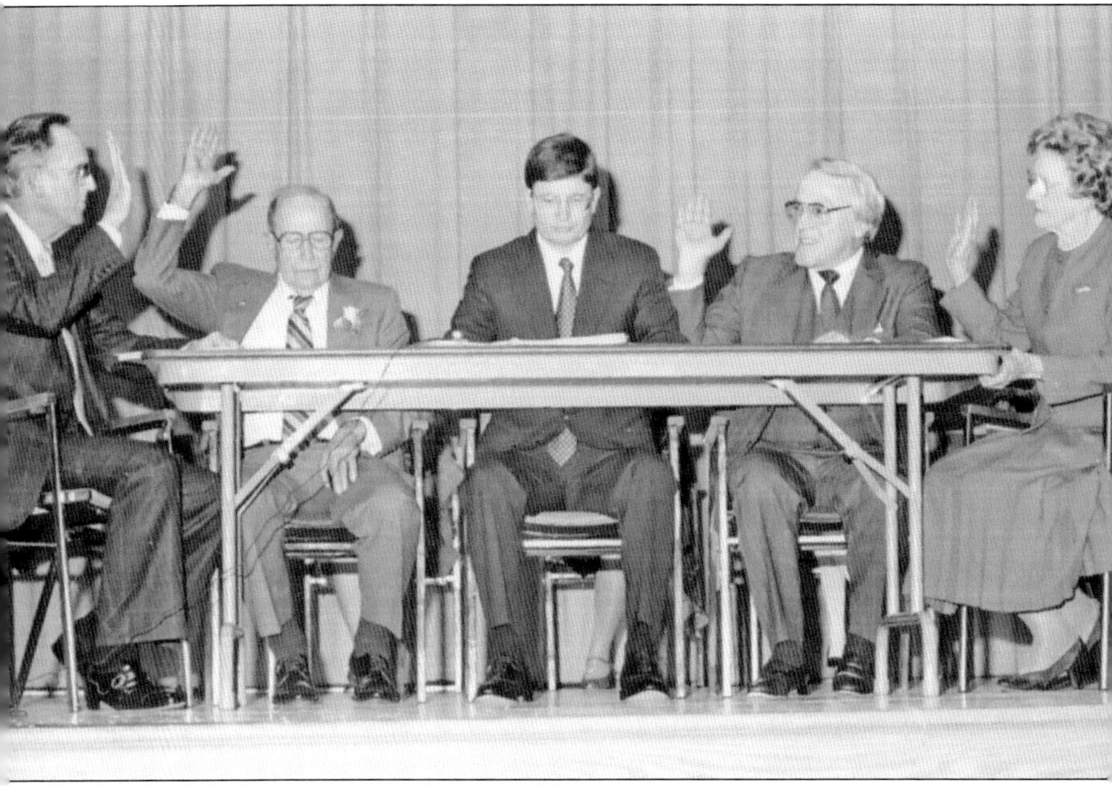

Clemmons residents voted to incorporate in November 1986 by a vote of 1,757 to 712. Clemmons officially became a municipality on December 3, 1986, when the first interim council was sworn in at ceremonies at Clemmons Elementary School. Council members included John F. Hunter, Dennis Brewer, Ron Willard, Bob Caudill, and Harriet Moody. One of the first actions the group took was to elect Ron Willard as its chairman. (Courtesy Village of Clemmons.)

Three
Places

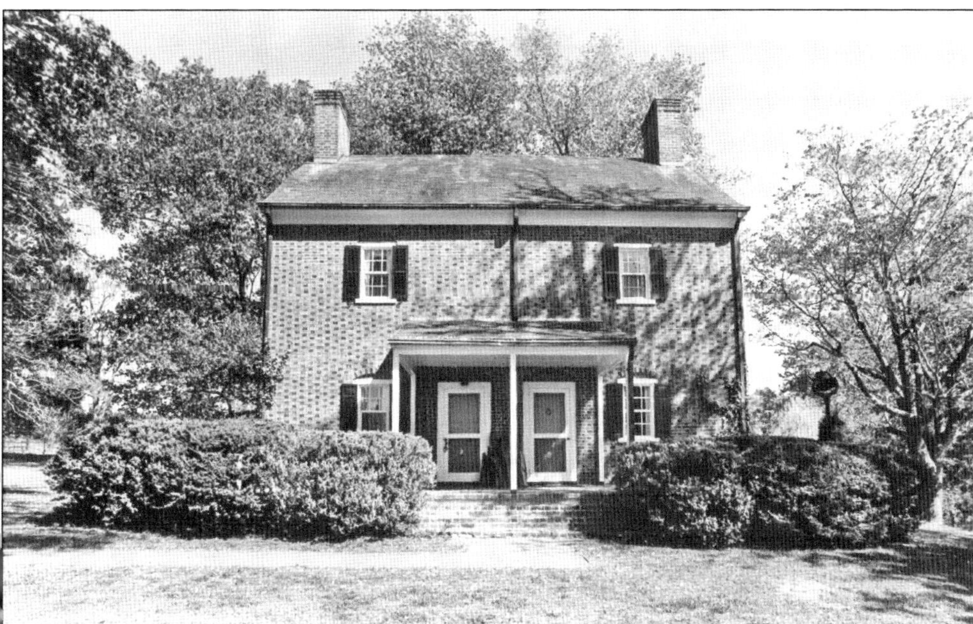

The Phillip Hanes house is the oldest standing structure in Clemmons. Built by Phillip Hanes (Hoehns) in 1789, it is on Middlebrook Drive. Hanes (1752–1820) was born in York, Pennsylvania, and was of German ancestry. He built this impressive home after his family relocated to the area in 1774. The exterior walls of the home are a foot thick and made of locally made bricks. One particular feature of the home was its two front doors, one for business use and one for family use. In the 1900s, the Womack family lived in the house, and P. Huber Hanes Jr. began restoring the house in 1948. Architect J. Frank Cook and his family moved into the house in 1966. The house has been rented to other families over the years but remains in the Hanes family today. (Courtesy Cookie Snyder Photography.)

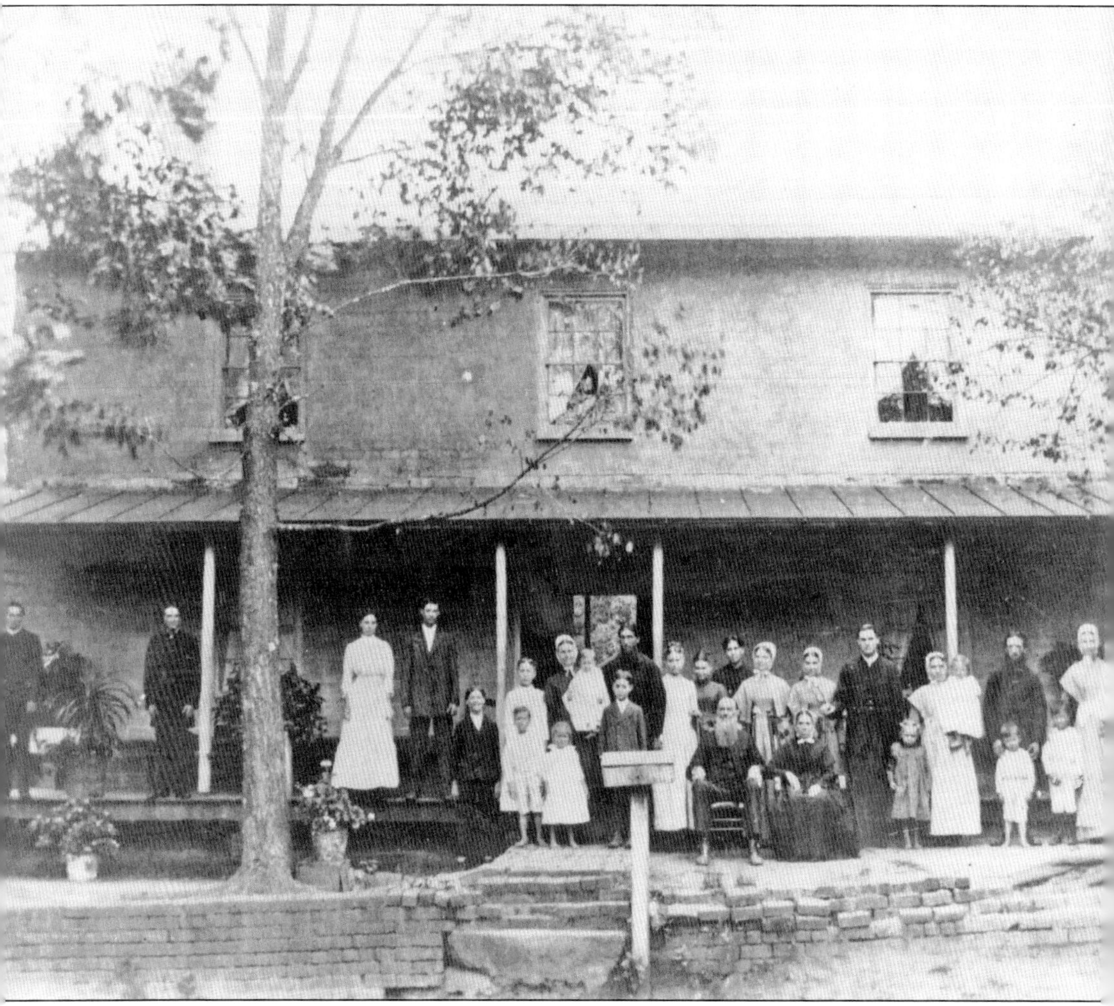

The Sides family relaxes at the home of Levi Sides around 1910. Levi and his wife, Nancy Faw, are at the front of the group. The home, which has since been remodeled, is on Highway 158 on the east side of the Muddy Creek Bridge coming into Clemmons from Winston-Salem. (Courtesy Genevieve Lesher.)

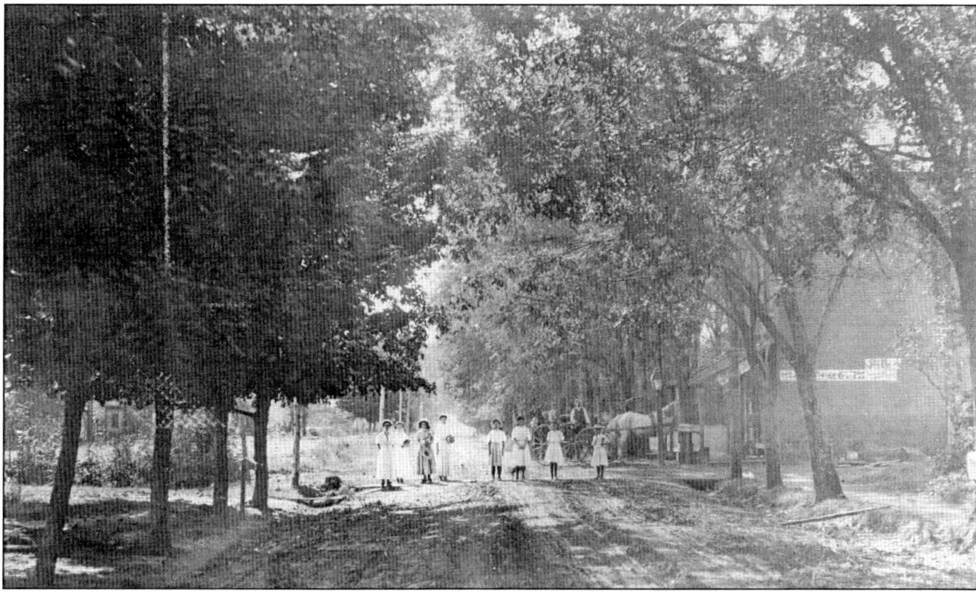

Children gather on Main Street in Clemmons to have their photograph taken in the late 1890s. Afterwards, they may have enjoyed a refreshing Coca-Cola at the Strupe store on the right. (Courtesy Cookie Snyder Photography.)

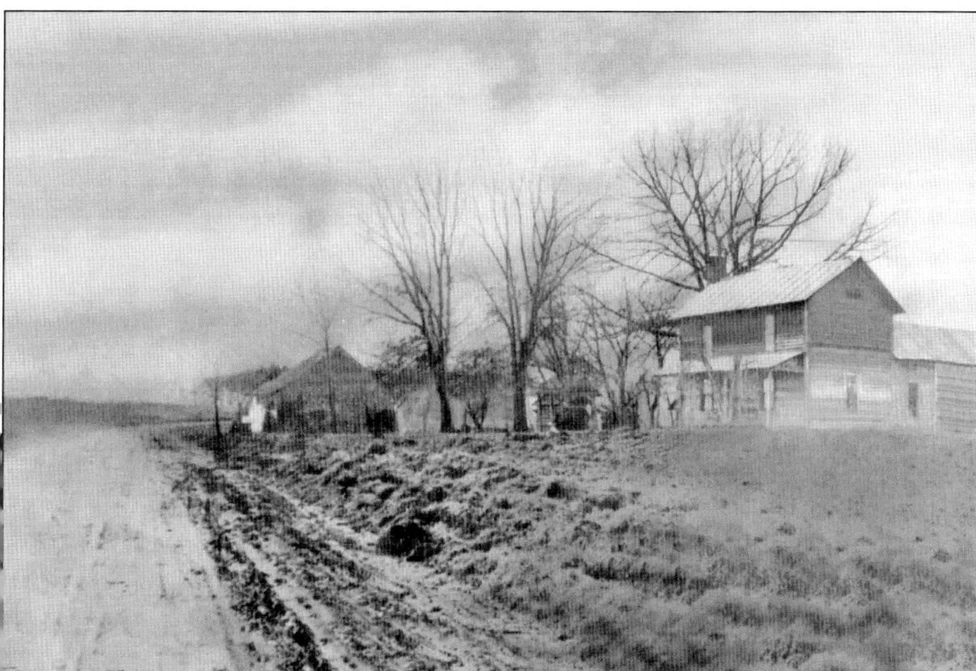

This 1900 view shows a farm on Hope Church Road, near the current Fraternity Church of the Brethren Church. The farm belonged to the Johnson family and then to the overseer for Christian Sides. The farm and buildings no longer exist. (Courtesy Jerry Johnson.)

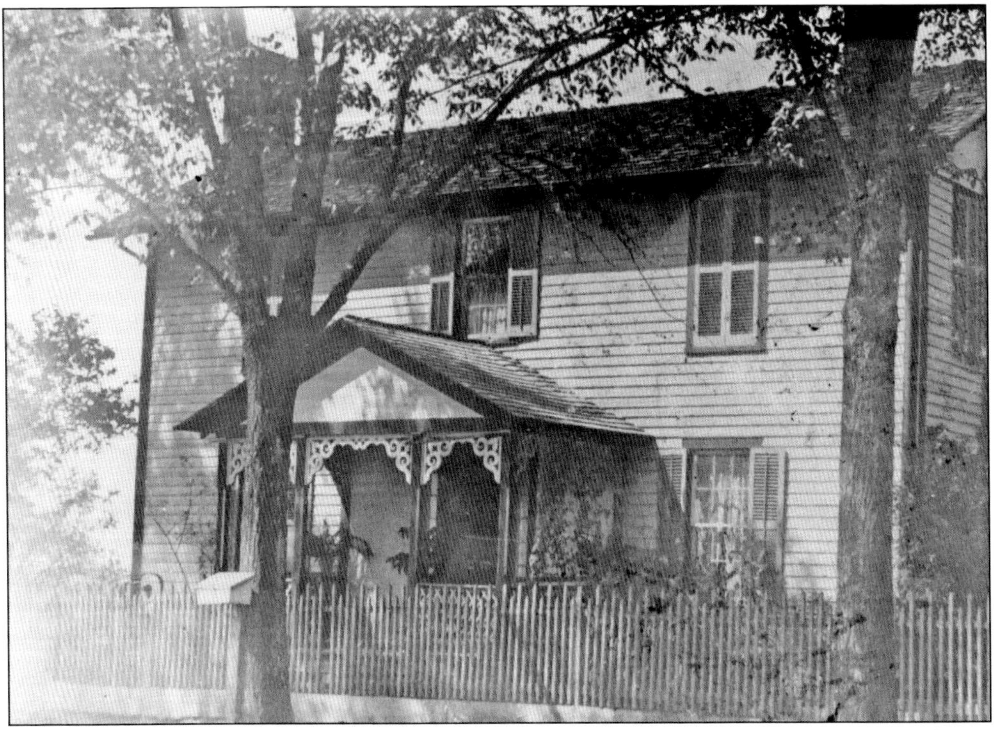

This impressive home, built around 1850, stood on Idol's Road near the Clemmons train depot. The home no longer exists. (Courtesy Cookie Snyder Photography.)

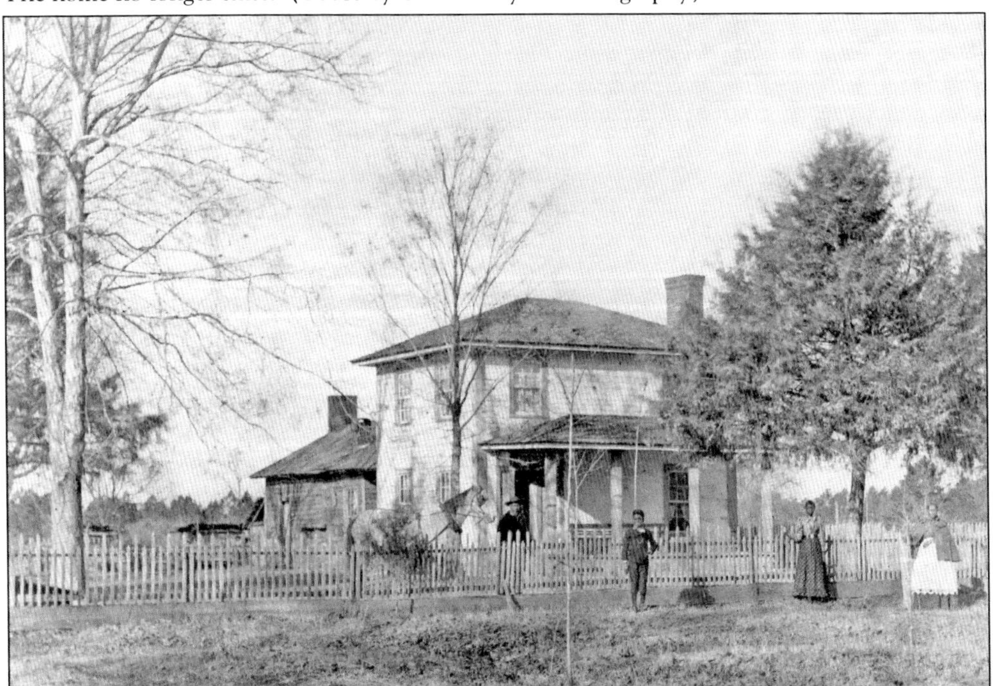

This home was built in the early 1800s on Idol's Road. The people in the foreground model the dress of the time period. (Courtesy Cookie Snyder Photography.)

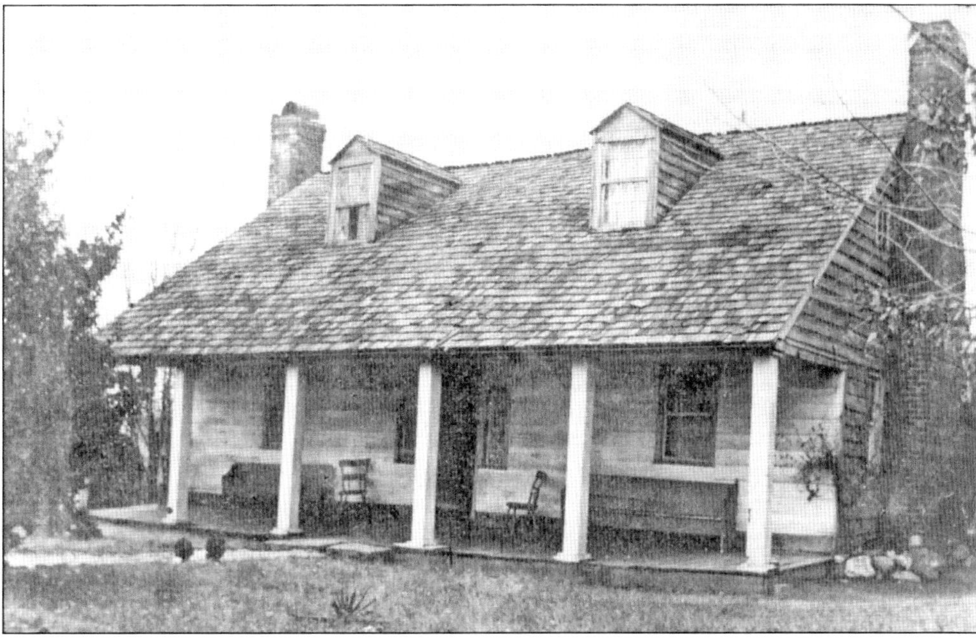

This home was built by William and Mary "Polly" Hanes Clemmons, the parents of E.T. Clemmons, who was born here. It was then owned by the Cooper family. The home was on the current site of the Clemmons United Methodist Church. (Courtesy Cookie Snyder Photography.)

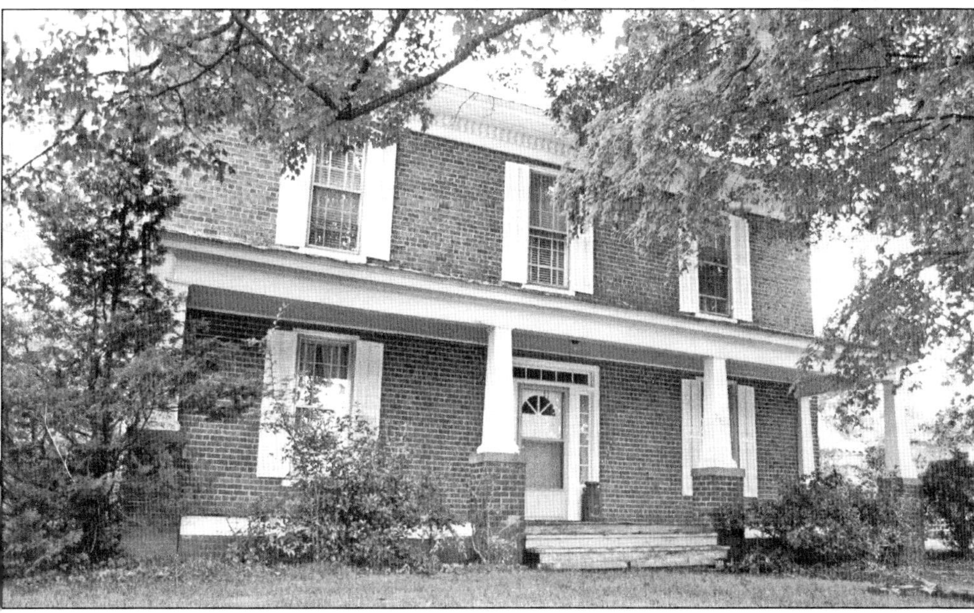

The Cook-Bingham house, a two-story Greek Revival home built in Clemmons around 1839, is seen here in the 1950s. The house is located at the intersection of Hampton Road and Cook Place, just off of Highway 158 and across the street from Clemmons First Baptist Church. It was originally owned by Jacob and Nancy Cook, who lived here until her death in 1919, when it was sold to the Hooper family. It was sold again in 1947 to the Bingham family, who lived there until the 1970s. The home has been vacant for several years but is a historic landmark in Clemmons. (Courtesy Cookie Snyder Photography.)

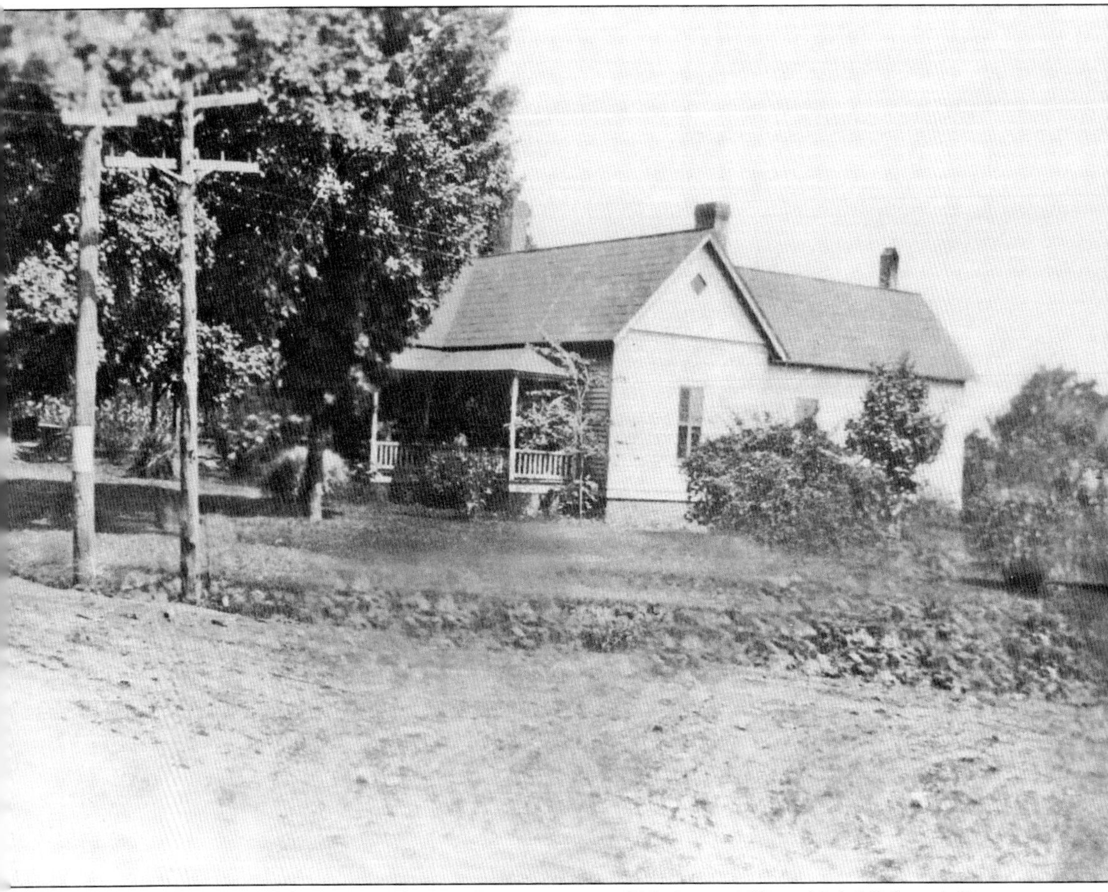

The Frank Cook home, on the southeast corner of Highway 158 and Middlebrook Drive, is seen here around 1940. The home was built in 1874 and torn down in the 1970s. Note the unpaved roads. (Courtesy Cookie Snyder Photography.)

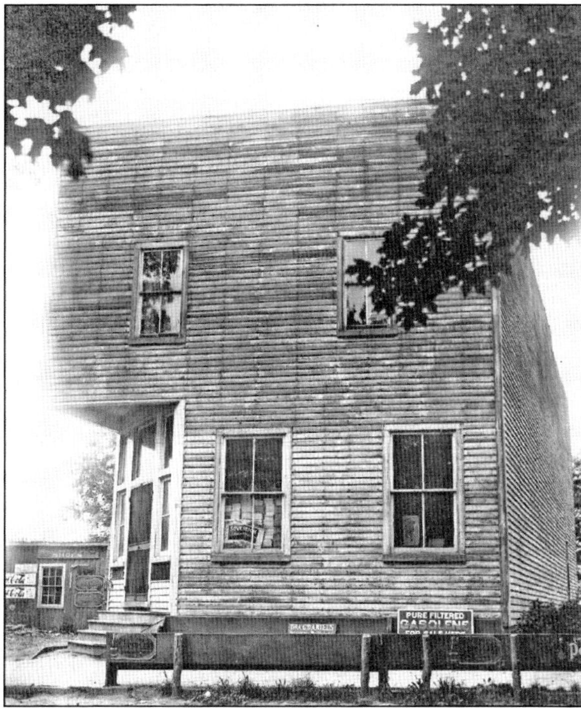

The Milton Blackburn store (right), on the northeast corner of the Highway 158 and Lewisville-Clemmons Road intersection, was built in the early 1900s and sold furniture and other goods to residents of Clemmons. The building was torn down in the 1950s. Below is an original receipt from the store from February 1913. (Right, courtesy Cookie Snyder Photography; below, courtesy Sammy Smith Conrad.)

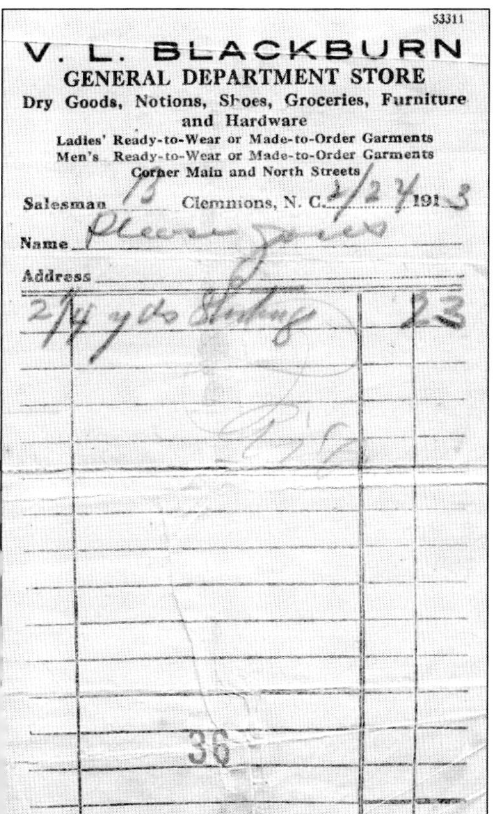

53311

V. L. BLACKBURN

GENERAL DEPARTMENT STORE

Dry Goods, Notions, Shoes, Groceries, Furniture and Hardware

Ladies' Ready-to-Wear or Made-to-Order Garments

Men's Ready-to-Wear or Made-to-Order Garments

Corner Main and North Streets

Salesman 13 Clemmons, N. C. 2/24 1913

Name

Address

36

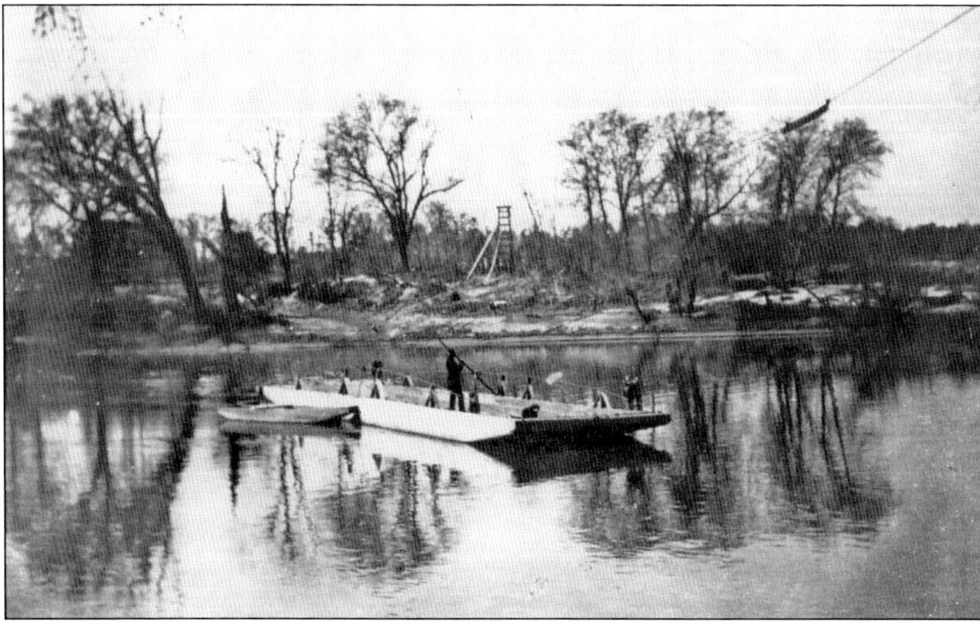

Hall's Ferry shuttled passengers over the Yadkin River from Clemmons to Davie County and back until 1914, when a new steel bridge was built. Running approximately where Highway 158 crosses the Yadkin River, the ferry was one of many local ferries. The first ferry at this spot was started by Peter Clemmons shortly after he moved here. (Courtesy Cookie Snyder Photography.)

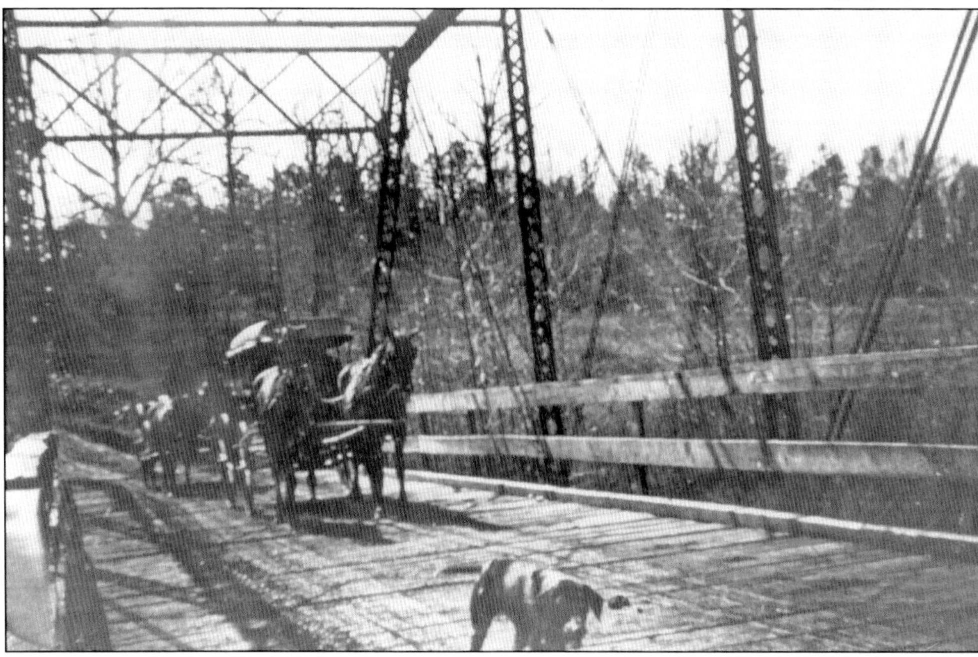

The steel bridge that was built over the Yadkin River between Clemmons and Davie County in 1914 is seen here before the widespread use of automobiles in the area. The bridge was later replaced by a two-lane concrete structure. In 2010, the bridge was replaced by an even larger four-lane structure. Here, on what appears to be a hot day, a weary dog leads the team of horses across the bridge. (Courtesy Cookie Snyder Photography.)

An adventurous person sits atop the new steel bridge where Hall's Ferry had been located. This sign reads, "No automobiles allowed on bridge while a team is crossing. No team allowed on bridge while an automobile is crossing." (Courtesy Caspar Howard.)

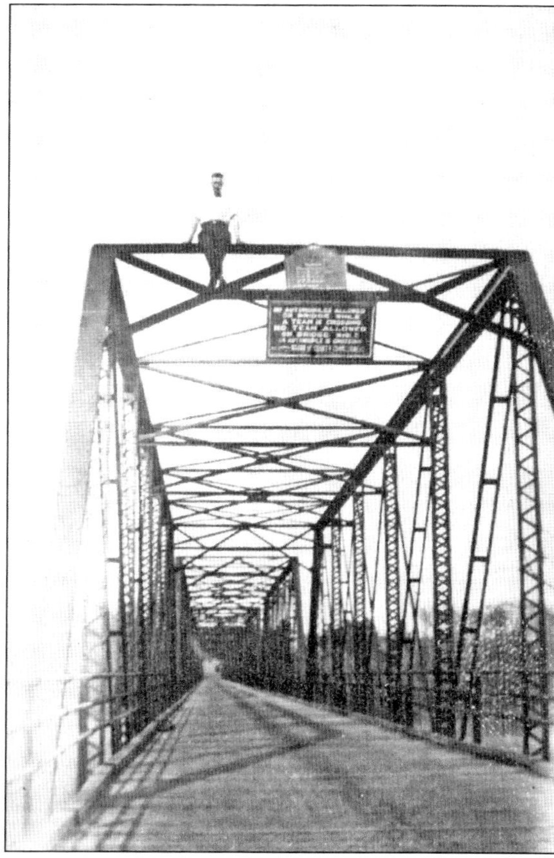

The wooden and steel bridge over Muddy Creek, where Highway 158 now crosses near the Sides Mill Road area, is seen below around 1900. (Courtesy Cookie Snyder Photography.)

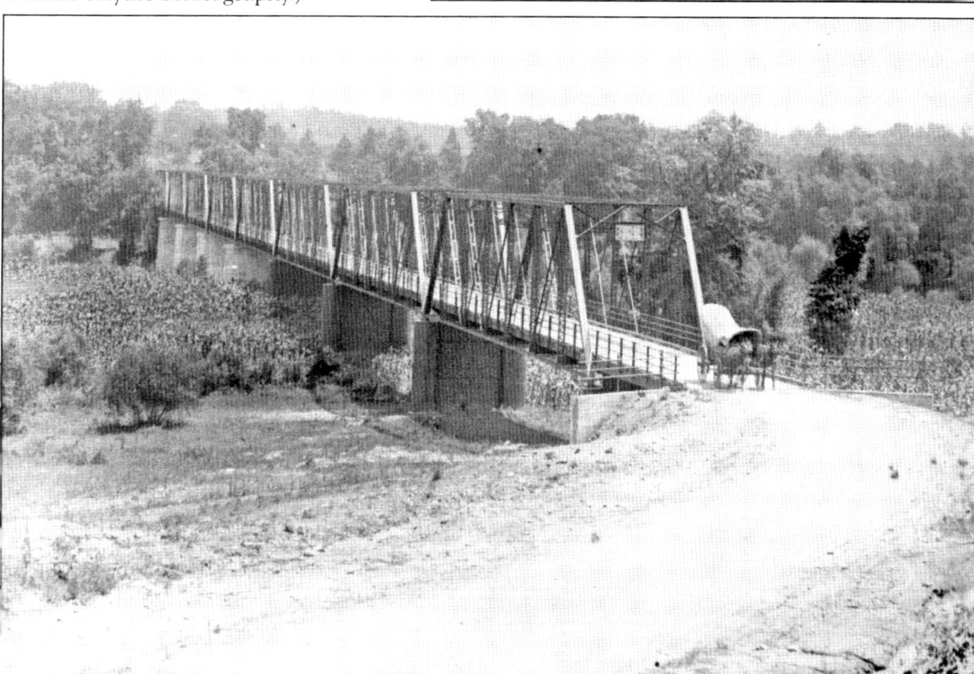

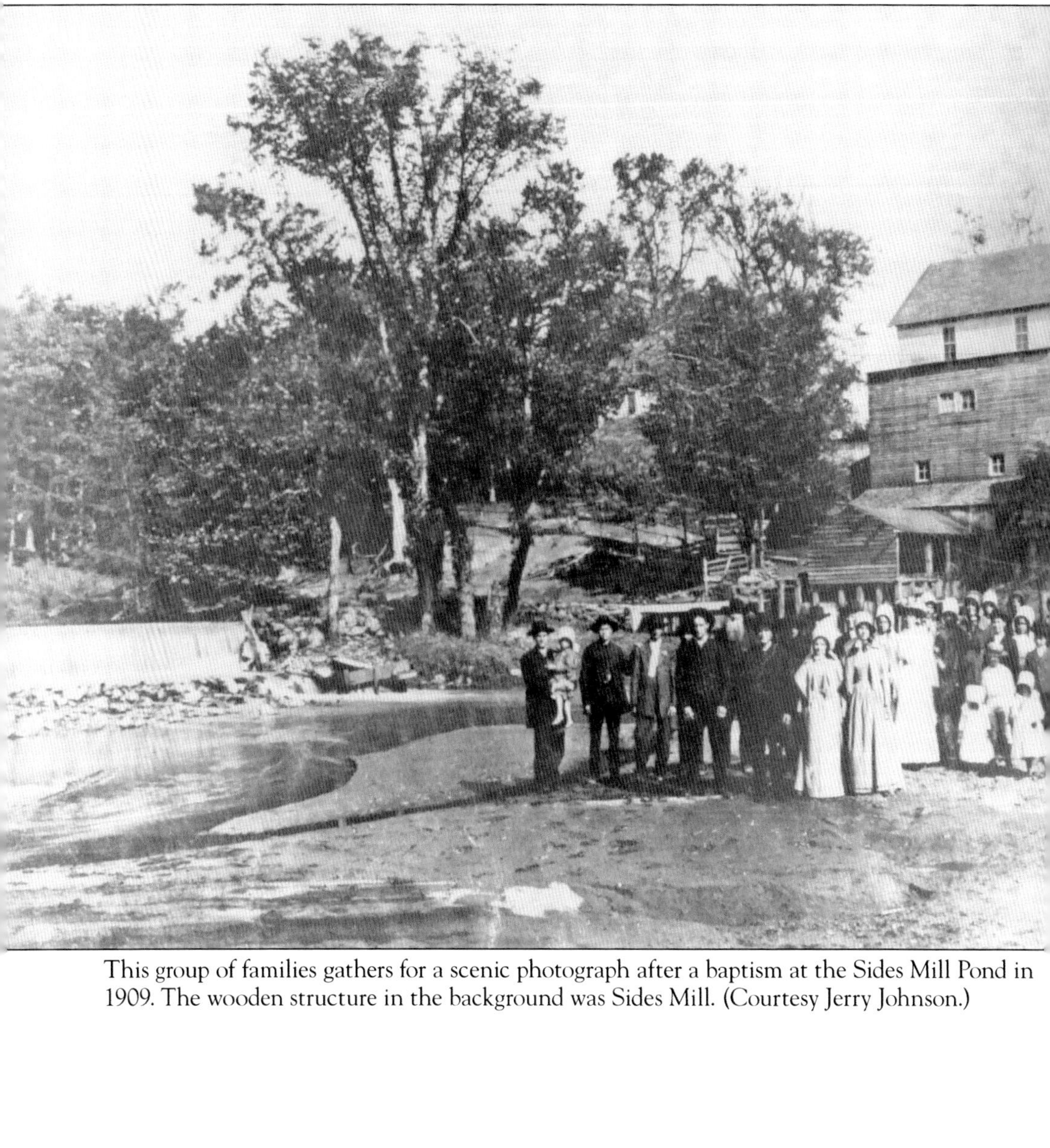

This group of families gathers for a scenic photograph after a baptism at the Sides Mill Pond in 1909. The wooden structure in the background was Sides Mill. (Courtesy Jerry Johnson.)

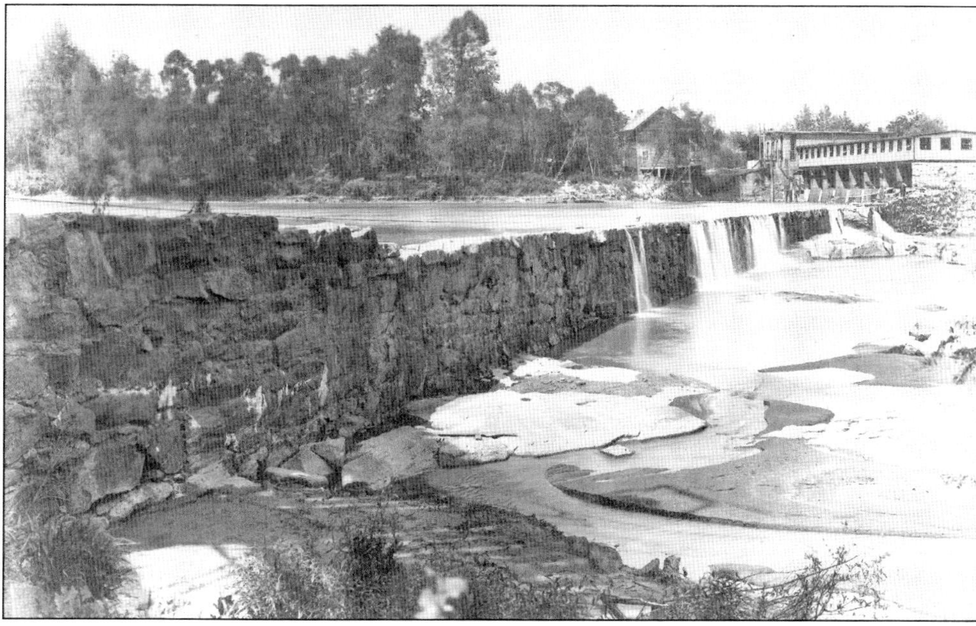

Idol's Dam and Power Plant is on the Yadkin River just south of Clemmons. Henry Fries, of Salem, who founded the Fries Manufacturing and Power Company in the 1890s, built the hydroelectric generating station plant in 1898 at the site of the old Idol's Ferry on the Yadkin River. The dam operated for many years and eventually came under the ownership of the Duke Power Company before closing in 1996. The dam is significant and important in local history, as it was the first hydroelectric generating station of its size in North Carolina to use the long-distance transmission of power. It provided power over a distance of 13 miles to various textile mills and other industries that ultimately assisted Winston-Salem in developing into a major industrial and manufacturing center in North Carolina. The plant also powered Winston-Salem's trolleys. Thomas Edison was a financial backer. (Above, courtesy Moravian Archives, Winston-Salem, NC; below, courtesy Forsyth County Public Library.)

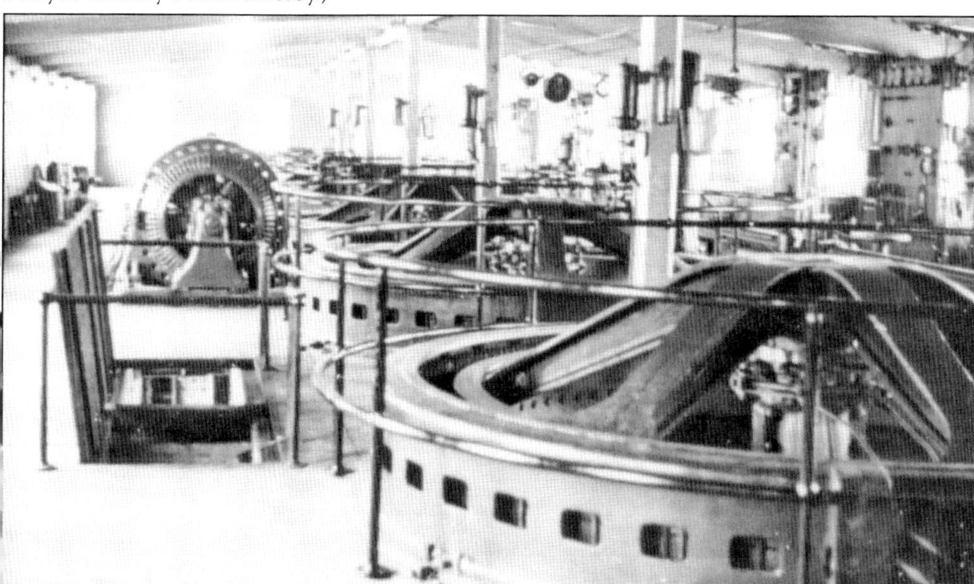

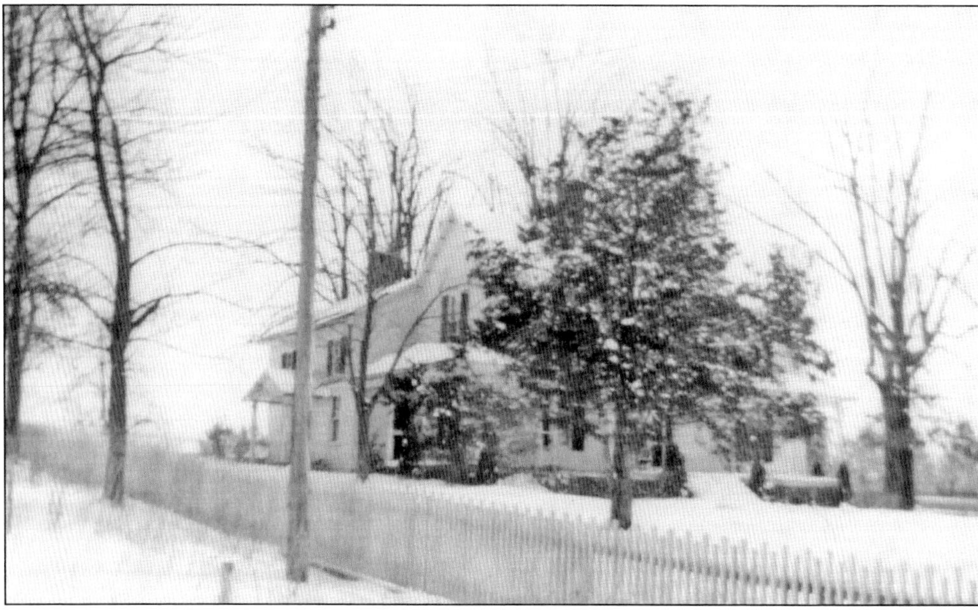

The J.F. Brower home was built in 1906 on Middlebrook Drive, across the street from the Clemmons Civic Club. Brower was a teacher and principal at the Clemmons School. The home still stands today. (Courtesy Pam Corum, Snyder Photography.)

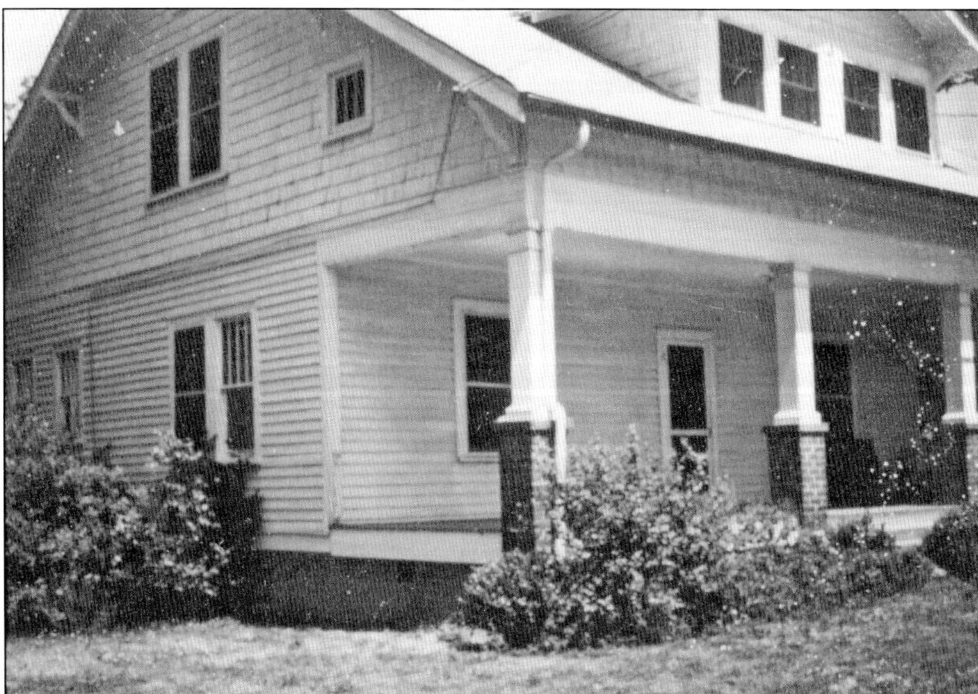

The Carlos Cooper house originally stood along Highway 158 where the Clemmons United Methodist Church parking lot is today. It was purchased from Cooper's widow in 1966 and became the church parsonage. In 1978, the house was razed to make room for the current church building and expansion. (Courtesy Clemmons United Methodist Church.)

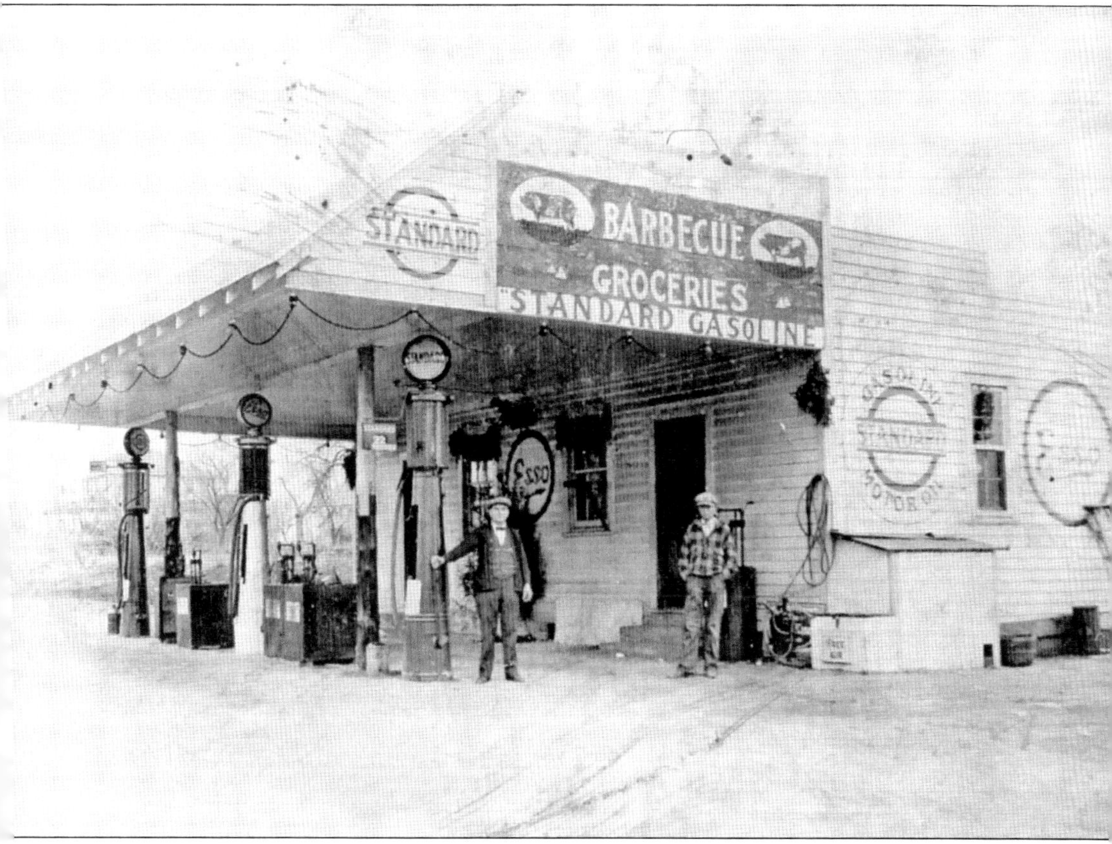

Jack White and Henly Ogburn operated this gas station and convenience store on Highway 158, where Littlebrook Drive is today. The store was on the right side of the road heading east toward Winston-Salem. This photograph is from 1929. The house on the left behind the store belonged to J. Dodd Linker Sr. The store has since been demolished, but the house remains occupied by the Linker family. (Courtesy Sammy Smith Conrad.)

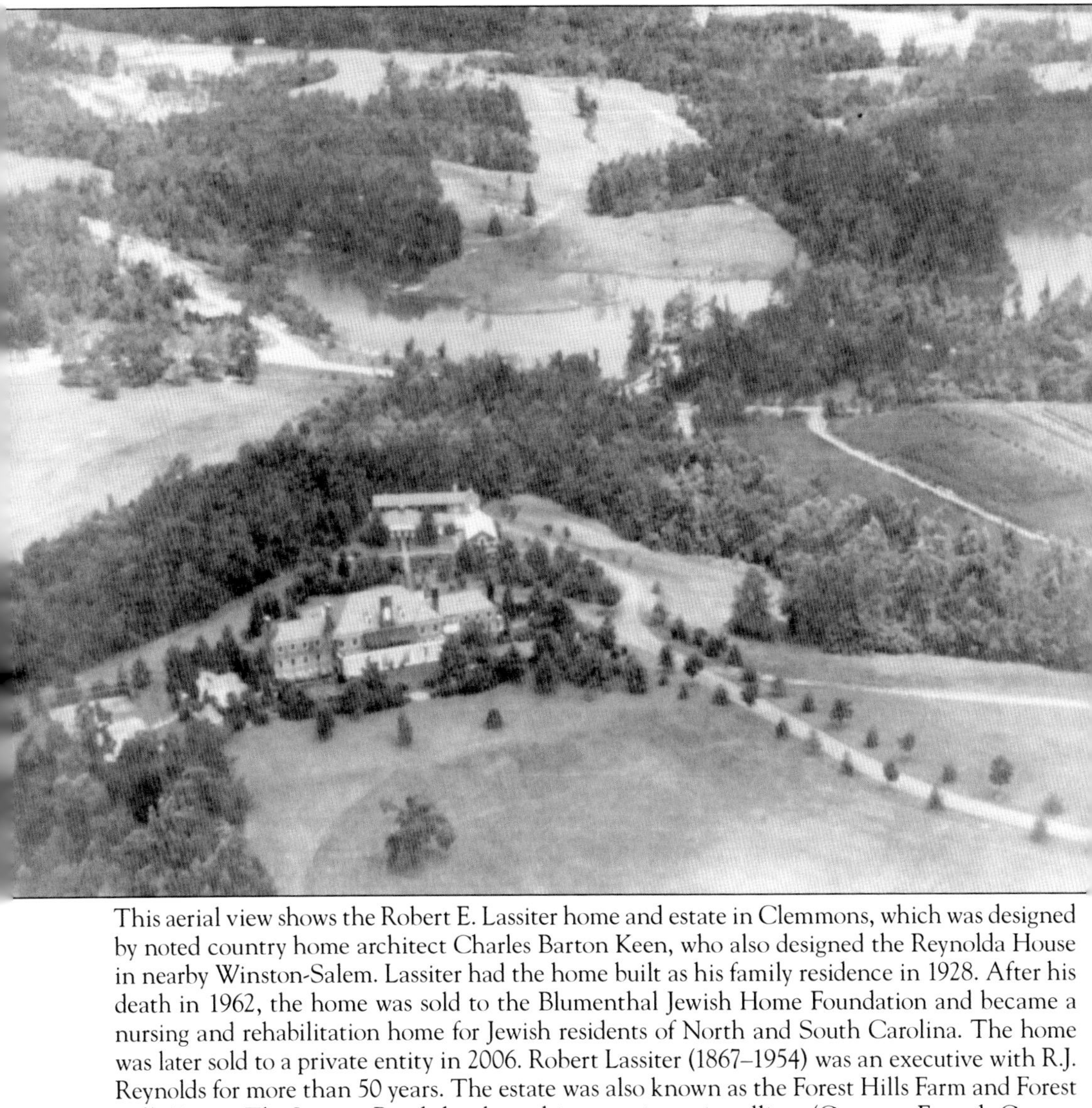

This aerial view shows the Robert E. Lassiter home and estate in Clemmons, which was designed by noted country home architect Charles Barton Keen, who also designed the Reynolda House in nearby Winston-Salem. Lassiter had the home built as his family residence in 1928. After his death in 1962, the home was sold to the Blumenthal Jewish Home Foundation and became a nursing and rehabilitation home for Jewish residents of North and South Carolina. The home was later sold to a private entity in 2006. Robert Lassiter (1867–1954) was an executive with R.J. Reynolds for more than 50 years. The estate was also known as the Forest Hills Farm and Forest Hills Estate. The Lasater Road that bears his name is a misspelling. (Courtesy Forsyth County Public Library.)

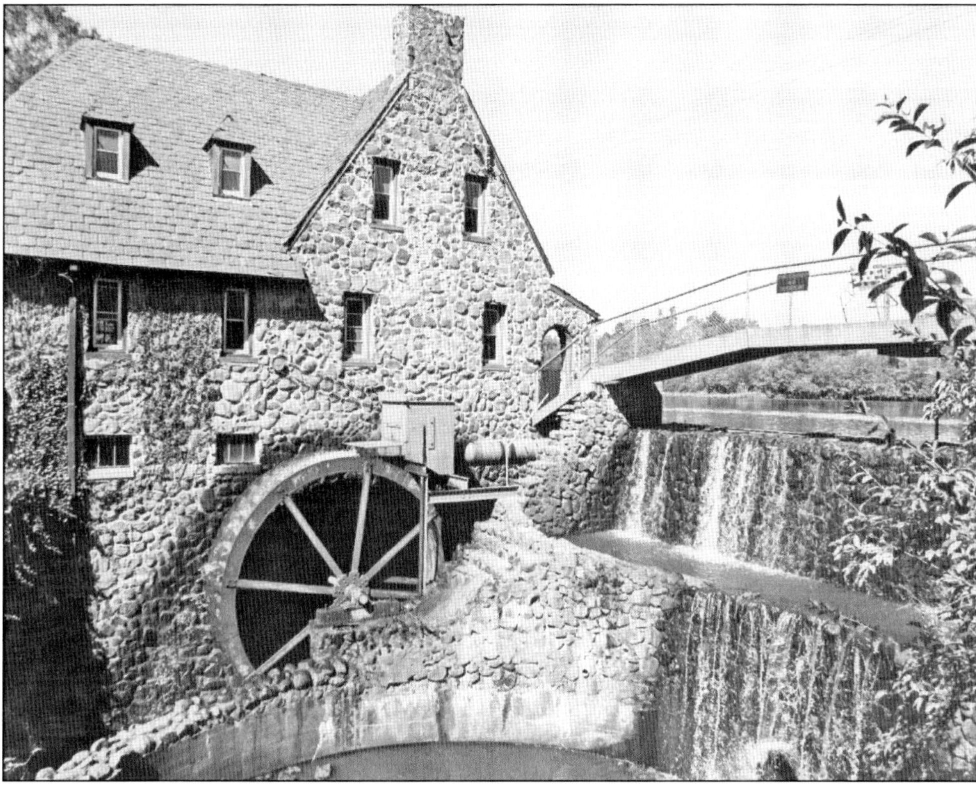

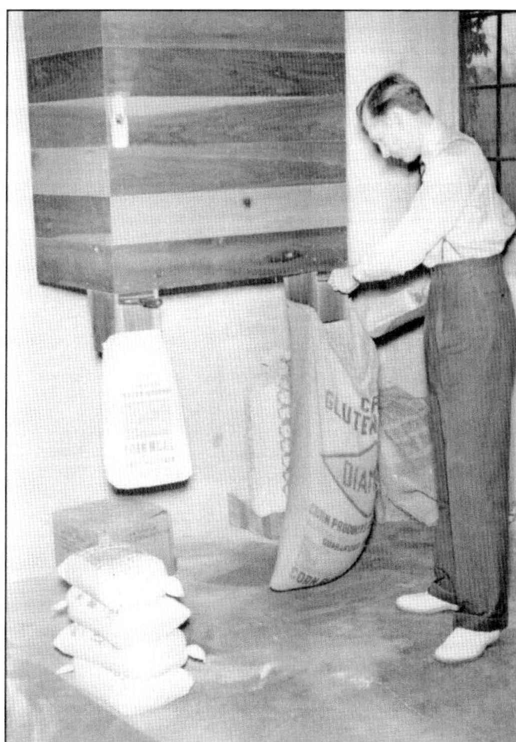

Lassiter Mill, also known as the Forest Hills Mill, was built in 1928 and operated as a grain grinding mill, providing flour to local residents. In the 1950s, it served as a summer home for various stock actors who performed at the Barn Theatre at Tanglewood Park. It is now a private residence whose owners offer a resident art program that supports aspiring artists from all over the world. (Above, courtesy David H. Hauser; right, courtesy Forsyth County Public Library.)

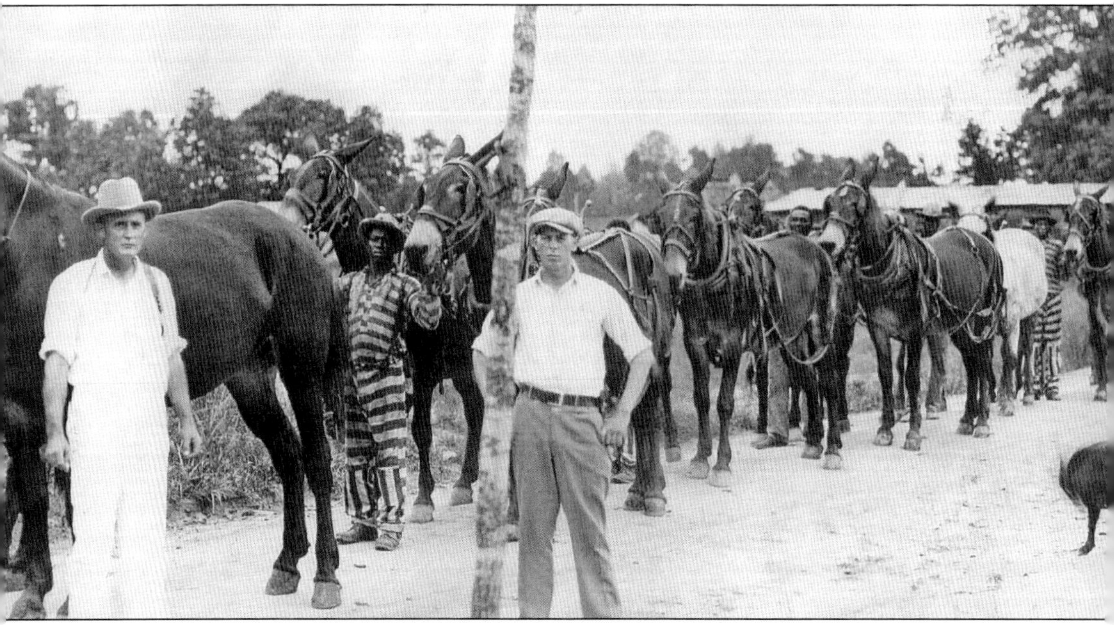

The Forsyth County road crew used prison labor to drag and level roads in the county before the state consolidated all county highway departments into the North Carolina Department of Transportation during the Great Depression. This photograph from about 1930 shows Capt. Henry Burke (left) and Clint Holder (right) leading the crew down Lewisville-Clemmons Road at the Peace Haven Road intersection, where the First Citizens Bank is currently located. (Courtesy Ed Brewer.)

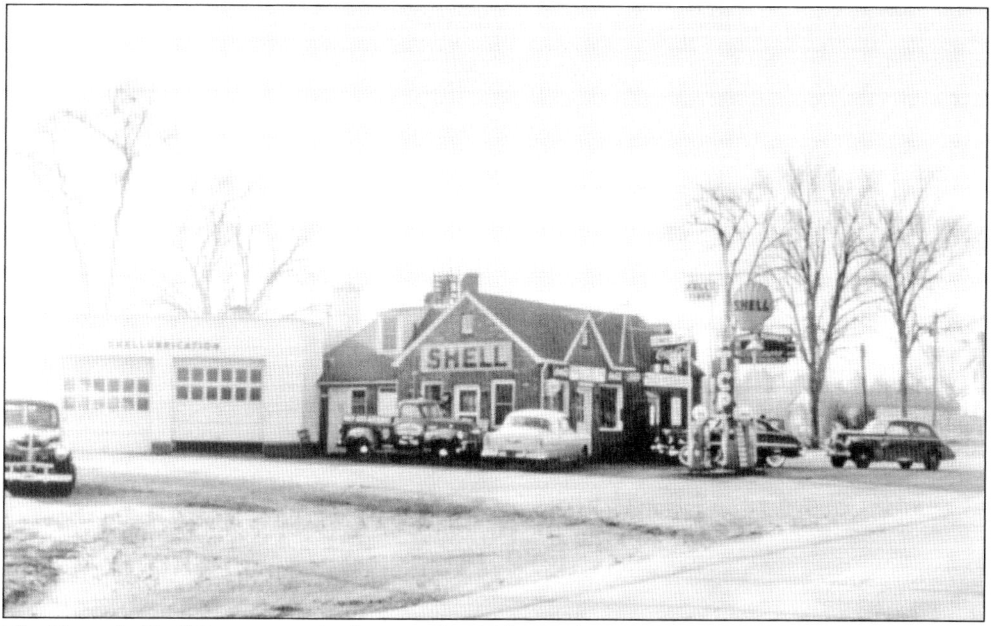

The Triangle Shell Station was built around 1935 for Carl Cooper Cook to operate. Cook, the son of Frank Cook, died in 1939. The building, known as the Triangle Shopping Center, was at the intersection of Highway 158 and Hampton Road. Brothers W.A. Hunter Jr. and John F. Hunter took over operation of the station in October 1945. This became the first location of Hunter Brothers Oil Company. The first fire truck in Clemmons was housed in the Shell station service bay at night until the Clemmons Fire Station was built next to what is now Clemmons Pallet and Skid Works. Clemmons Pharmacy was in the front, and Dr. Frank Nifong's office and the Clemmons post office were in the rear of the triangle. (Courtesy Forsyth County Public Library.)

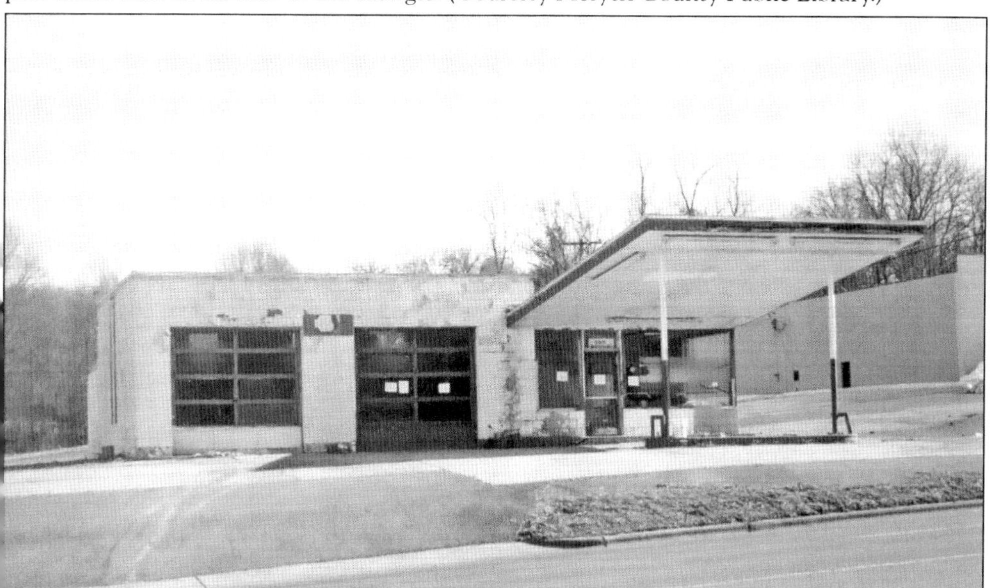

The Clemmons Union 76 gas station and garage was last operated by Arnold Rose. The business closed and the building was torn down in 2011. It was at the intersection of Lewisville-Clemmons Road and Stoney Drive. (Courtesy Mike Parks.)

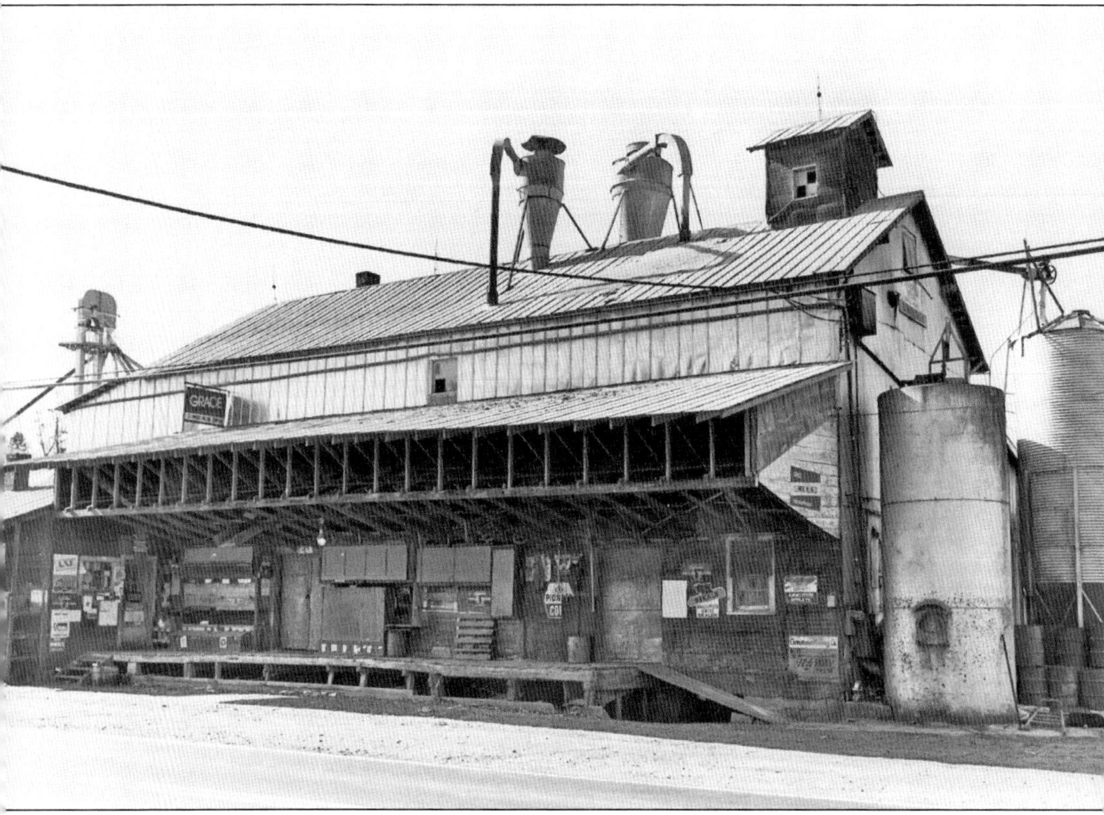

Clemmons Mill on Hampton Road has served residents and farmers in Clemmons since 1920. Also called the Brewer Mill, for the Brewer family who ran it for more 70 years, it has long been a gathering place for farmers to conduct business and purchase farming necessities. In 1944, a mixing room and basement were hand-dug by German prisoners of war. It is Clemmons's oldest continuously operating business. (Courtesy Cookie Snyder Photography.)

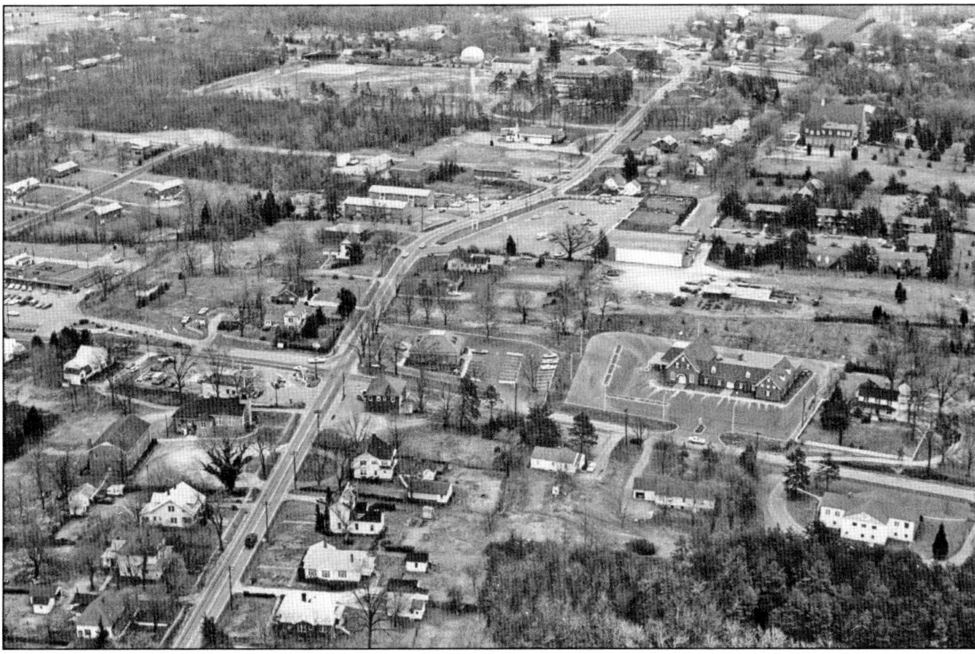

This aerial view of Clemmons was taken about 1970 from the southwest corner of the Highway 158 and Lewisville-Clemmons Road intersection, looking east toward Winston-Salem. Clemmons Moravian Church is in the top right corner and the United Methodist Church building (1920–1979) is in the northwest corner. (Courtesy Cookie Snyder Photography.)

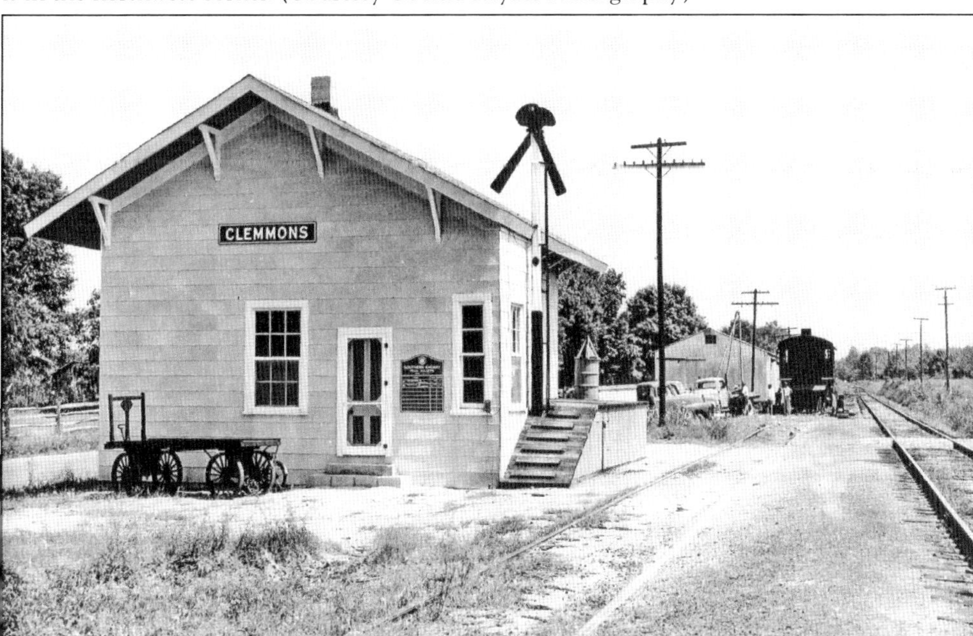

The Clemmons train depot, seen here, stood at the intersection of Middlebrook Drive and Idol's Road before it was demolished about 1960. In this 1954 photograph, engine 542 of the Southern Railway is in the background. The engine was on its way to the new Tanglewood Park to be installed as an attraction for the park guests. (Courtesy Forsyth County Public Library.)

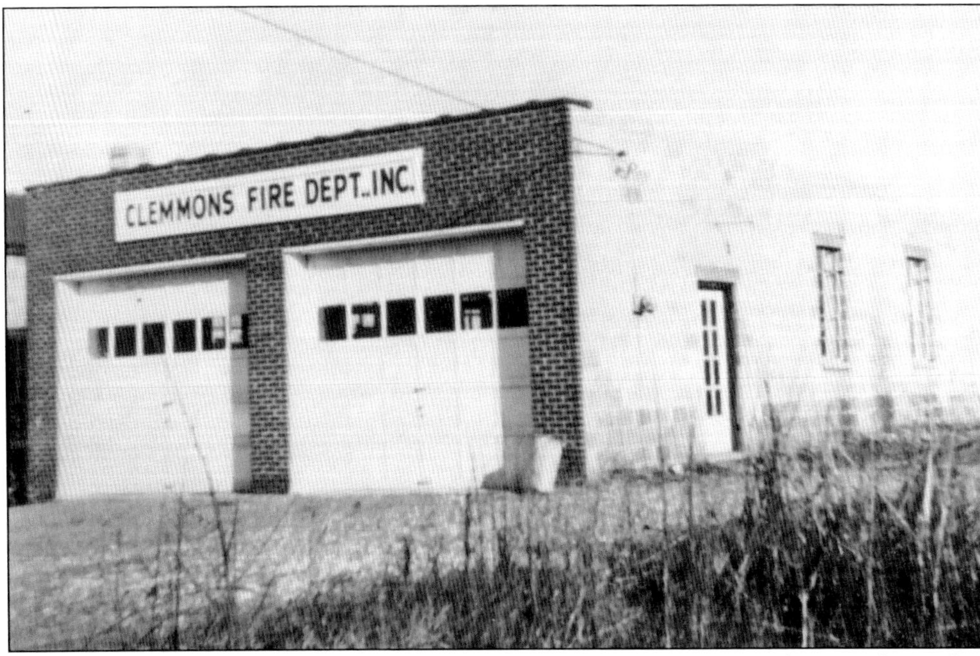

The Clemmons Fire Department was organized as a volunteer organization by a North Carolina charter in 1952. Originally located on Clemmons Road just east of the Clemmons First Baptist Church, it is now on James Street. The first building is above, and the department's first fire truck is below. Originally under the jurisdiction of chief W.A. Hunter Jr., the department had four divisions, with each including a driver and an alternate for the truck, a lieutenant, "someone qualified to render first aid," and at least two traffic men. In its first year, the assets of the fire department were $17,572, a figure that included the land, the building, the truck, equipment, and insurance and legal fees. According to record, the first fire call handled by the newly formed department was a fire that destroyed a barn valued at $100 at the time. (Both, courtesy Clemmons Fire Department.)

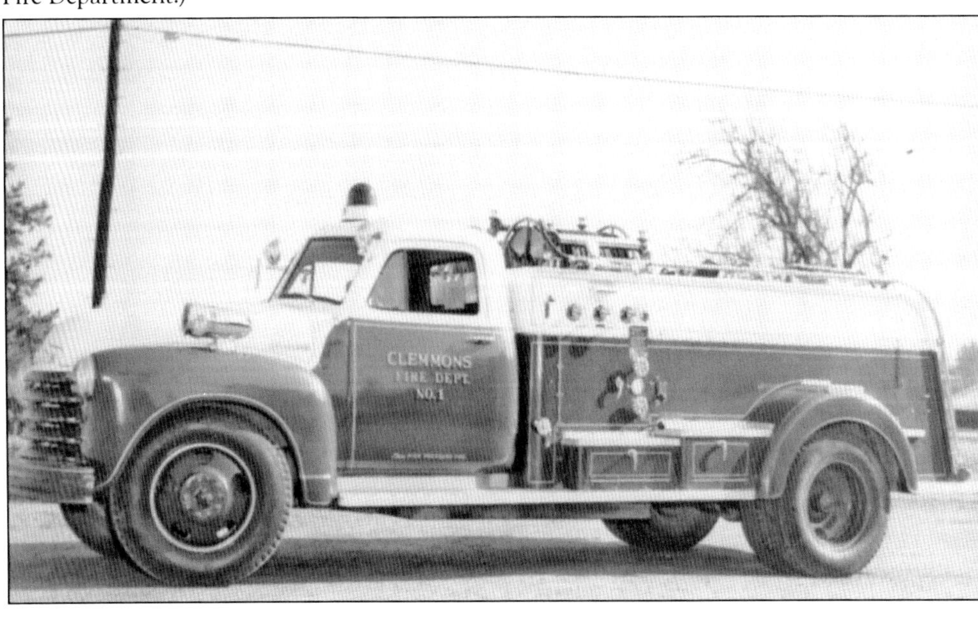

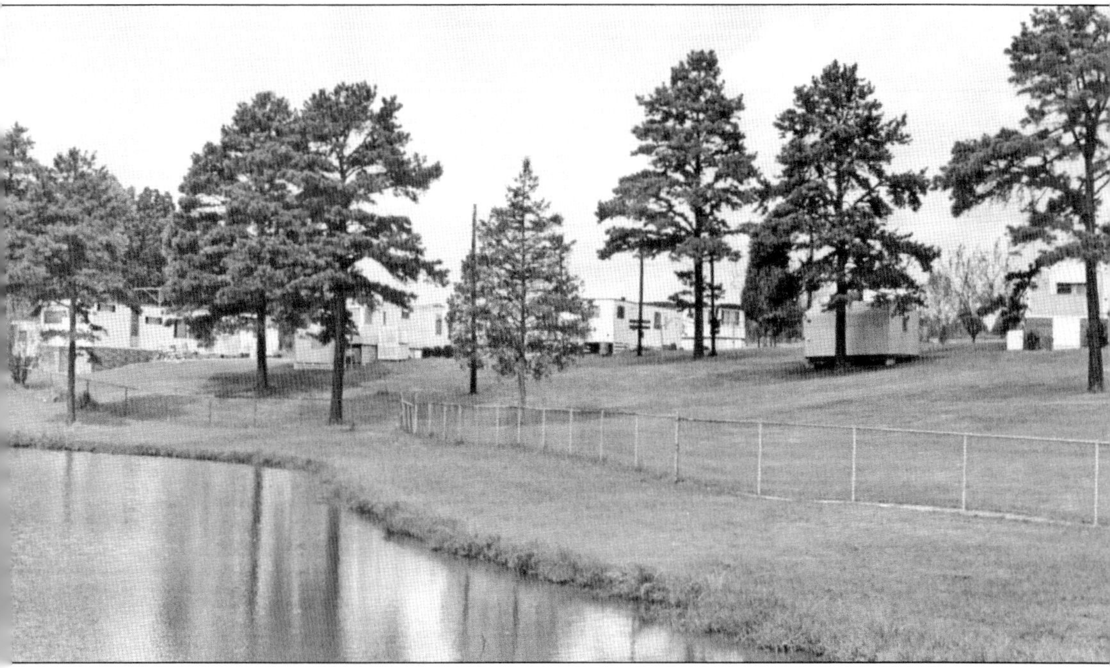

The Hauser mobile home park and pond were originally situated on what is now the Westwood Village shopping center on Lewisville-Clemmons Road. The area was rezoned for commercial use in the late 1970s. (Courtesy David H. Hauser.)

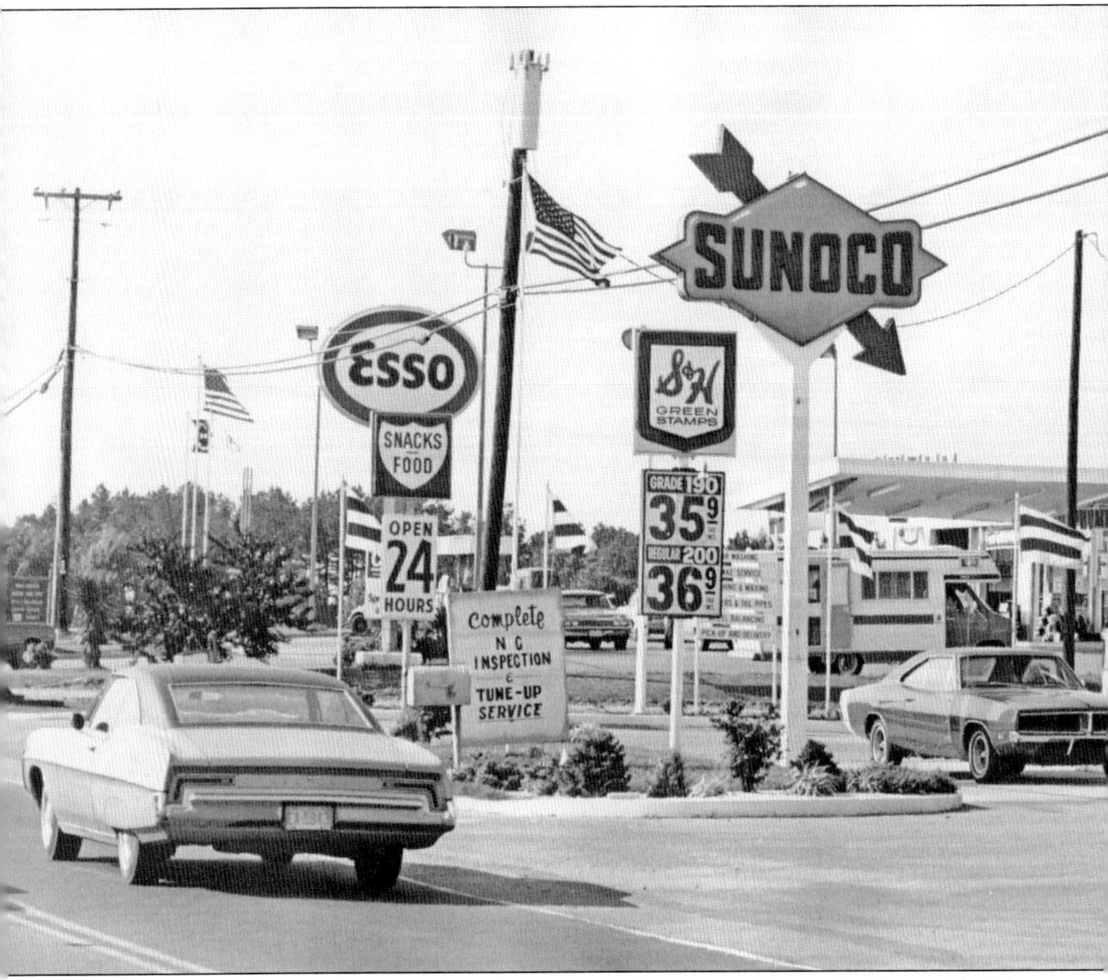

The Esso and Sunoco gas stations of Clemmons seen here originally stood on Lewisville-Clemmons Road just before the on ramp to Interstate 40 East during the 1970s. Literally a sign of the times, gas was only 35¢ a gallon. (Courtesy David H. Hauser.)

Four

SCHOOL DAYS

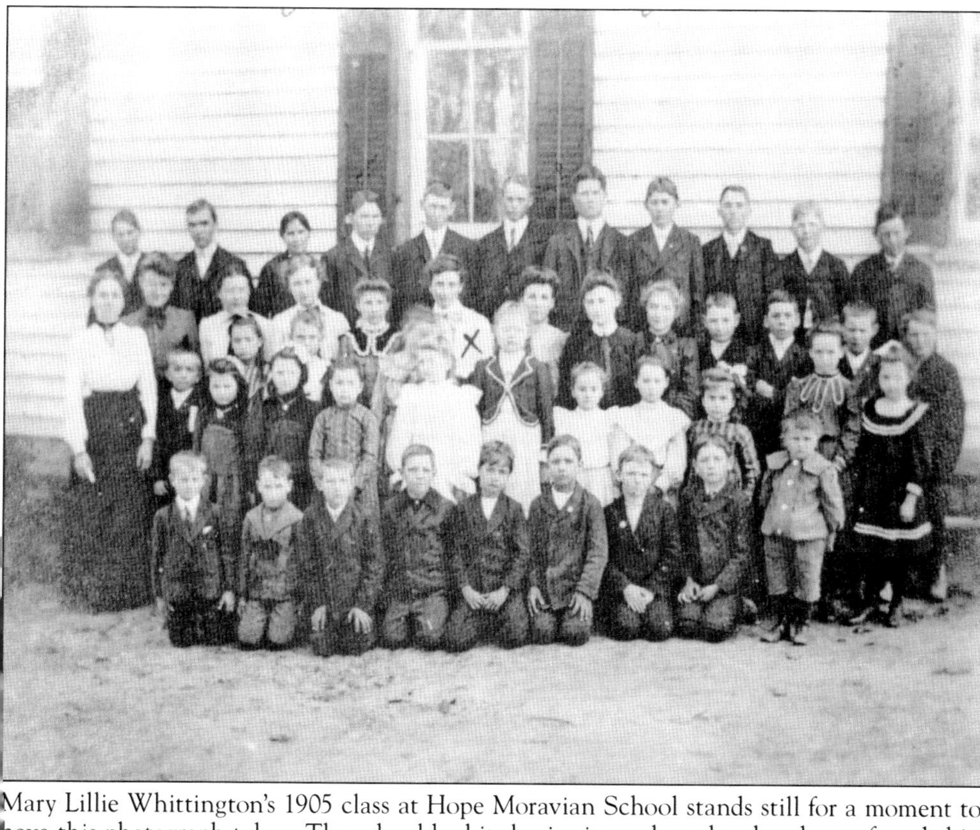

Mary Lillie Whittington's 1905 class at Hope Moravian School stands still for a moment to have this photograph taken. The school had its beginnings when the church was founded in 1775. This photograph shows the front the 1896 building, on Hope Church Road. (Courtesy Jerry Johnson.)

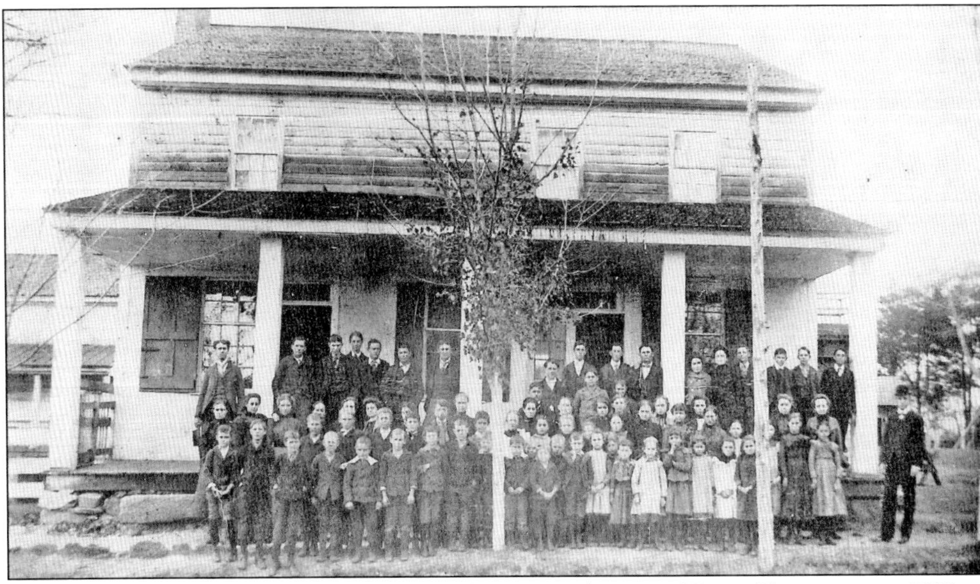

Clemmons Academy was built by Benton Clemmons, the son of Peter Clemmons, in 1833 on Highway 158, near the front corner of his family's home place. He was the largest financial supporter of the school and was also in charge of hiring the various headmasters. The academy was eventually closed to make way for the new Clemmons Moravian School. The school used the upper level of this building for the 1900–1901 school year while construction was completed on the new building. Rev. J. Kenneth Pfohl was its first principal. A store was also operated on the main level of the building by Henry E. Fries and later by the Douthit family. The foundation stones are all that remain today and can be seen along the edge of the road. In the photograph below, students and teachers gather on the front porch of the Peter Clemmons home for the first commencement celebration in 1901. Seated in the first row from left to right are Rev. James E. Hall, Dr. Edward Rondthaller, John W. Fries, Bessie Whittington, Nanny Bessent, and Rev. J. Kenneth Pfhol. (Above, courtesy Forsyth County Public Library; below, courtesy Hill Hunter.)

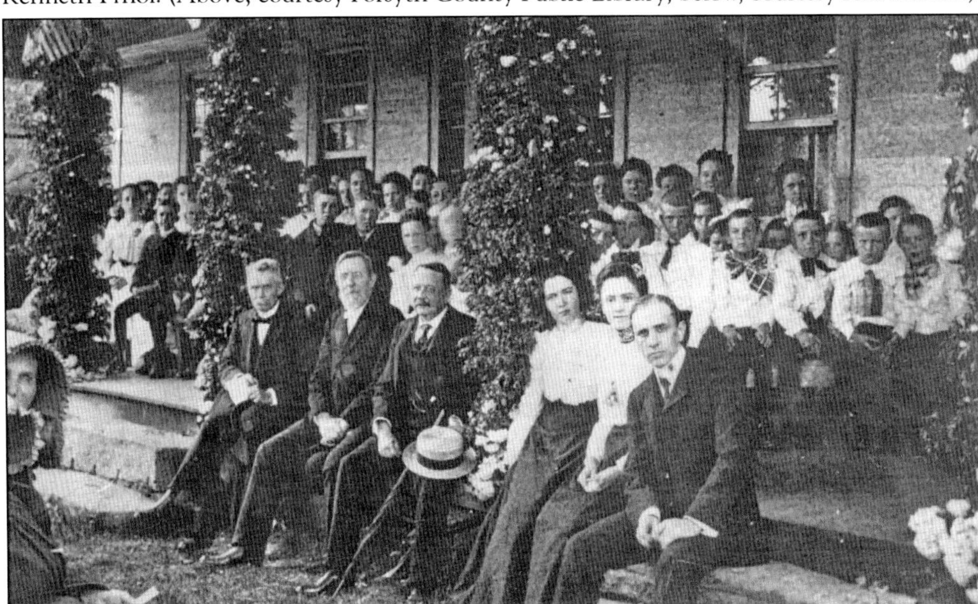

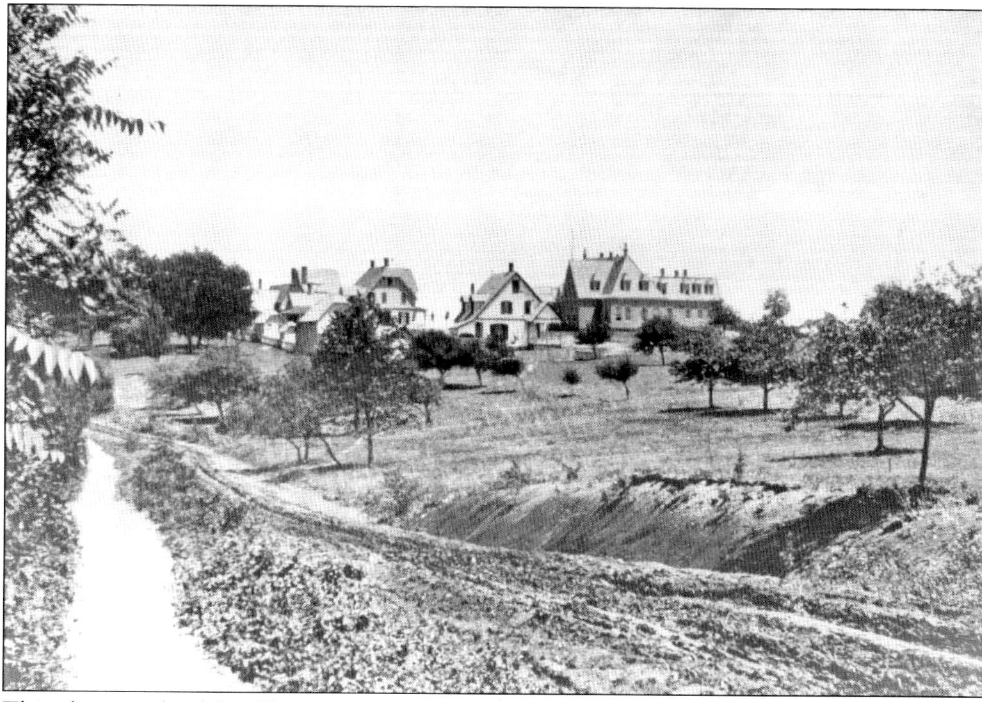

This photograph of the Clemmons Moravian Church and School was taken around 1910. The dirt road in the foreground is now Highway 158. (Courtesy Forsyth County Public Library.)

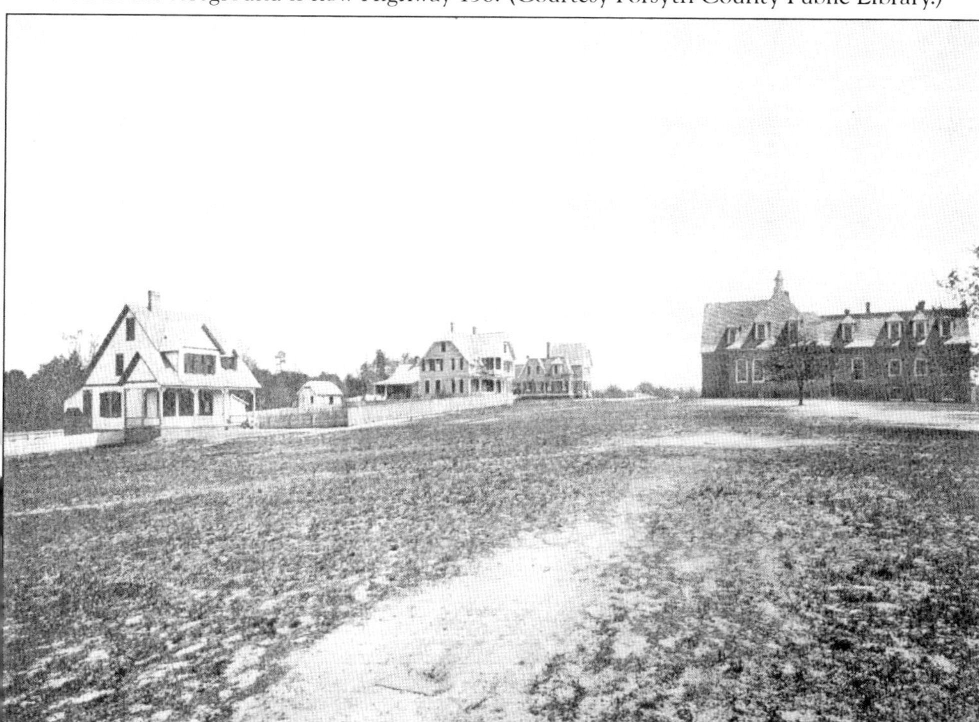

This is an early view from the southwest of the Clemmons Moravian Church and School (right) and the grounds. (Courtesy Forsyth County Public Library.)

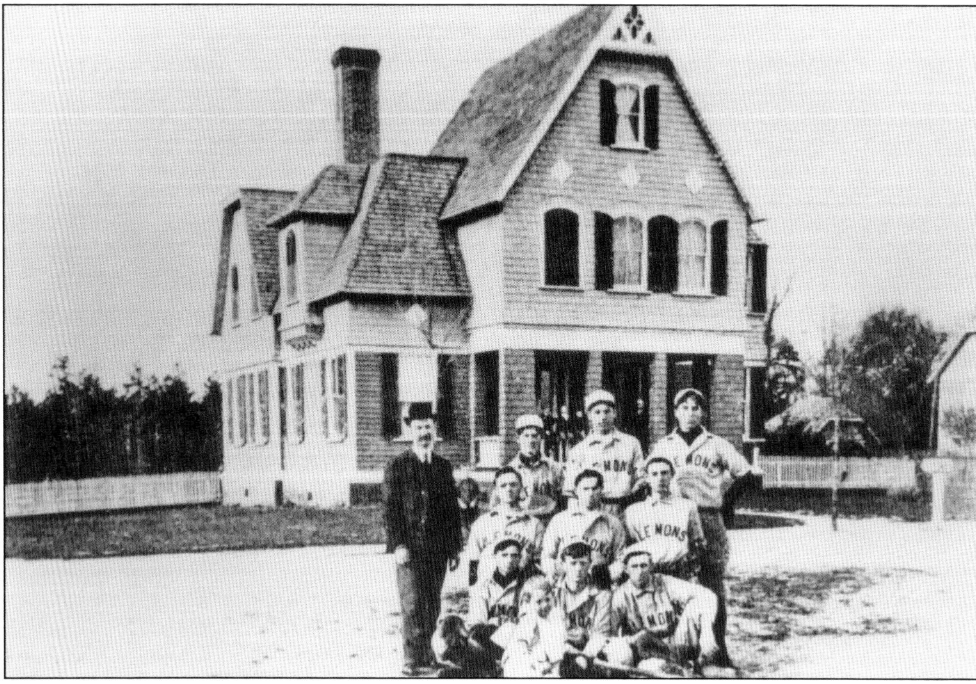

The Clemmons baseball team poses in front of the home of the Clemmons Moravian School's principal around 1905. The home later became the parsonage at Clemmons Moravian Church and is now the church office. (Courtesy Pam Corum, Snyder Photography.)

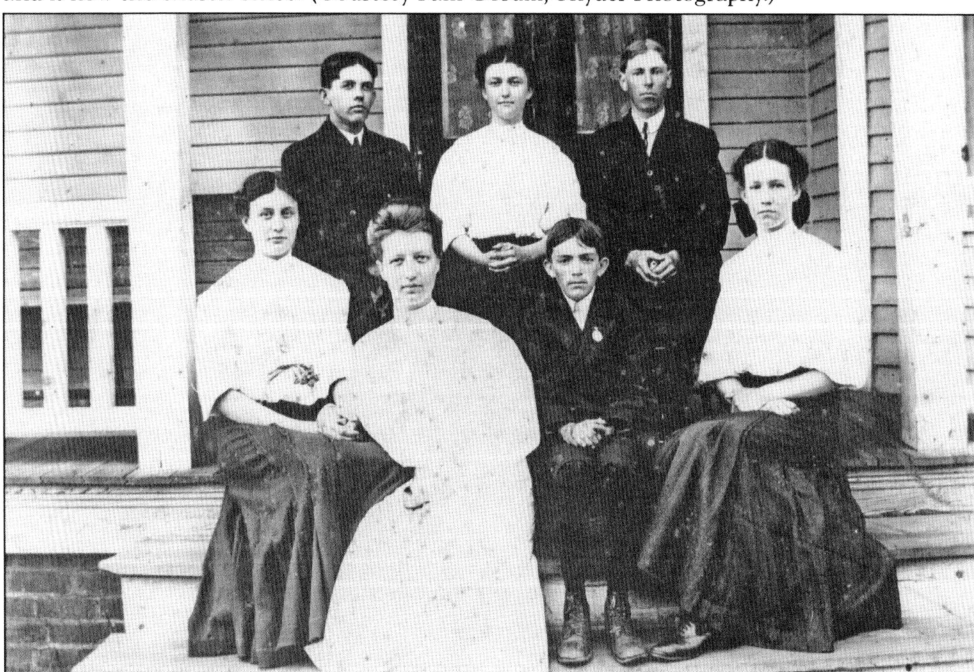

The Clemmons School class of 1906 poses on the steps of the ladies dormitory. Bertie Sprinkle Cook (1888–1954) is in the front row in the white dress and her sister, Fannie Sprinkle Ogburn (1889–1985), is on the far right. (Courtesy Cookie Snyder Photography.)

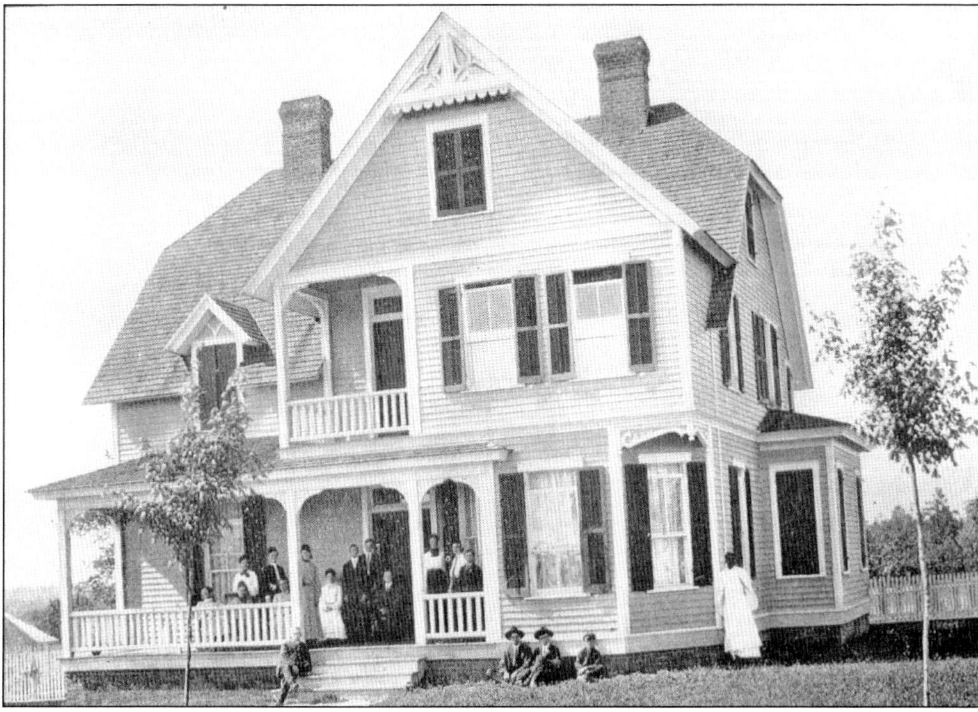

The ladies dormitory of the Clemmons Moravian School is seen here in the early 1900s. (Courtesy Forsyth County Public Library.)

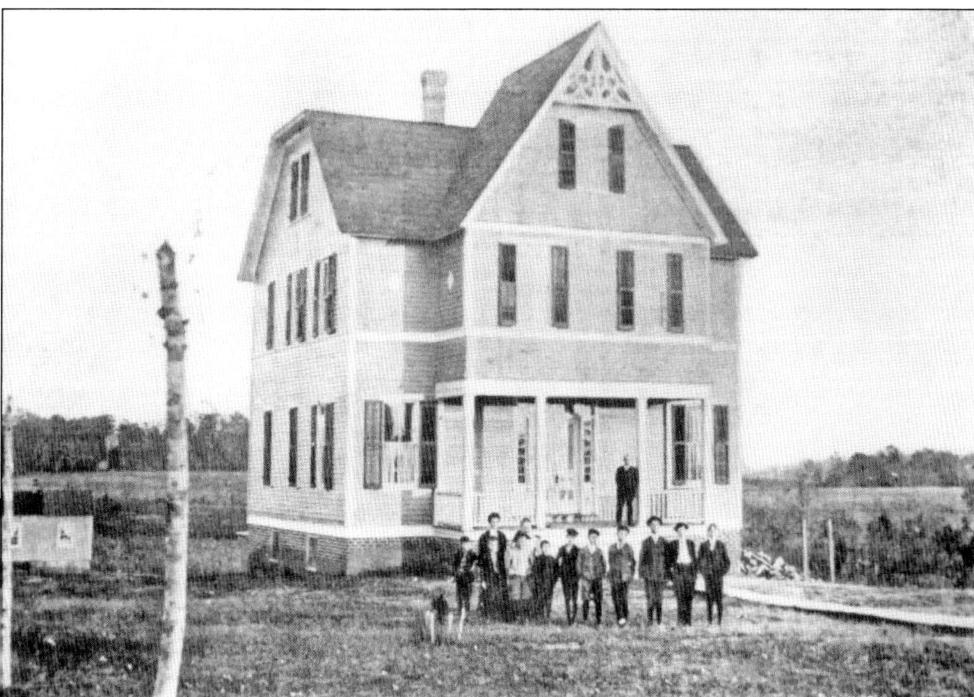

This view shows the boys dormitory at Clemmons Moravian School in the early 1900s. This building no longer stands. (Courtesy Pam Corum, Snyder Photography.)

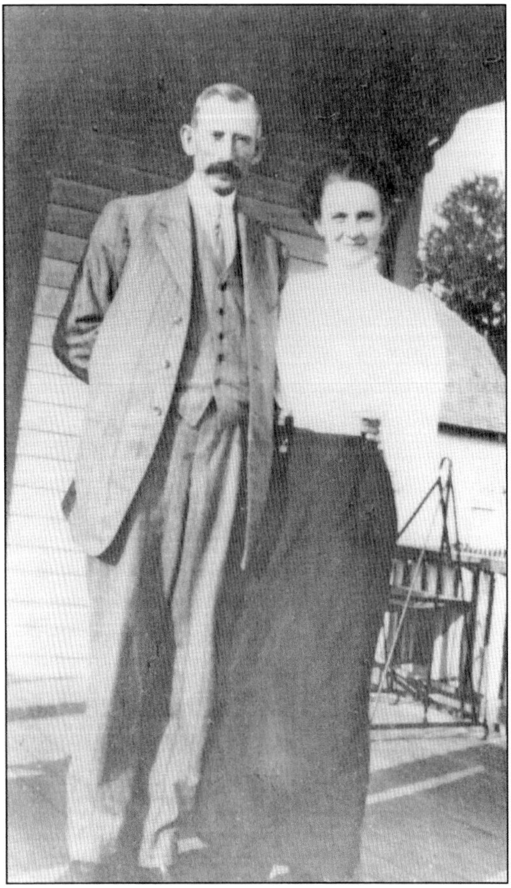

James Fletcher "J.F." Brower and his wife, Annie Brower, are seen here around 1920 in front of their home. Mr. Brower (1856–1937) was the first principal of Clemmons School and was highly regarded by his colleagues and students. He was educated at Trinity College (now Duke University), where he earned both bachelor's and master's degrees. He was an educator for more than 50 years. Mrs. Brower was the Clemmons School librarian. (Courtesy Cookie Snyder Photography.)

A Forsyth County Consolidated School bus stands ready to go in the 1924 photograph below. This bus and others like it took the children of Clemmons to and from school. (Courtesy Neal Harper.)

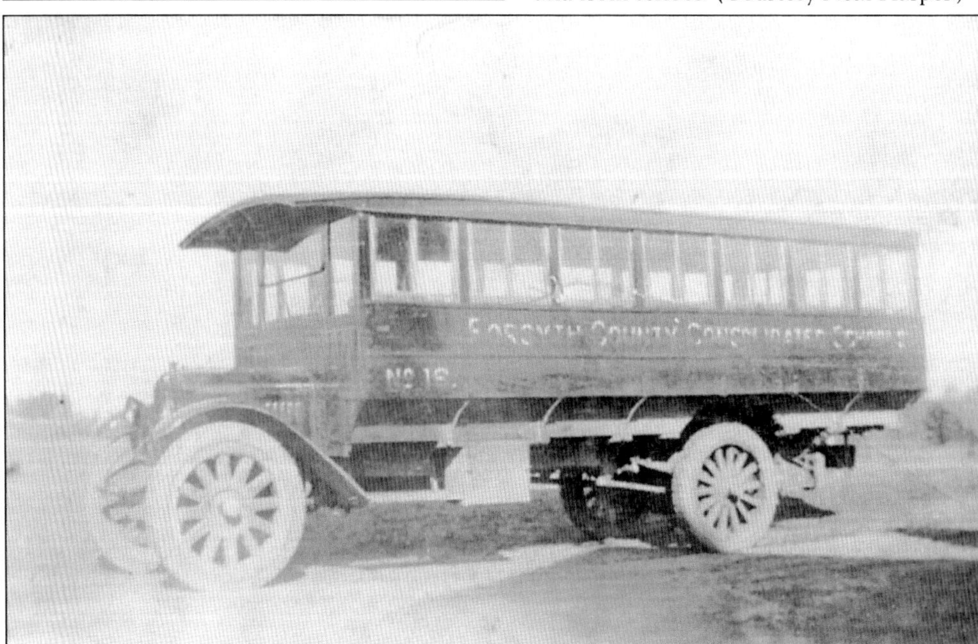

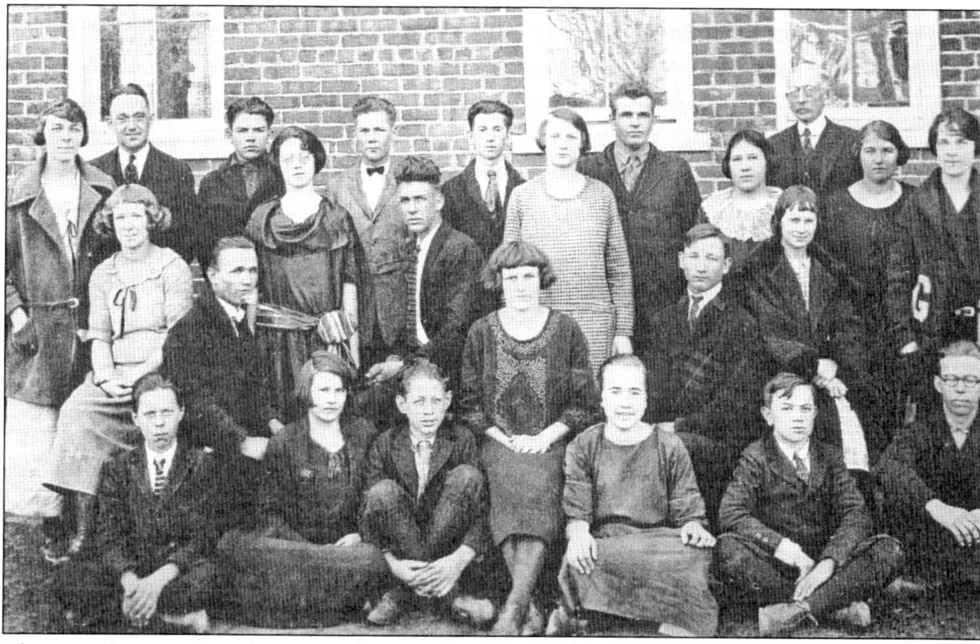

These students and teachers, seen here in the fall of 1925, were part of the first class at the new Clemmons School. Professor J.F. Brower was the first principal of the school and is seen in the back row on the far right. At the far right of the second row, wearing her Guilford College sweater, is first-year teacher Josephine (Crews) Mock, who taught English and French at the school. (Courtesy Jane Crews Meekins.)

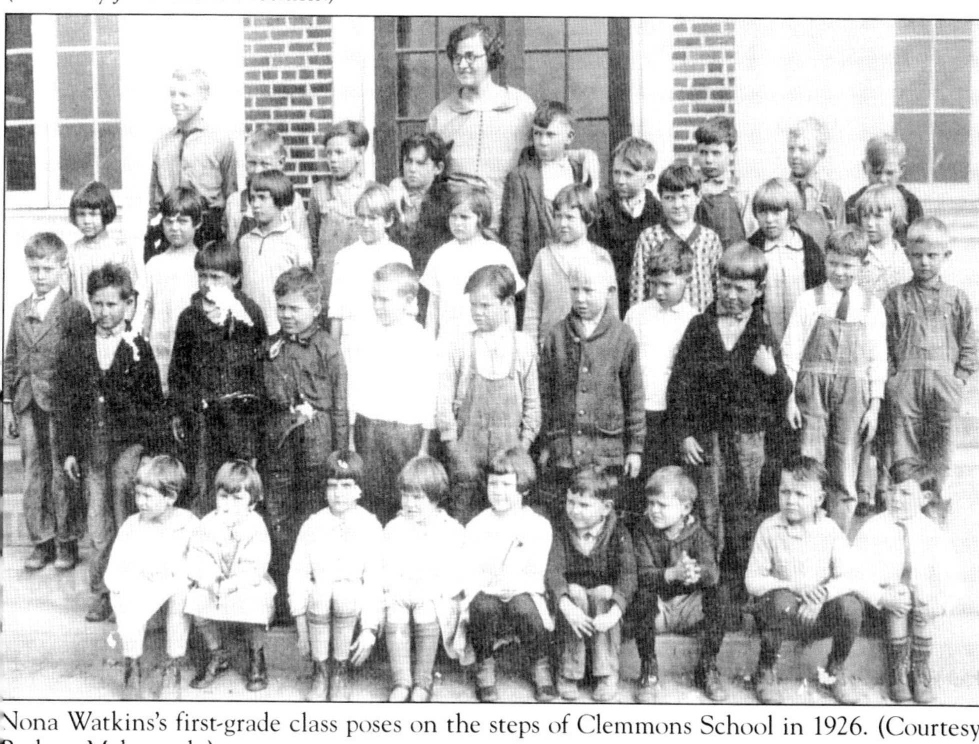

Nona Watkins's first-grade class poses on the steps of Clemmons School in 1926. (Courtesy Barbara Mahannah.)

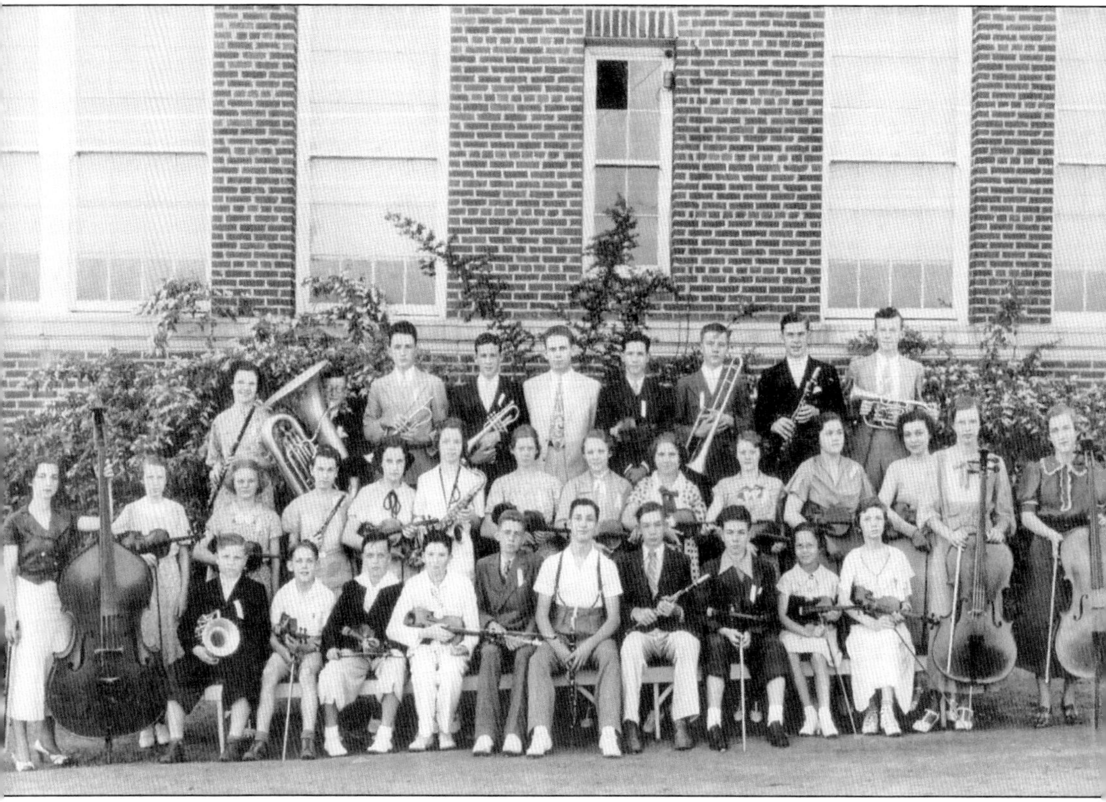

Forsyth County's high school orchestra won the North Carolina High School Class C State Championships every year from 1932 to 1937. More than half of the students were from Clemmons High School. The orchestra posed for this group photograph in 1936 outside the Clemmons School. (Courtesy Anna-Lena Cooper.)

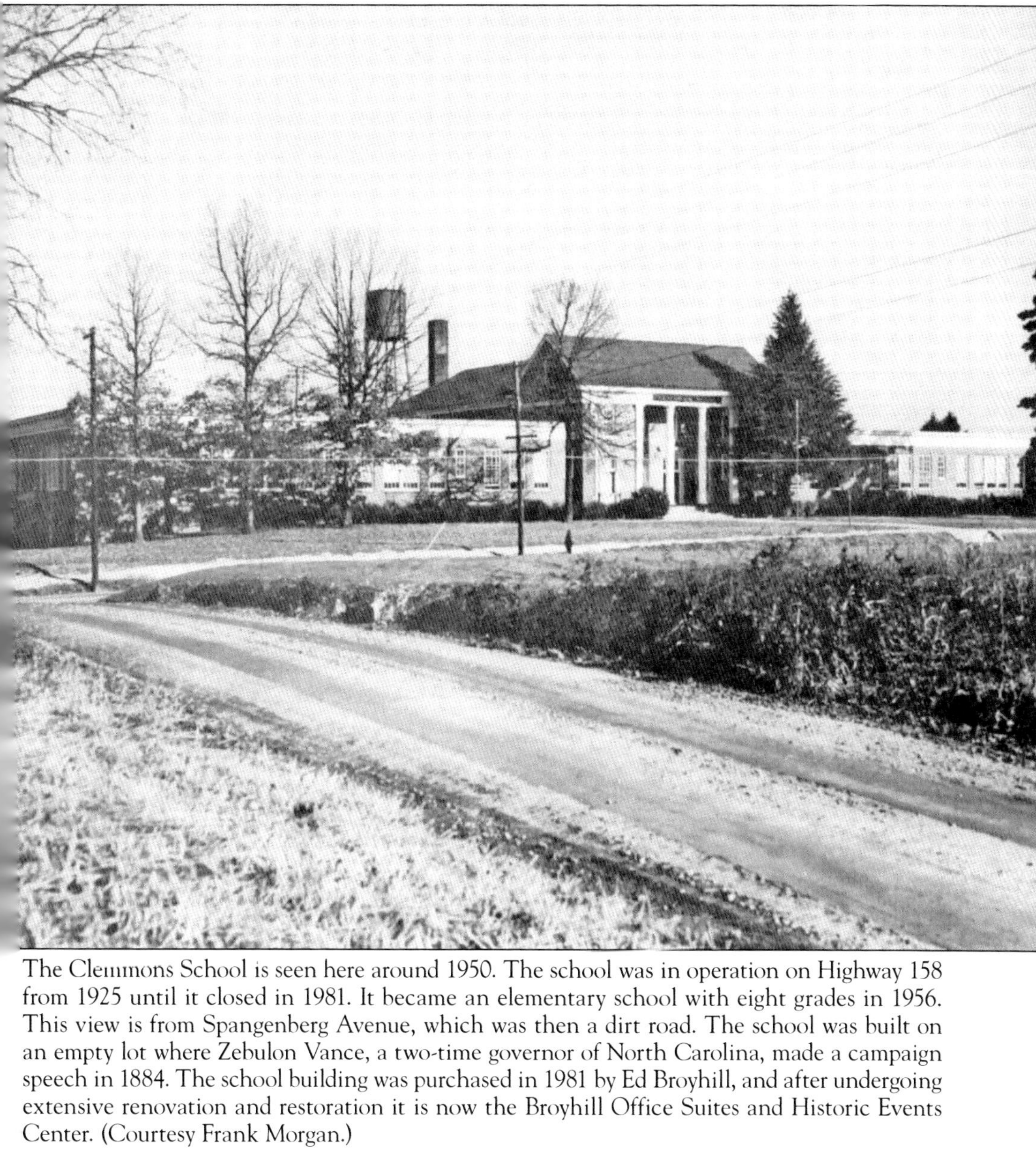

The Clemmons School is seen here around 1950. The school was in operation on Highway 158 from 1925 until it closed in 1981. It became an elementary school with eight grades in 1956. This view is from Spangenberg Avenue, which was then a dirt road. The school was built on an empty lot where Zebulon Vance, a two-time governor of North Carolina, made a campaign speech in 1884. The school building was purchased in 1981 by Ed Broyhill, and after undergoing extensive renovation and restoration it is now the Broyhill Office Suites and Historic Events Center. (Courtesy Frank Morgan.)

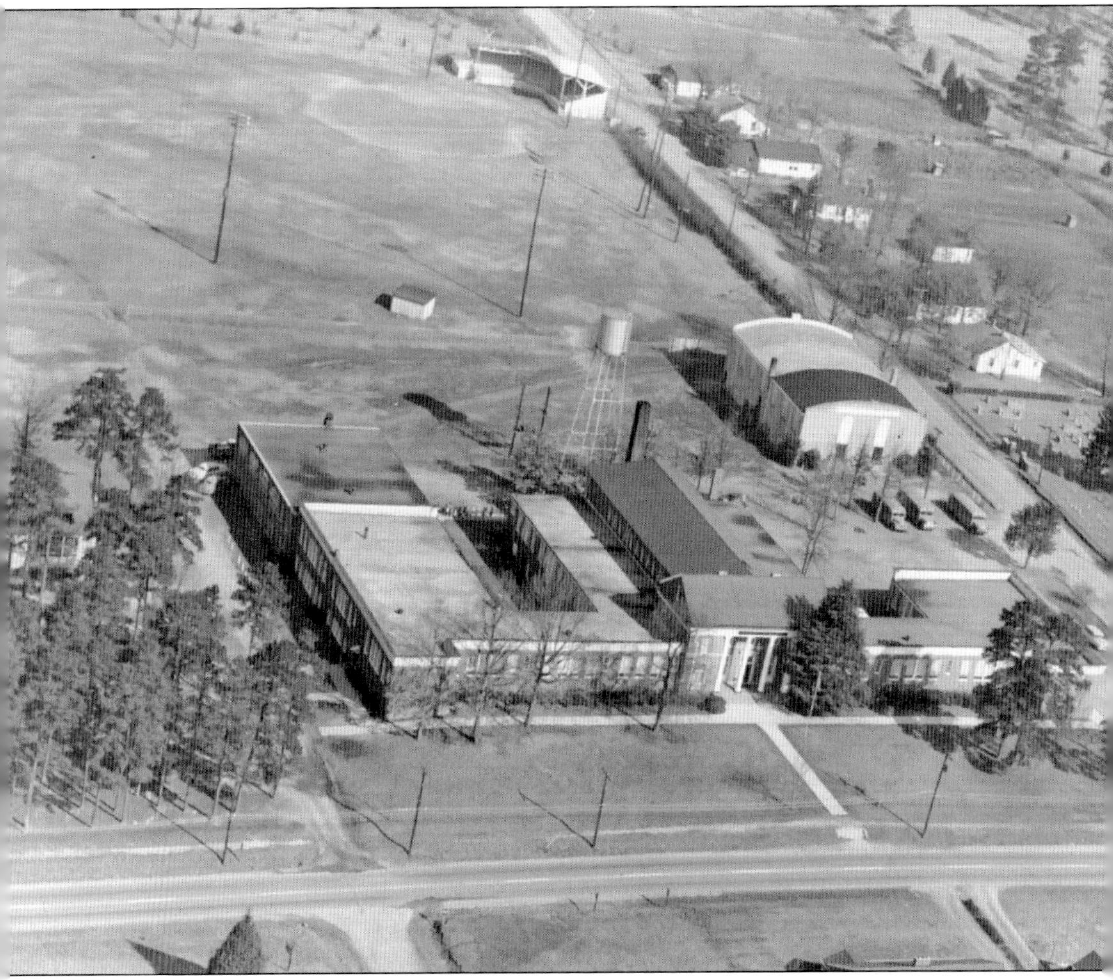

This aerial view of Clemmons School shows the gymnasium that was built in 1940 by the Works Progress Administration (WPA) with money raised by students and residents of the community. The football field, the baseball stadium with bleachers, outdoor lights, and a chain-link fence were ready for use in 1950. Dennis Brewer, of the class of 1929, headed up fundraising for the project, which cost $30,000. Half of the money was donated by William N. Reynolds, the owner of Tanglewood. Forsyth County gave $6,000 and Clemmons citizens raised $9,000. (Courtesy Clemmons Public Library.)

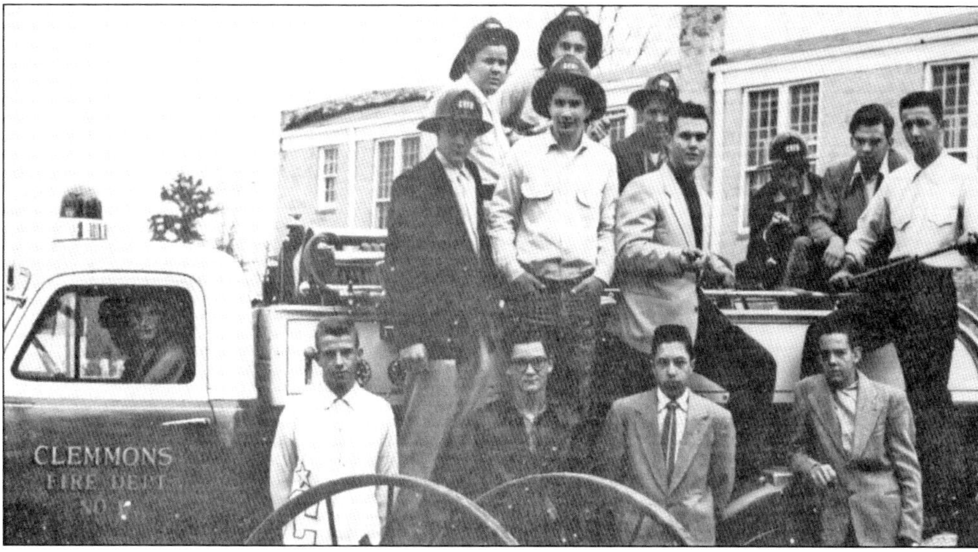

The Clemmons School fire squad poses on the back of the first Clemmons Fire Department truck in 1954. (Courtesy Frank Morgan.)

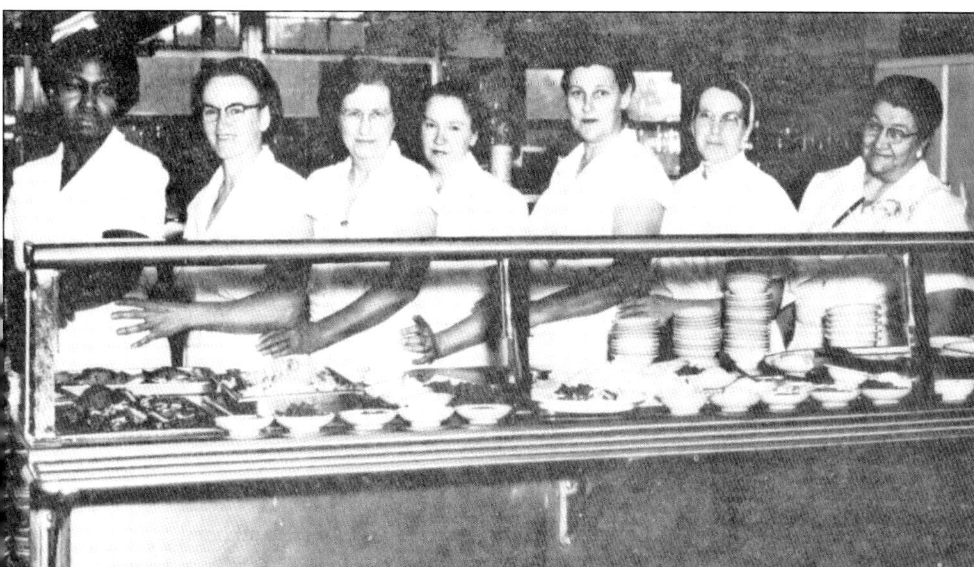
The Clemmons School cafeteria staff paused from serving tasty lunches for this photograph in 1953. From left to right are Mary Watson, Lucille Nelson, Vergie Stimpson, Lois Berrier, Juanita Holton, Rosa Beckner, and Alma "Ma" Hampton. (Courtesy Frank Morgan.)

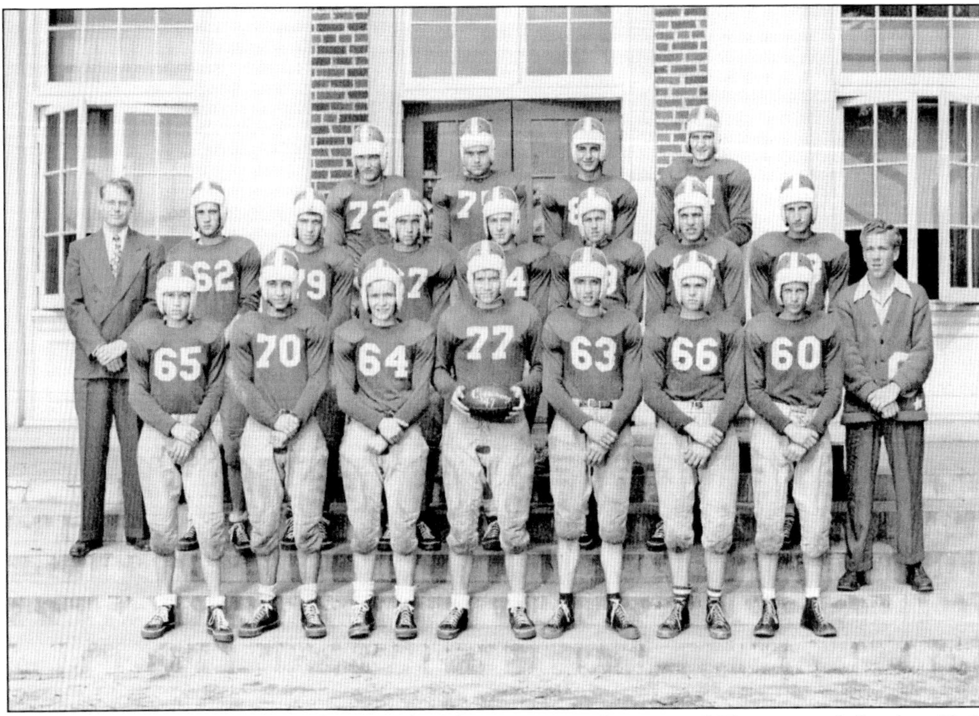

The Clemmons School football team, the Blues, pose on the steps of Clemmons School in 1947, in the era before facemasks. (Photograph by Copedge & Talton, courtesy Barbara Mahannah.)

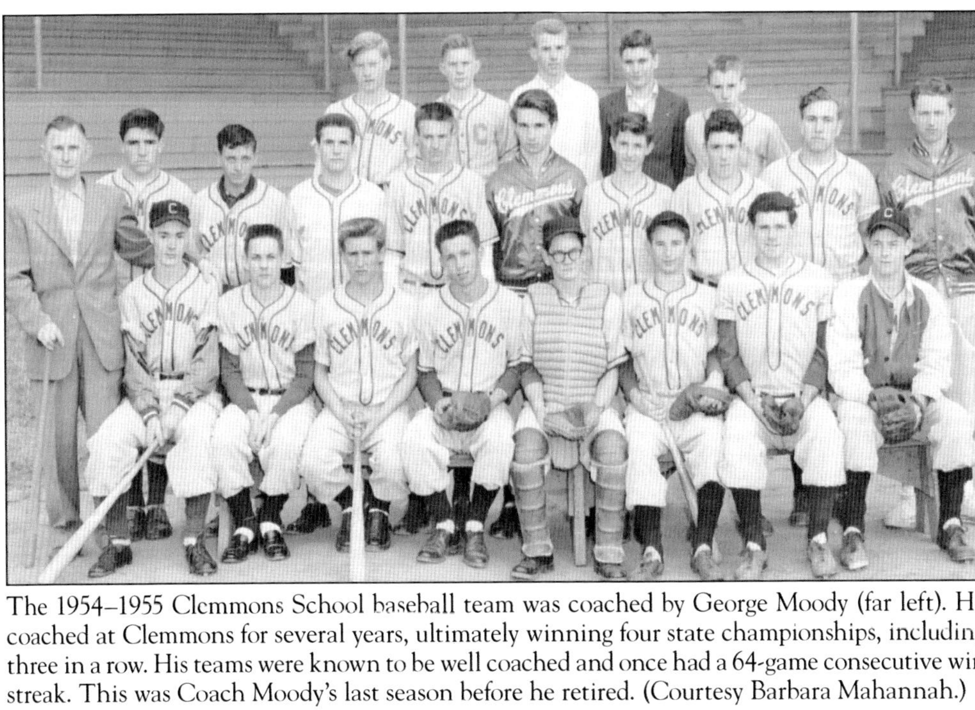

The 1954–1955 Clemmons School baseball team was coached by George Moody (far left). He coached at Clemmons for several years, ultimately winning four state championships, including three in a row. His teams were known to be well coached and once had a 64-game consecutive win streak. This was Coach Moody's last season before he retired. (Courtesy Barbara Mahannah.)

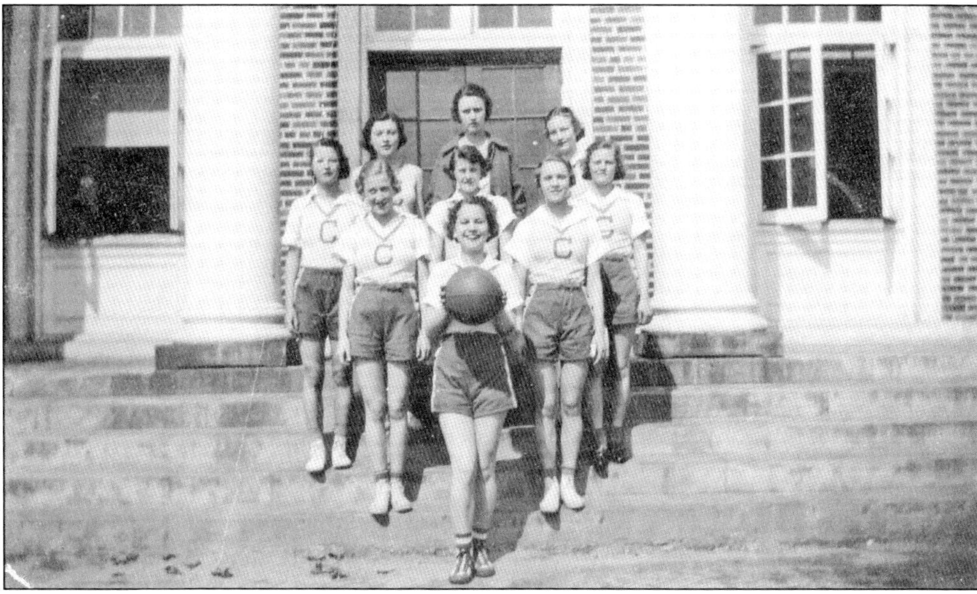

The 1937 Clemmons High School girls' basketball team included, from left to right, (first row) Treva Nifong; (second row) Ruth Miller and Dorothy Robertson; (third row) Virginia Grubbs, Helen Sides, and Irene Sides; (fourth row) Hill Alspaugh, an unidentified, and Hazel Pegram. (Courtesy William A. Hunter III.)

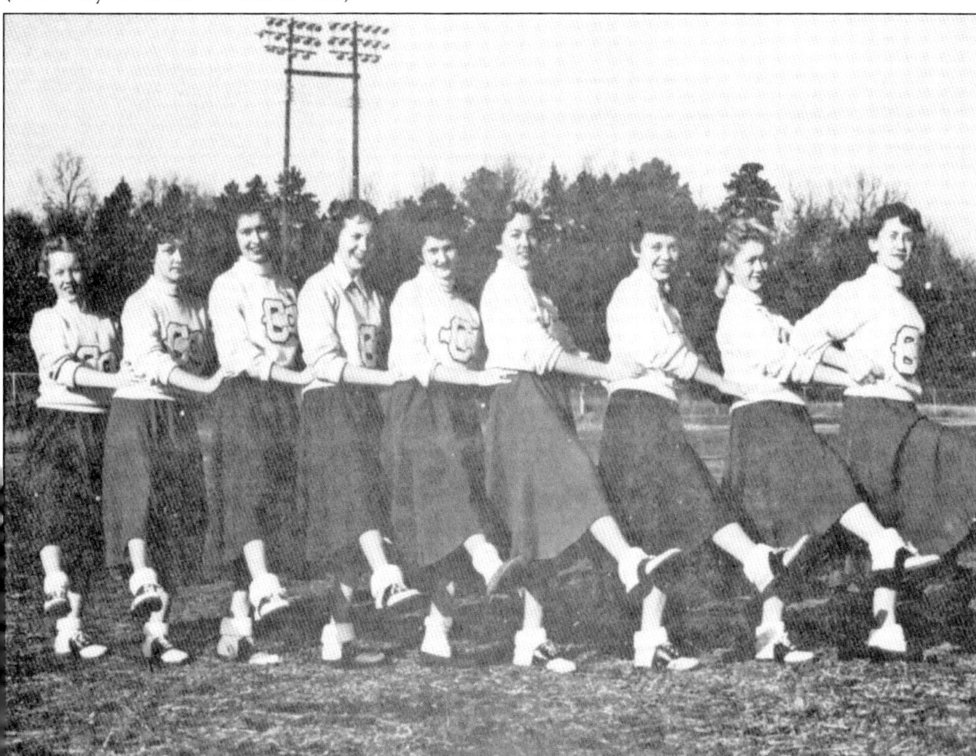

Clemmons School cheerleaders show off their bobby socks and saddle shoes before a 1953 Blues game. (Courtesy Frank Morgan.)

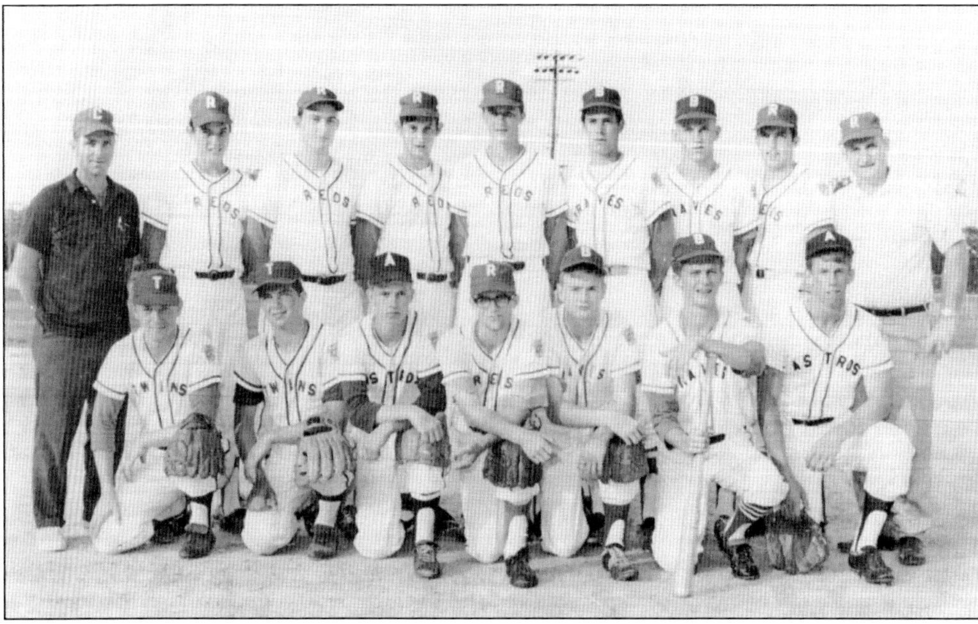

In 1968, the Southwest Forsyth Big League Tournament was held in Winston-Salem with players from Southwest High School in Clemmons. The team included, from left to right, (kneeling) John VanHoy, Mike Vogler, Stanley Brown, Roger Taylor, Steve Carter, Marty Hauser, and Steve Jones; (standing) coach Richard Vogler, John Cline, Jerry Howell, Johnny Harrington, Keith Lawson, Robert Fulton, Jimmy Hunt, Tim Gurganus, and manager Bud Spaugh. (Courtesy Bud Spaugh.)

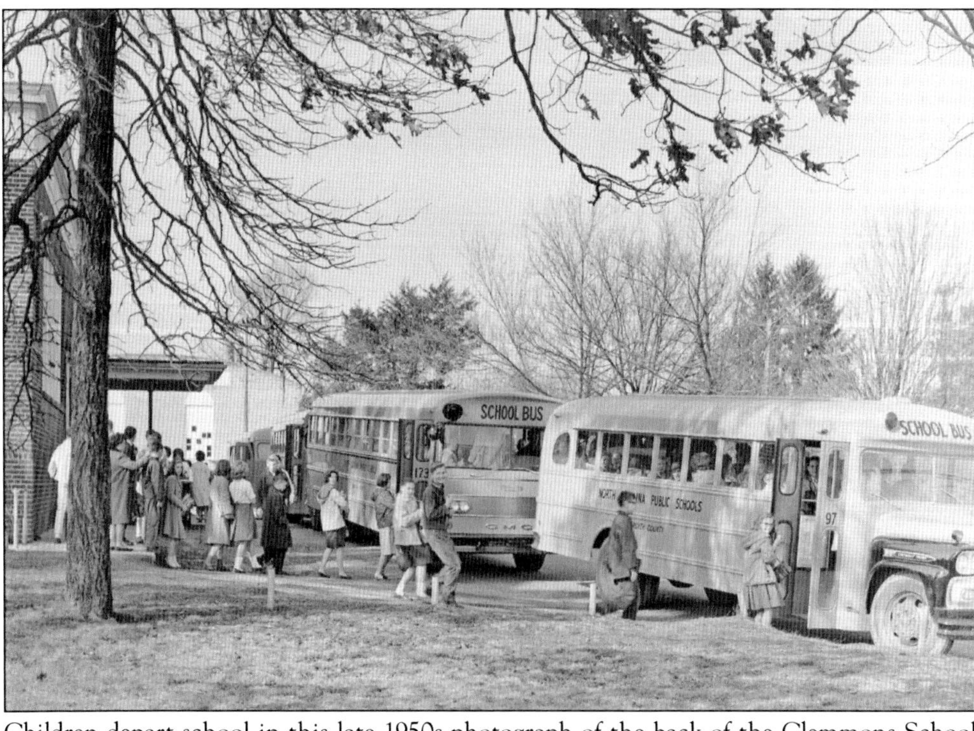

Children depart school in this late 1950s photograph of the back of the Clemmons School. (Courtesy Barbara Mahannah.)

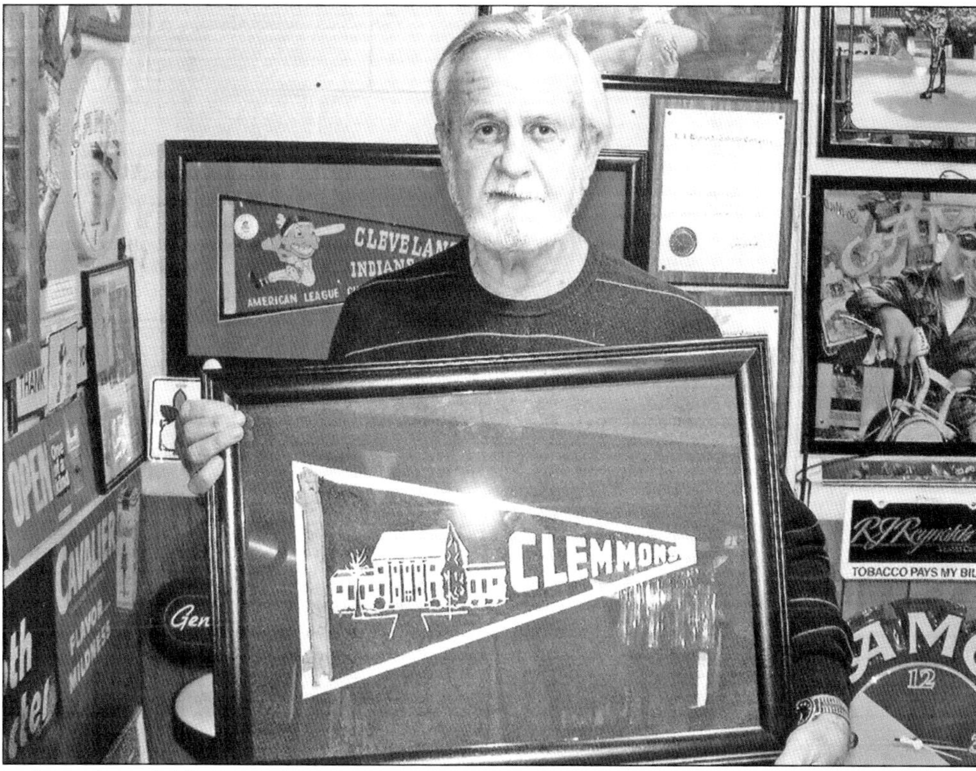

Mike Parks, a lifelong resident of Clemmons, displays the Clemmons School pennant he has owned since he was a student. Parks attended 12 grades at the school and graduated in 1955. The 1956 class was the last high school graduating class at Clemmons School before it became an elementary-only school. (Courtesy the *Clemmons Courier*.)

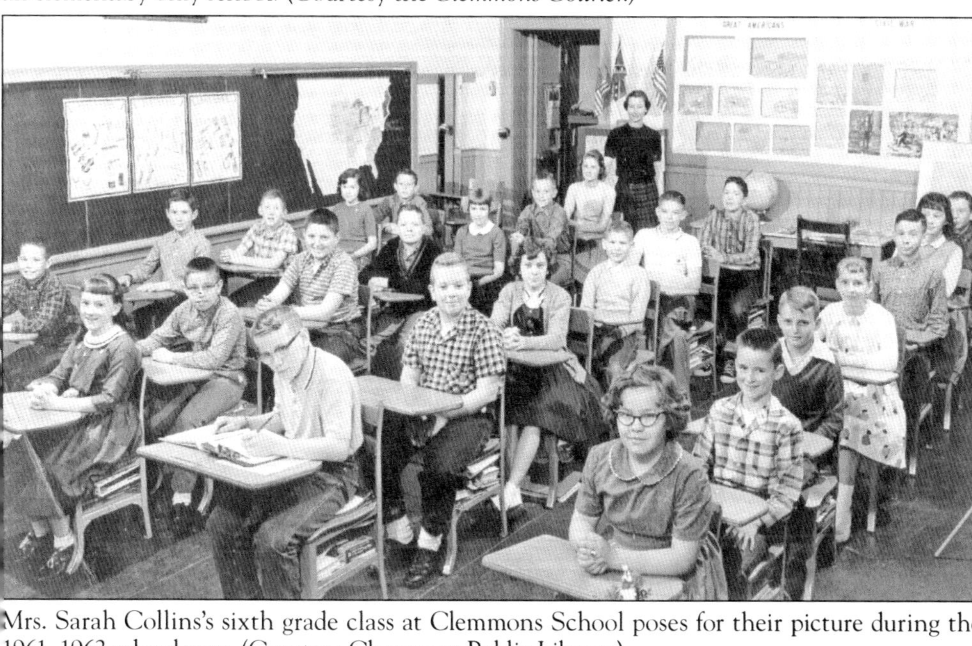

Mrs. Sarah Collins's sixth grade class at Clemmons School poses for their picture during the 1961–1962 school year. (Courtesy Clemmons Public Library.)

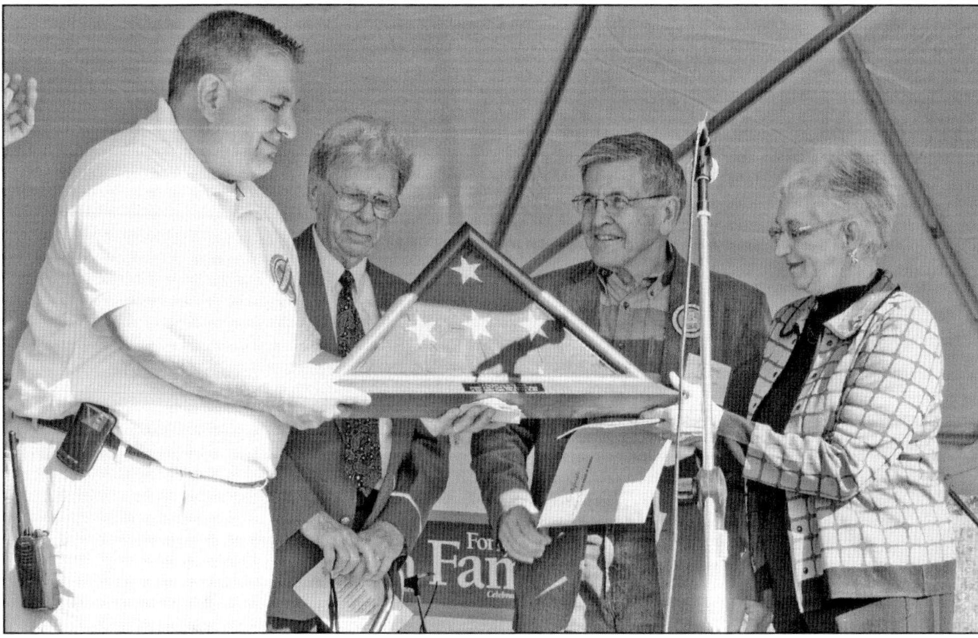

The Village of Clemmons celebrated its 25th anniversary of incorporation in 2011. Throughout the year, several events were held to celebrate the occasion. A special celebration to honor Clemmons schools was held on October 22 at the new W. Frank Morgan Elementary School on Harper Road. The school's namesake began teaching at Clemmons High School in 1951. By 1955, he was principal, and when the high school closed the next year, he became principal of Clemmons Elementary School, a position he held for 30 years until retiring in 1984. Before his teaching and school career, Morgan served in World War II and was captured in Germany after his aircraft was hit by enemy fire. He was held by Axis forces as a prisoner of war until 1945. In the photograph above, current Morgan Elementary principal Mike Hayes receives an American flag that had been flown over the US Capitol from North Carolina representative Virginia Foxx. Below, Clemmons mayor John Bost shares a moment with Mr. Morgan prior to the ceremony. (Both courtesy Anne Grant, The Village Photographer.)

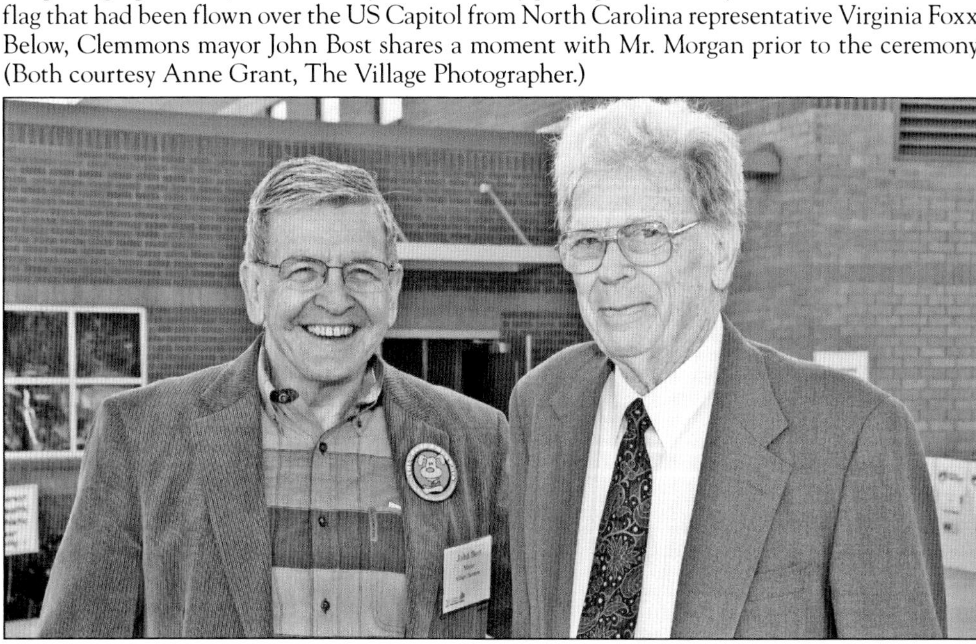

Five
CHURCHES

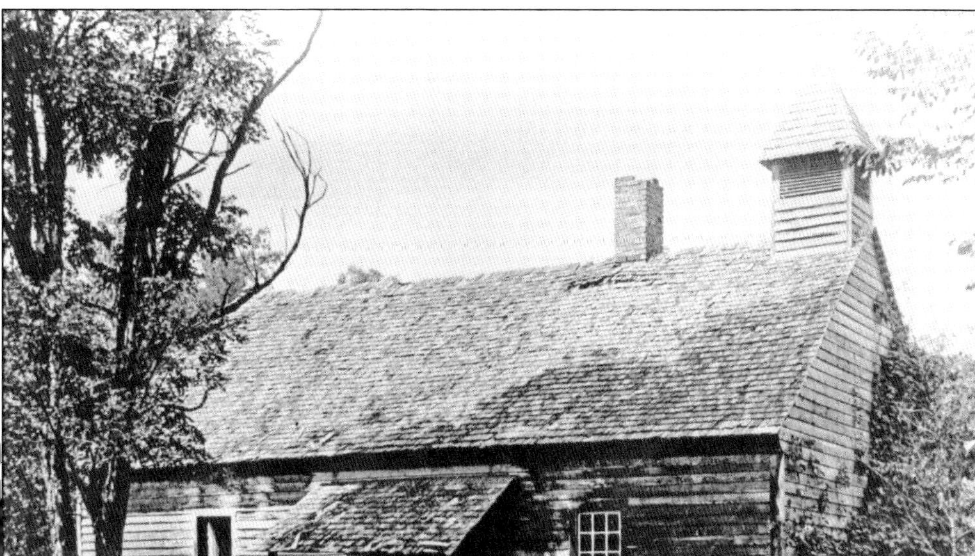

The Hope Moravian Church began in 1775 as the first English-speaking Moravian church in the Clemmons area; other services at the time were still in German. The congregation met in this building, seen here in 1870, at the forks of Muddy and Little Creeks until the new structure was built in 1896. This building no longer stands. (Courtesy Jerry Johnson.)

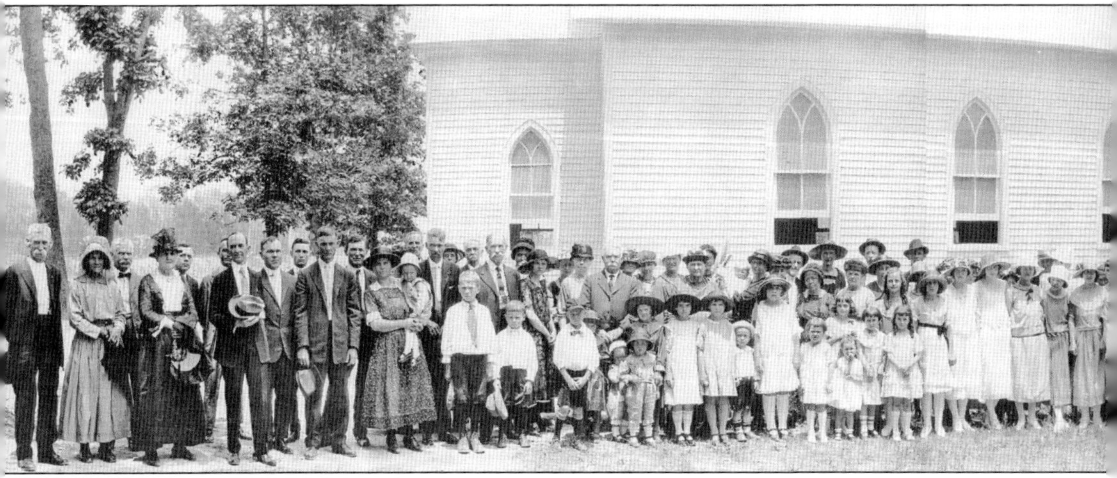

The congregation at Hope Moravian Church gathered for this photograph outside the church

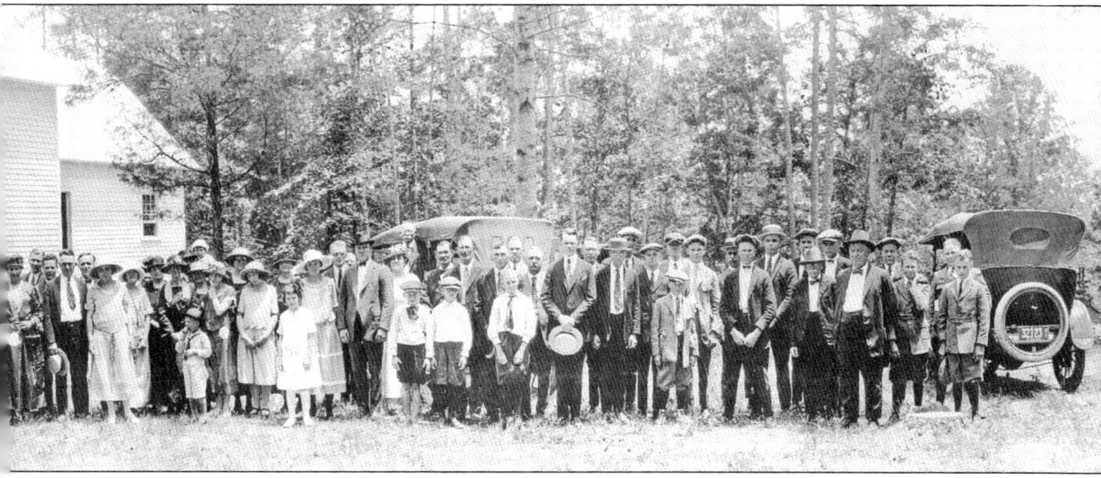

building around 1925. (Courtesy Jerry Johnson.)

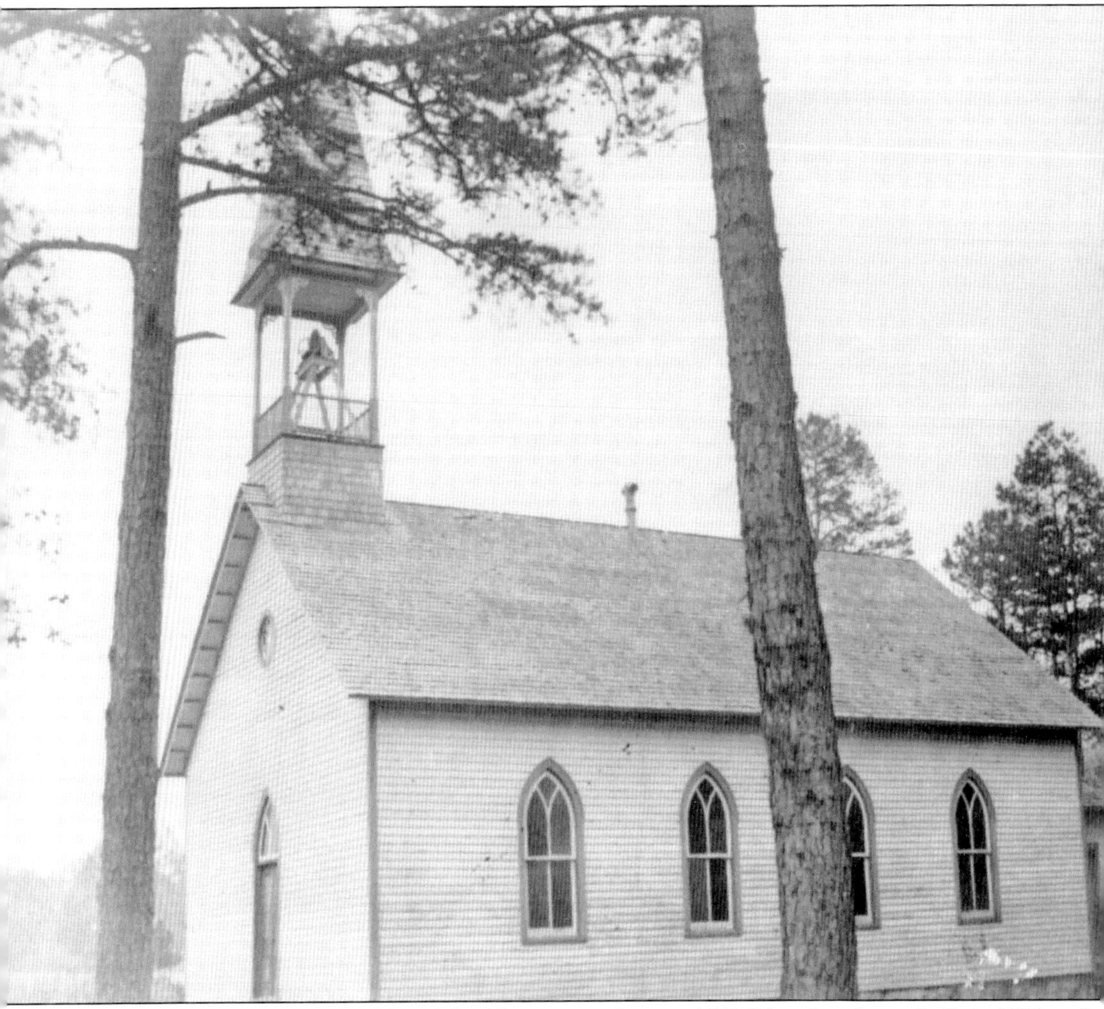

The new Hope Moravian Church building is seen here in 1910. The church was built in 1896 and remodeled and expanded in the 1920s and 1970s. It is now on Hope Church Road just outside Clemmons, in the area recently annexed by Winston-Salem. (Courtesy Jerry Johnson.)

Bishop Francis Asbury (1745–1816) was one of the first two bishops of the Methodist Episcopal church (now United Methodist Church). A traveling preacher, Asbury visited George McKnight's meetinghouse just off Highway 158 to preach in 1787. After that, he returned to the area and to McKnight's meetinghouse from 1789 to 1791 to hold the annual Methodist Episcopal Church Conferences. These conferences were important during the formation of the Methodist Church in early America. Members of McKnight's meetinghouse made up the area's first church congregations and eventually grew to the point where a formal church was needed. Mount Pleasant Church at Tanglewood was erected in 1809 to serve that purpose. (Courtesy Library of Congress, Prints & Photographs Division [LC-USZ62-132587].)

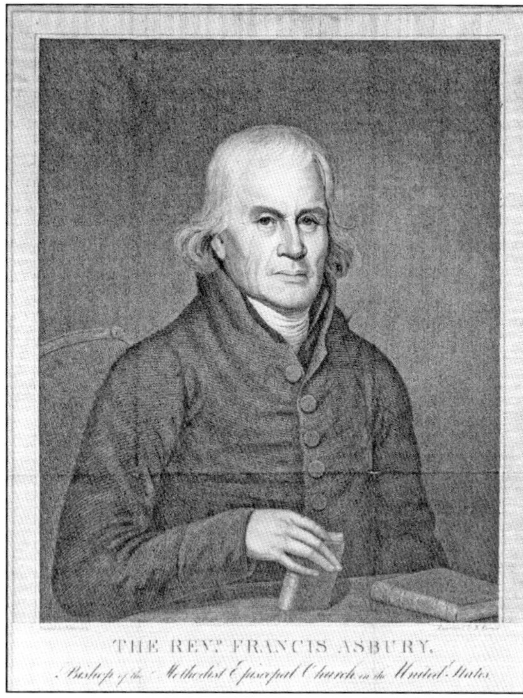

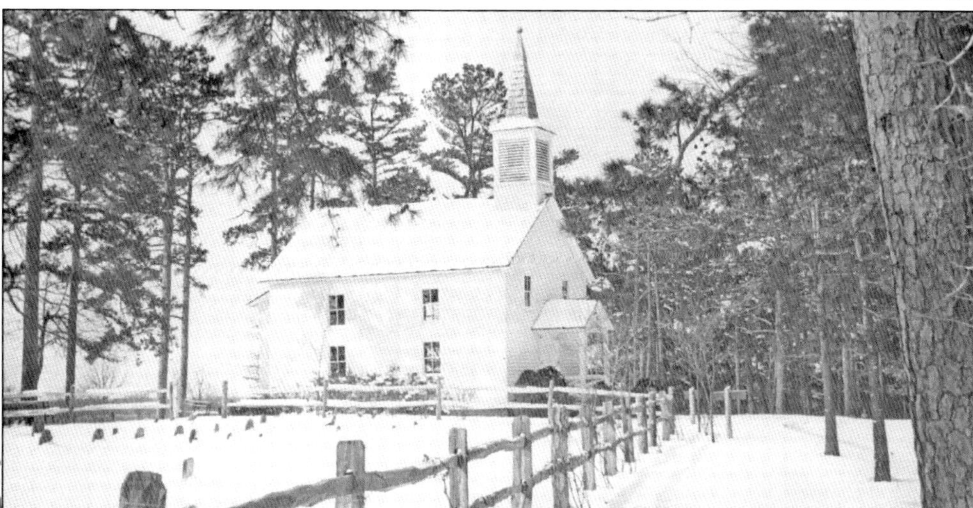

Mount Pleasant Methodist Church at Tanglewood Park was built in 1809 by Henry Eccles and served as home for several local congregations that had combined and previously met at McKnight's meetinghouse. The church is the oldest standing Methodist church in Forsyth County and held services from 1809 until the late 1800s, when Methodist membership began to decline and move to the Clemmonsville Methodist (now Clemmons United Methodist) Church. In 1921, the property was sold to William Reynolds and became part of his Tanglewood estate. Shortly afterwards, the steeple was removed and the entire building was moved downhill, close to where the current locomotive display is, and was used as a granary. In the mid-1950s, Senah Critz Kent, a niece of Reynolds, had the old church building moved back to its original location, where it remains today. Although services are no longer regularly held, special services and weddings do occur from time to time. (Photograph by Gardner Gidley, courtesy Tanglewood Photograph Collection.)

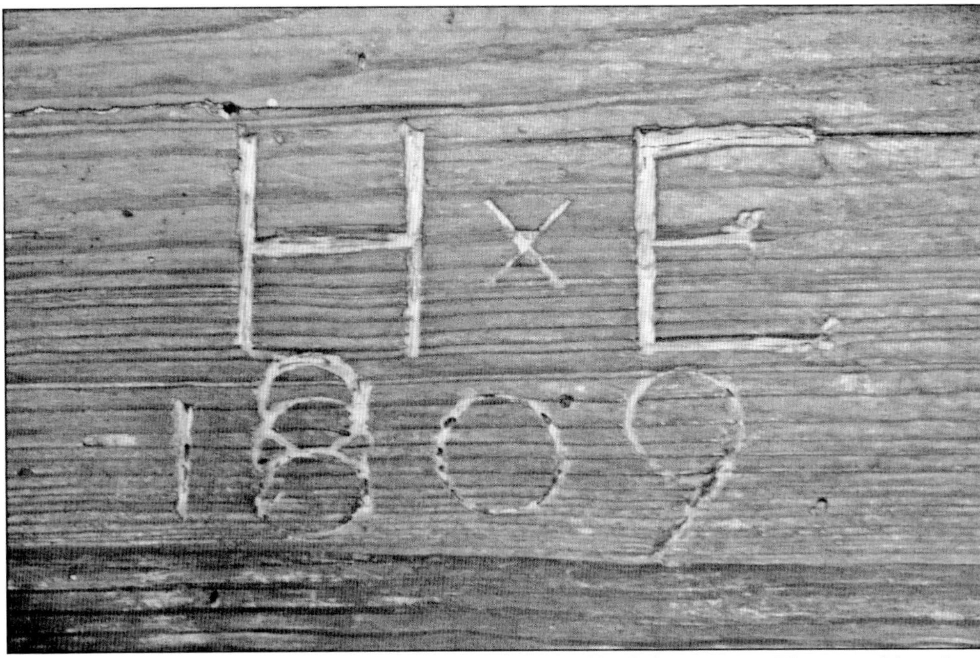

Henry Eccles carved his initials on the wooden wall of the Mount Pleasant Church at Tanglewood Park when he built it in 1809. The engraving is still visible today. (Courtesy Alyson Shulz Photography.)

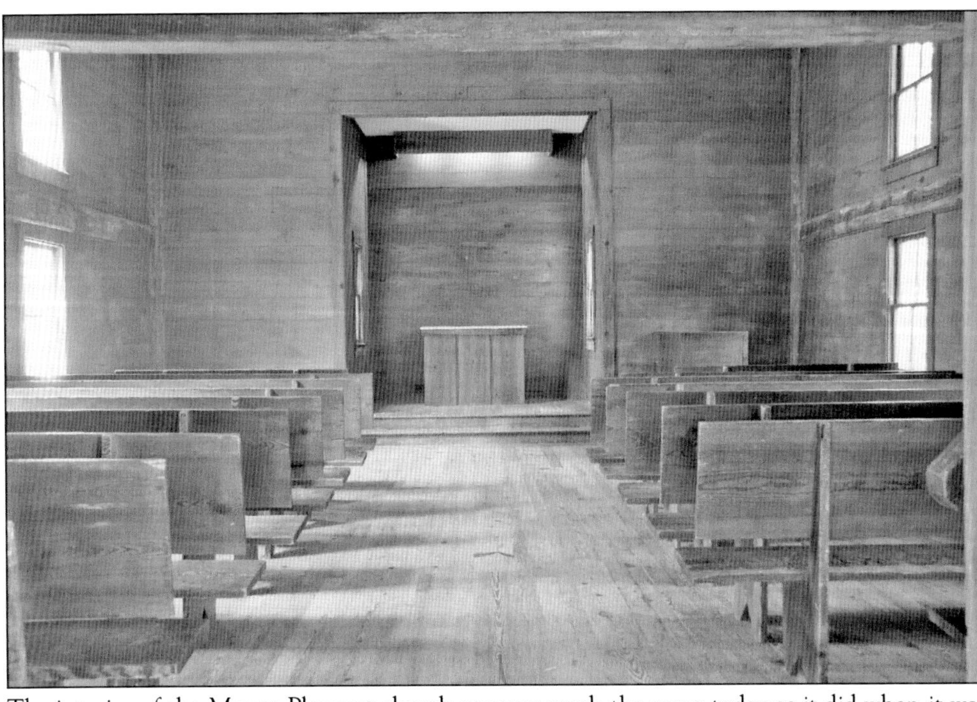

The interior of the Mount Pleasant church appears much the same today as it did when it was built. It still exhibits a sense of rustic simplicity. (Courtesy Alyson Shulz Photography.)

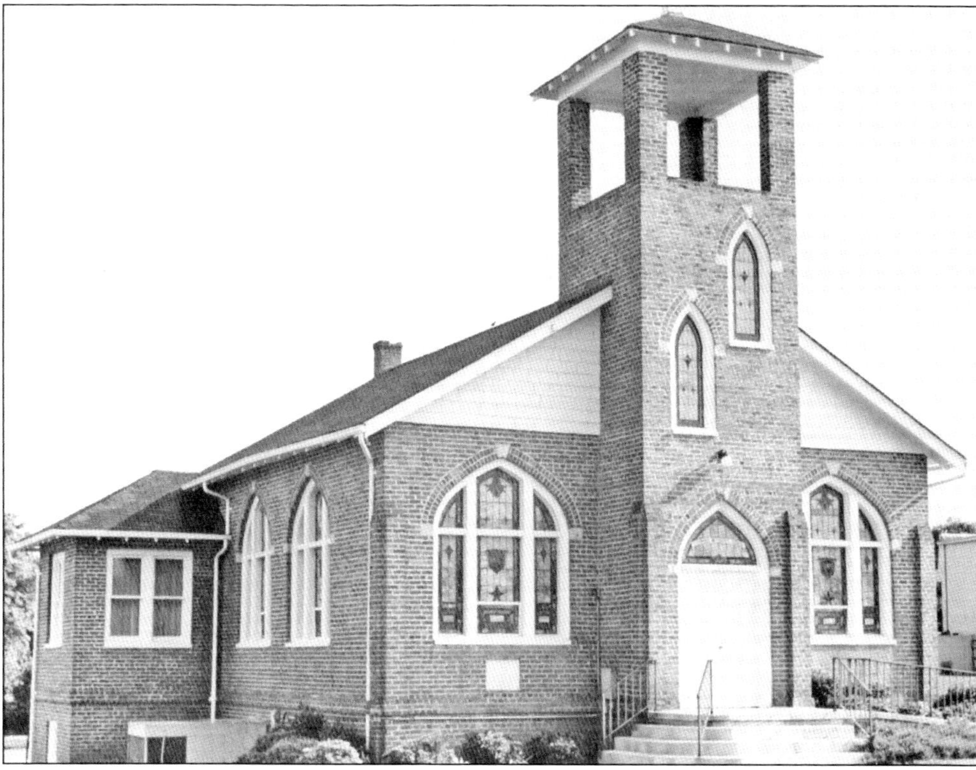

The Clemmons United Methodist Church began in the area in the late 1700s, first holding meetings at McKnight's meetinghouse before moving to Mount Pleasant and finally to its current location on Highway 158. The original building was built in 1874 and was destroyed by a storm in 1901. An attempt to rebuild the church was halted by a second storm. By then, membership declined until 1920, when the remaining 13 faithful members built the structure above. It was in use until 1979, when it was replaced by the current church. At right, the Clemmons United Methodist Church stands tall in the 1970s. (Above, courtesy David H. Hauser; right, photograph by Cookie Snyder Photography, courtesy Clemmons United Methodist Church.)

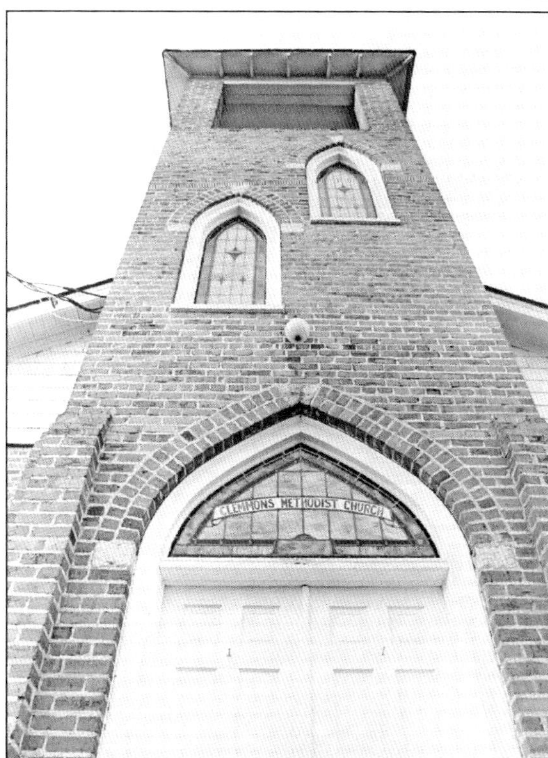

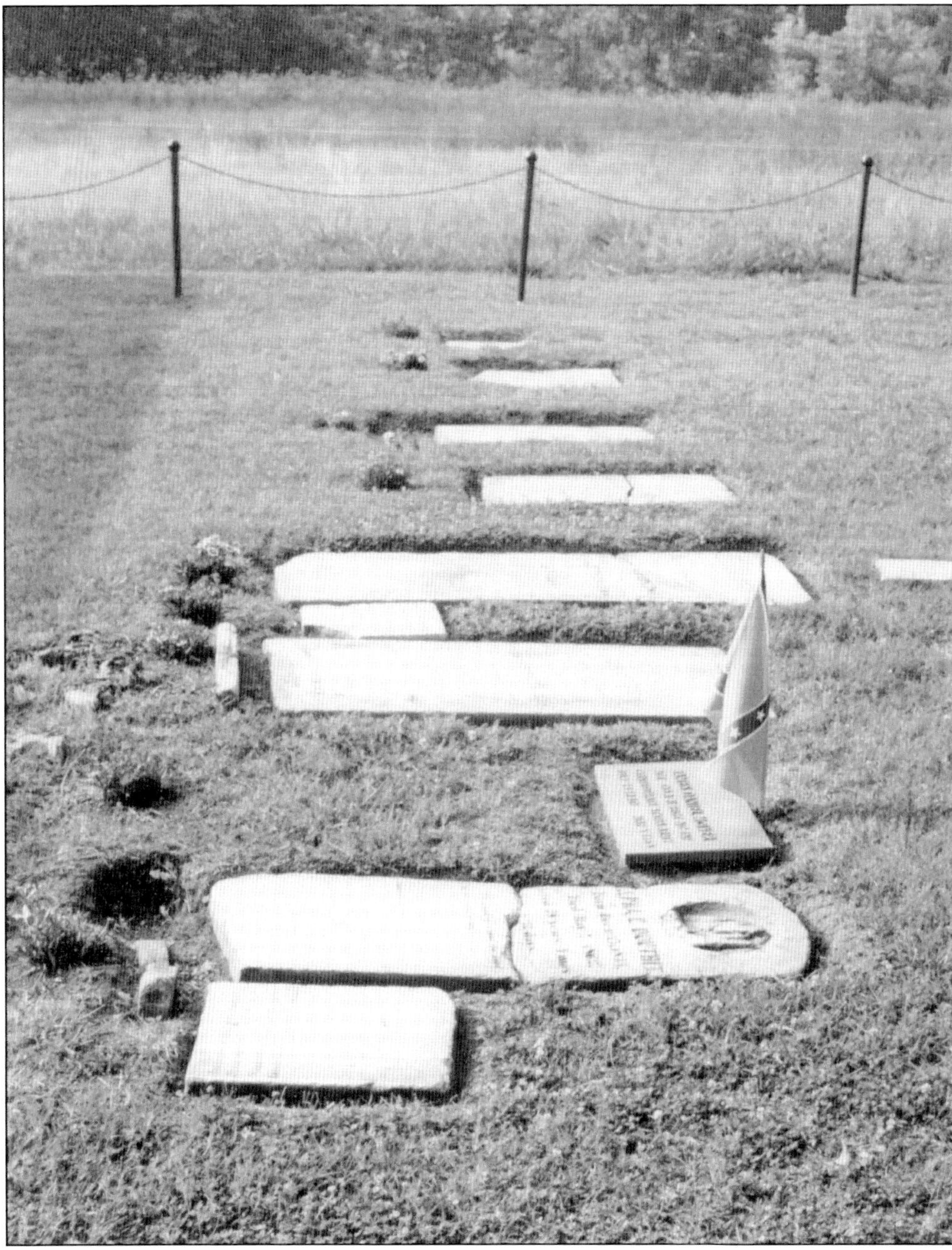

This old cemetery is adjacent to Clemmons United Methodist Church and behind the Peter Clemmons home. The remains of the original members of Eccles family, who settled in Clemmons, are here. Legend also says that Peter Clemmons and his wife, Comfort, are buried here, but it is difficult to confirm because their graves are not marked. The plaque seen with the flag memorializes Peter Clemmons's great-grandson, Confederate soldier James Daniel McIver (1840–1863). McIver was a first lieutenant with the 21st Regiment of North Carolina troops. According to records, he was wounded at Chancellorsville, Virginia, and died shortly afterwards at Fredericksburg. His body was returned to Clemmons and buried in this cemetery; however, the actual location is uncertain as the original marker has been removed. (Courtesy Clemmons United Methodist Church.)

The oldest German Baptist, or "Dunker," congregation in North Carolina was founded in 1775 just east of Clemmons in the Muddy Creek area on Fraternity Church Road. The Dunkers get their name from their method of baptizing believers. Dunker is based on the original German word *tunker*, meaning "to dip." The church baptized members three times for the Holy Trinity. The congregation met in homes until this church was built in 1860. It was expanded twice and the original structure is still standing and was in use until 2005, when the small remaining congregation moved to another area. This photograph was taken in 1910. (Courtesy Jerry Johnson.)

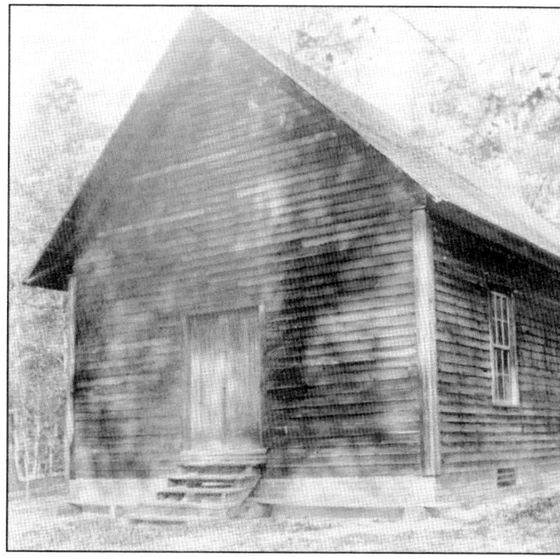

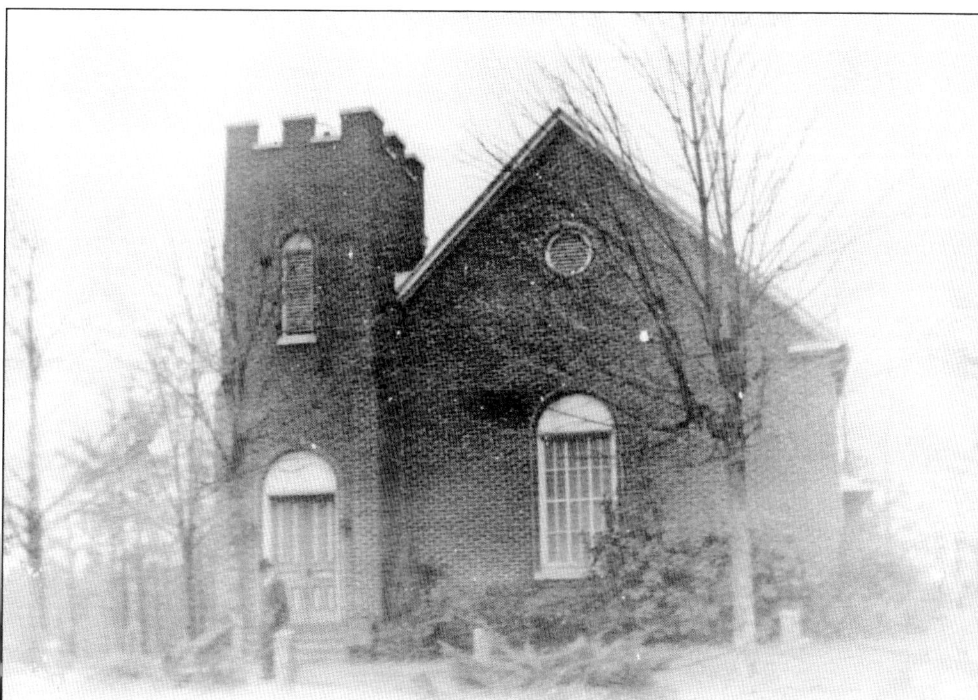

The congregation of the Fraternity Church of the Brethren, as the German Baptist church became known, split in 1885 when about one-third of the members withdrew under the leadership of Jacob Faw to form the Old Order Brethren. The remaining members of the church were led by Jacob Faw's grandson, Rufus Faw, and J. Frank Robertson. The two congregations shared the original building until 1900, when this building was constructed about a mile north of the original building. The new church originally had a white clapboard exterior but had a brick veneer applied in 1931, when this photograph was taken. (Courtesy Fraternity Church of the Brethren.)

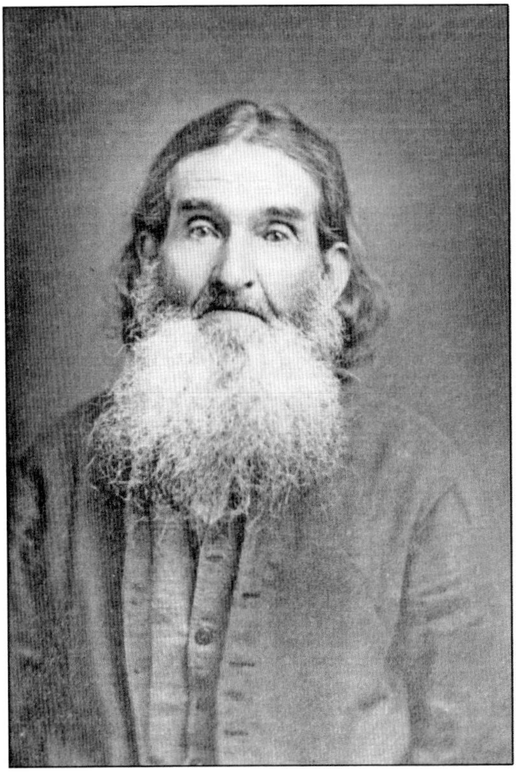

Jacob Faw (1810–1887) was grandson of the first Jacob Pfau, who arrived in the area in 1778. Faw became the leader of the church around 1845, following the death of his father, Isaac, and led it until his own death in 1887. He is buried in the old church cemetery off of Shady Acres Lane. (Courtesy Fraternity Church of the Brethren.)

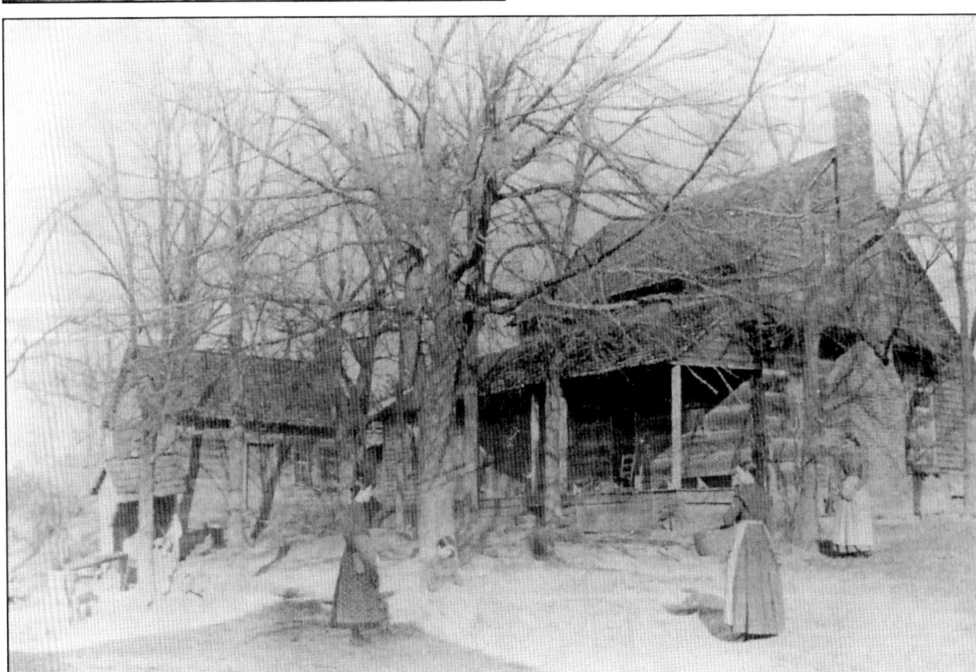

The Faw family farmstead is seen here in the late 1800s. The woman at the front right is Rebecca Sides, the wife of Amos Faw, who was the son of Dunker leader Jacob Faw. The house was built around 1840 near the old Dunker church. (Courtesy Peggy Chapell.)

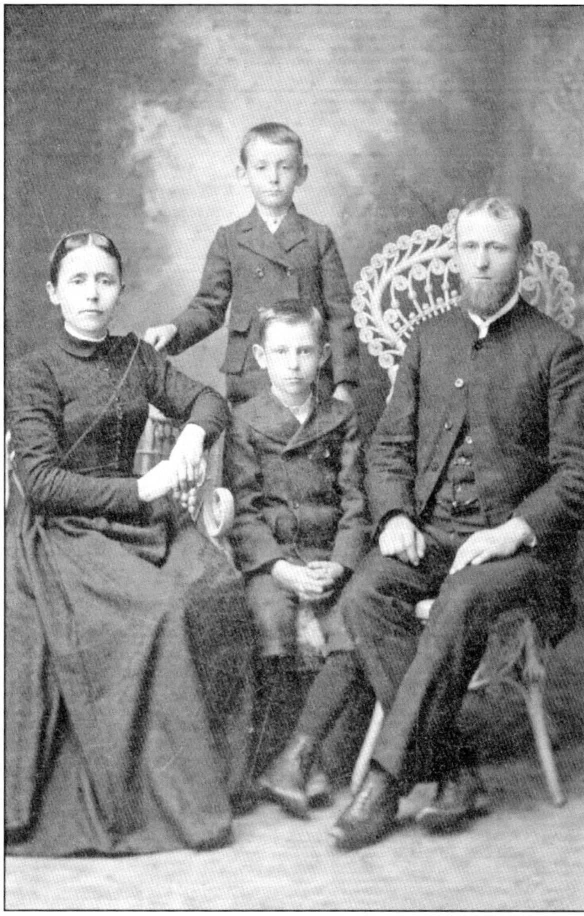

Charles Rufus Faw (1863–1930) is seen at right around 1900 with his wife, Rosa, and his sons Paul and Ross. The grandson of Jacob Faw, Charles assumed leadership of the original congregation after the Old Order split off in 1885. With the help of J. Frank Robertson, Faw led the church until his death, guiding the congregation through expansion and the building of the new church structure. He is seen below baptizing Howard Robertson in the Sides Mill pond in November 1909. (Right, courtesy Maxine Kiser; below courtesy Jerry Johnson.)

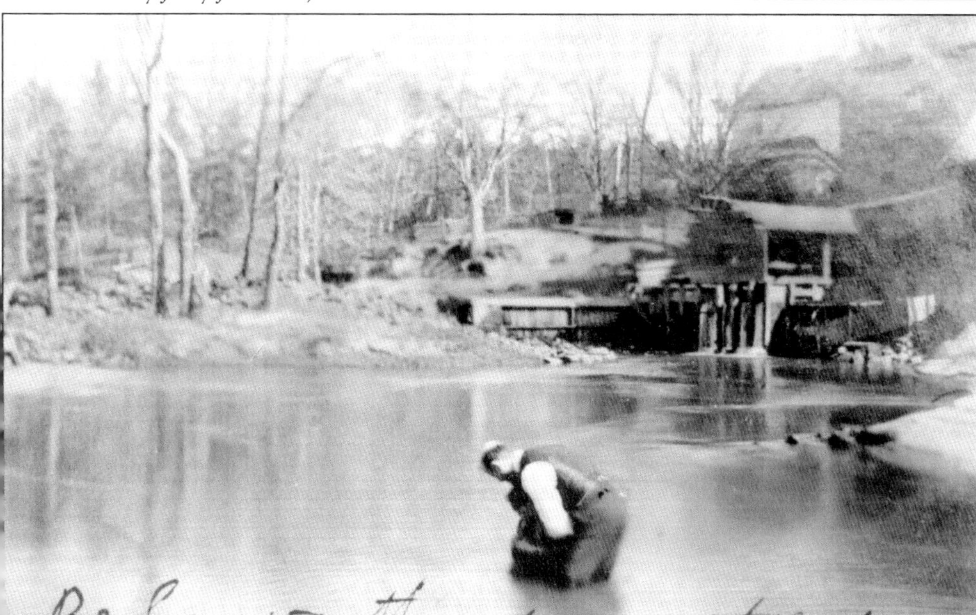

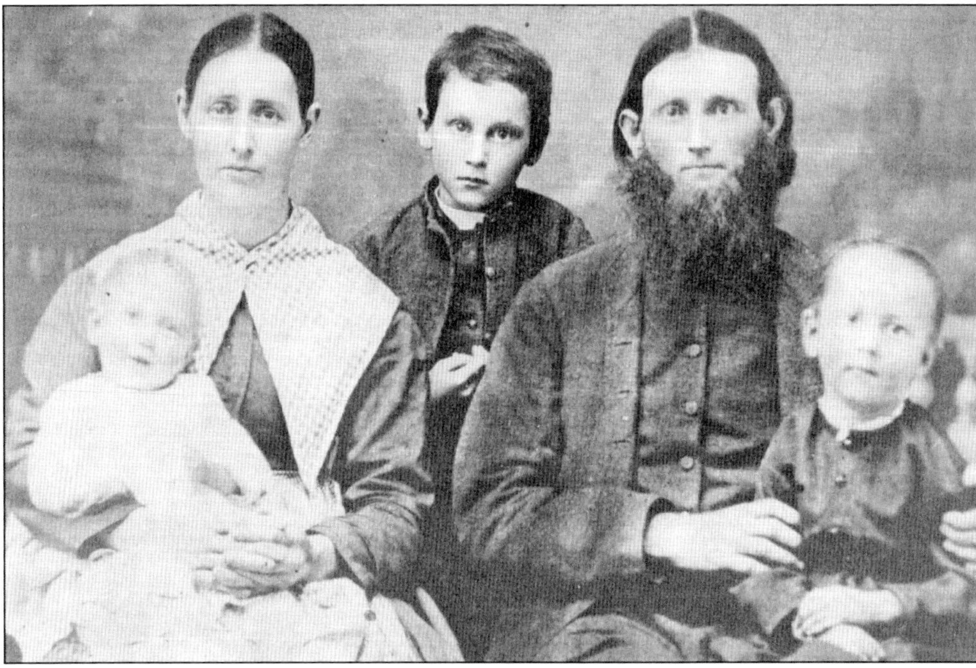

William Francis Sides (1845–1884) is seen here with his wife, Antoinette, and family around 1880. Sides was the son of Christian Seitz and the brother of Levi Sides. The Dunker leader and minister died in 1884, four days before his 39th birthday. (Courtesy Jerry Johnson.)

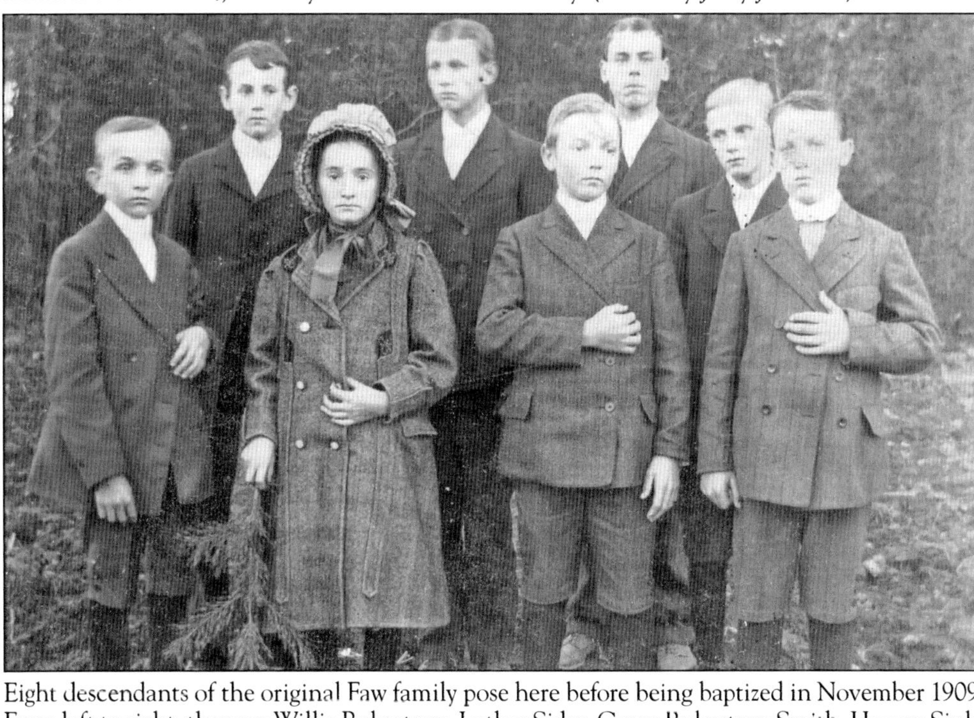

Eight descendants of the original Faw family pose here before being baptized in November 1909. From left to right, they are Willie Robertson, Luther Sides, Grace Robertson Smith, Harvey Sink, Russell Robertson, Marvin Daniels, Ross Sides, and Howard Robertson. (Courtesy Fraternity Church of the Brethren.)

Henry J. Woodie (left, 1868–1955) and J. Frank Robertson (1863–1927) are seen here in 1915. Both men were early leaders of the Fraternity Church of the Brethren. (Courtesy Fraternity Church of the Brethren.)

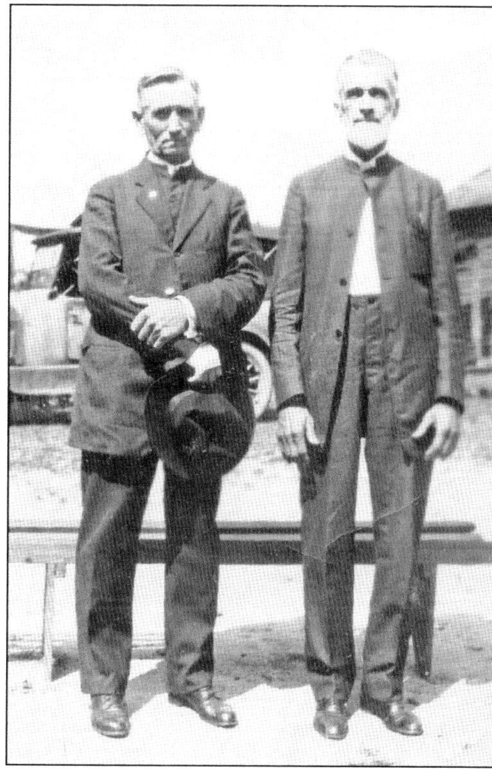

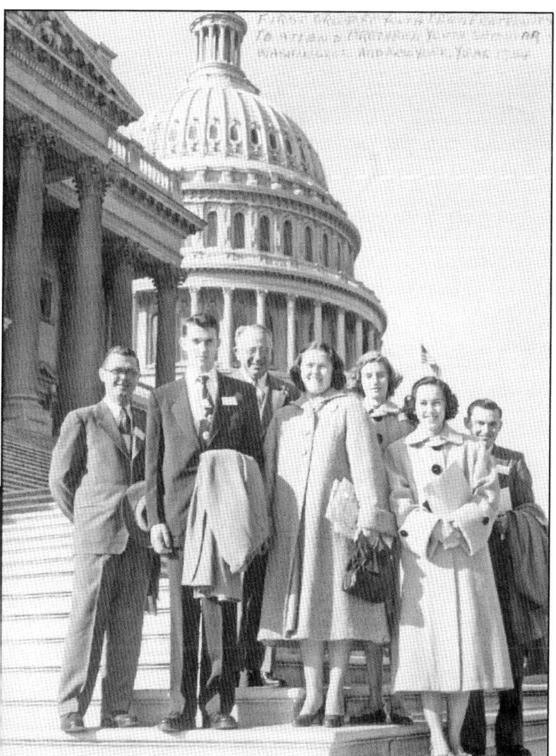

In 1954, a group of youths from the Fraternity Church of the Brethren was afforded the opportunity to visit and tour Washington, DC during a youth seminar. During the visit, the group met on the steps of the Capitol and had their picture taken. (Courtesy Fraternity Church of the Brethren.)

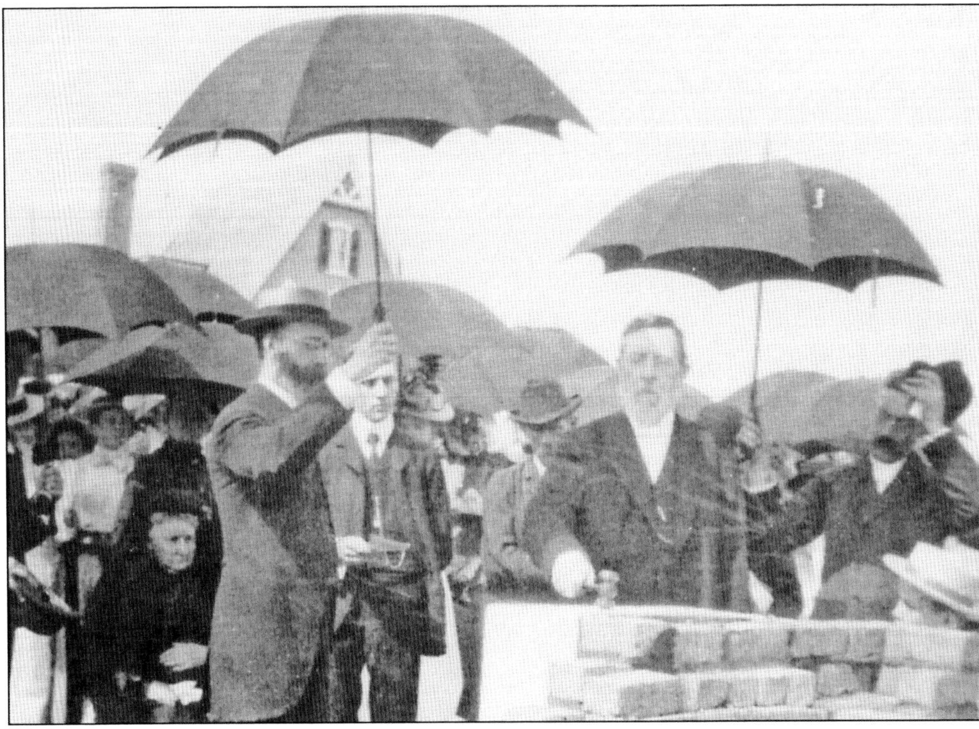

Clemmons Moravian Church was founded because E.T. Clemmons wished to benefit the Moravian Church as well as the community his ancestors had settled. In his will, he bequeathed funding to support the building of a church and school. In 1901, construction began on the school and church building. In the above photograph, from May 1901, the cornerstone for the school and church building is laid. Bishop Edward Rondthaler, the pastor of Home Moravian Church in Winston-Salem, placed the gavel on the cornerstone to set it into place, a symbolic gesture of the time. Hattie Butner, the wife of E.T. Clemmons, is seated in the wheelchair to the left. Holding the umbrellas are Rev. George Bahnson and Rev. John Clewell. (Courtesy Clemmons Moravian Church.)

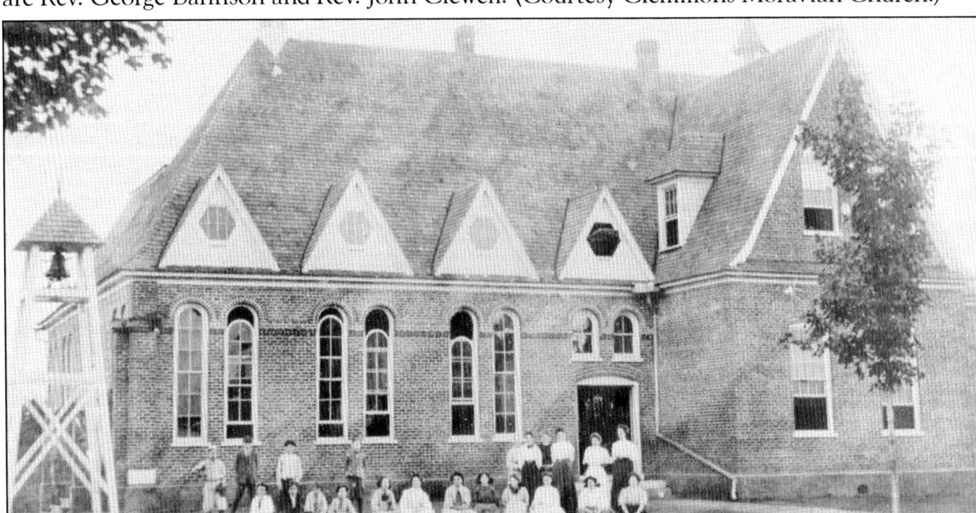

This 1909 photograph shows Founders Hall of Clemmons Moravian Church and School, with its bell tower, on the left. (Courtesy Hill Hunter.)

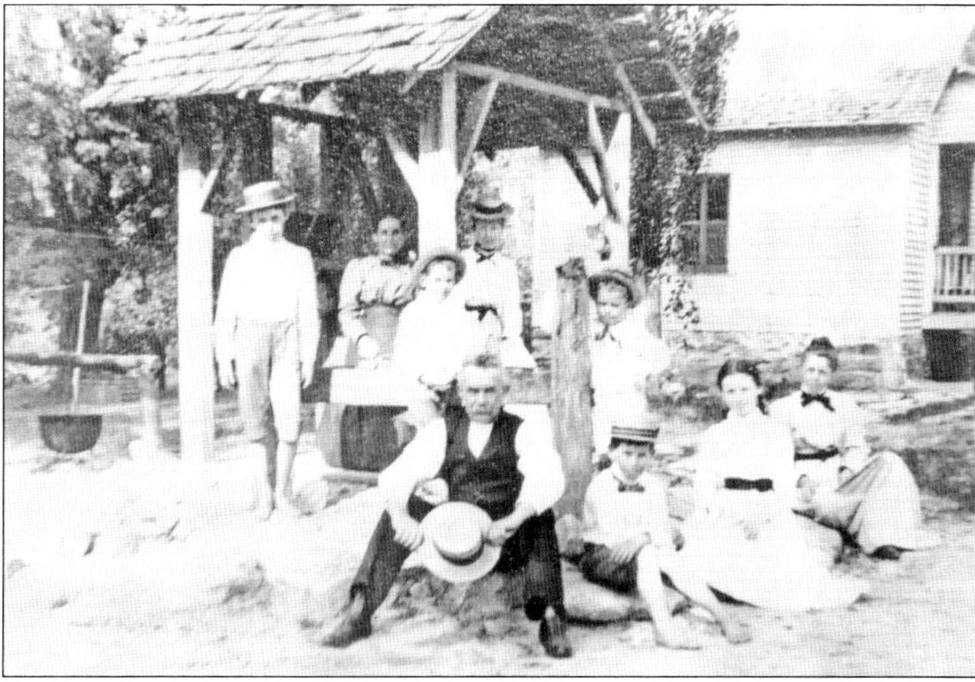

Rev. James E. Hall and his family pose for a photograph about 1910. Reverend Hall was the first pastor of the Clemmons Moravian Church and served in that role for 20 years before leaving in 1921. He also served at the Hope and Friedberg Moravian churches. (Courtesy Jerry Johnson.)

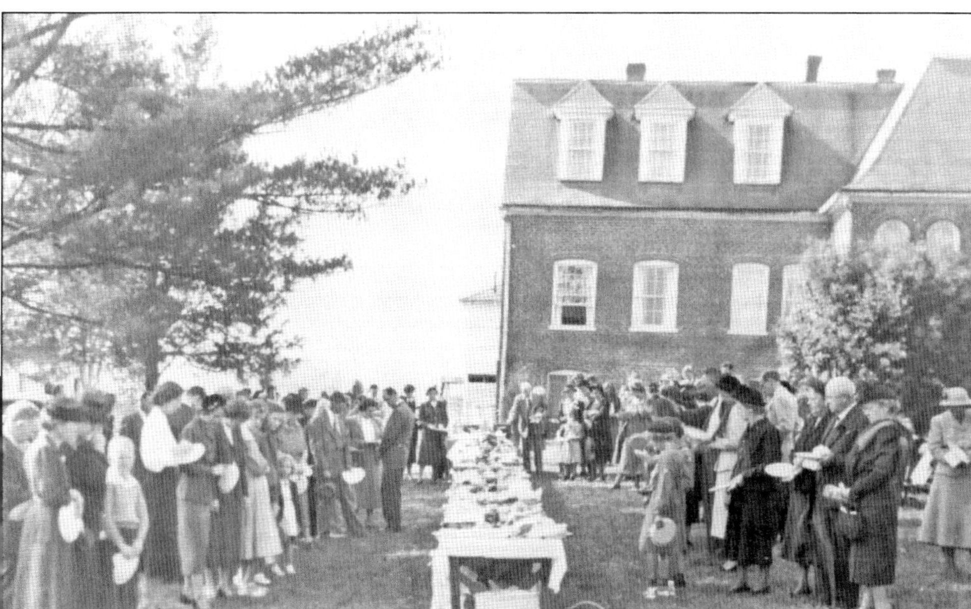

Friends and family gather together on the lawn of Clemmons Moravian Church at a 1950s homecoming. (Courtesy Pam Corum, Snyder Photography.)

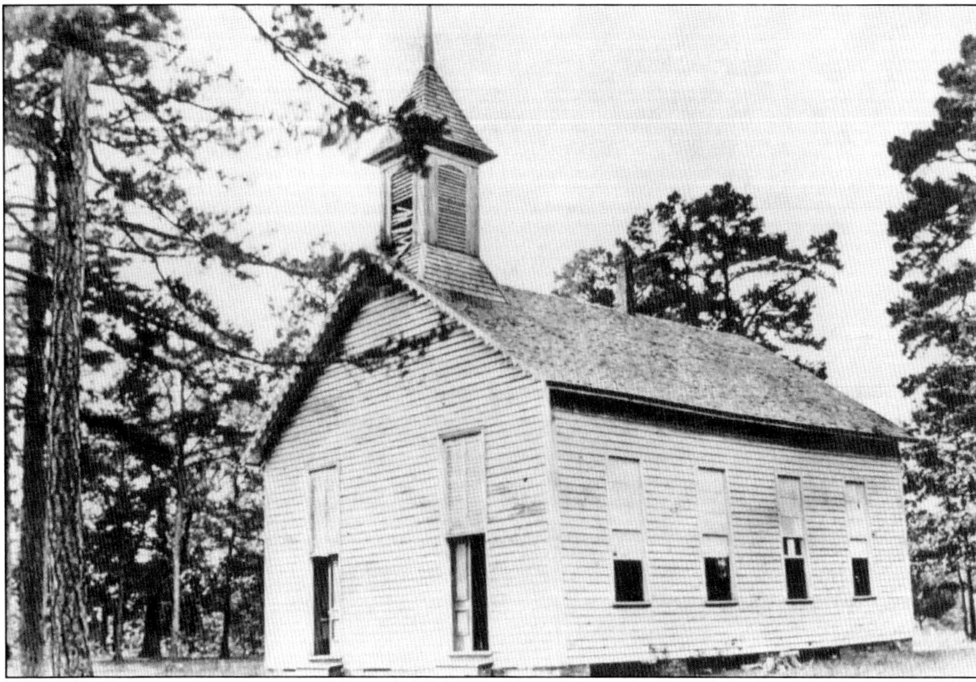

The first building erected by the Muddy Creek Baptist Church was on land donated to them by Nancy Cook in 1874. When the Muddy Creek congregation moved to Clemmons, they changed their name to Clemmons Baptist Church. This building was used until the first brick church was built on the same property. The interior photograph below shows the layout and comforts provided to its members. (Courtesy Clemmons First Baptist Church.)

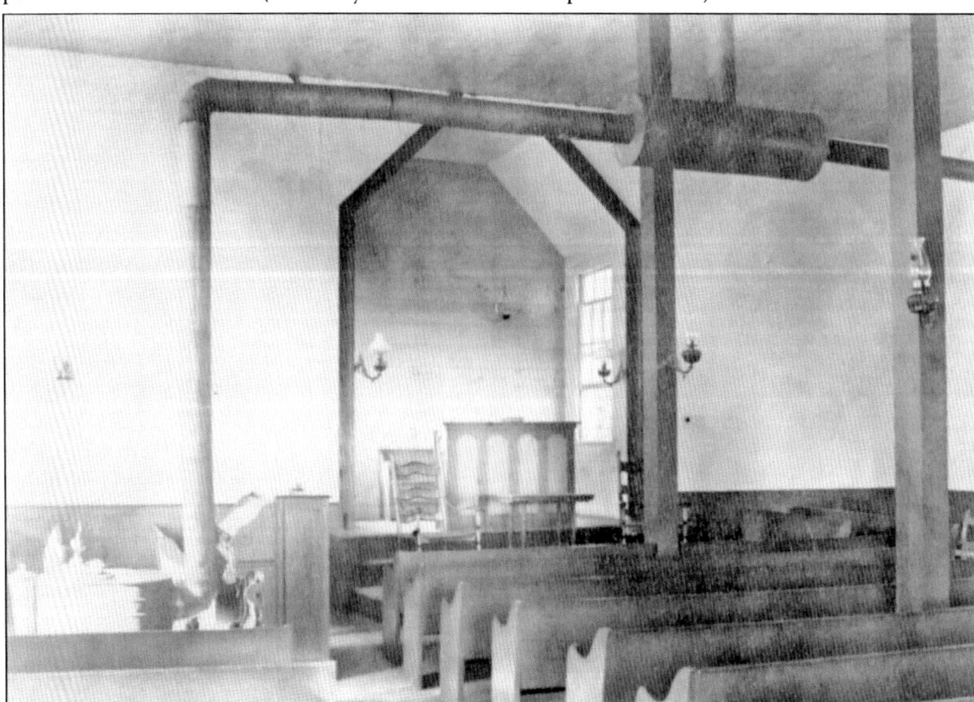

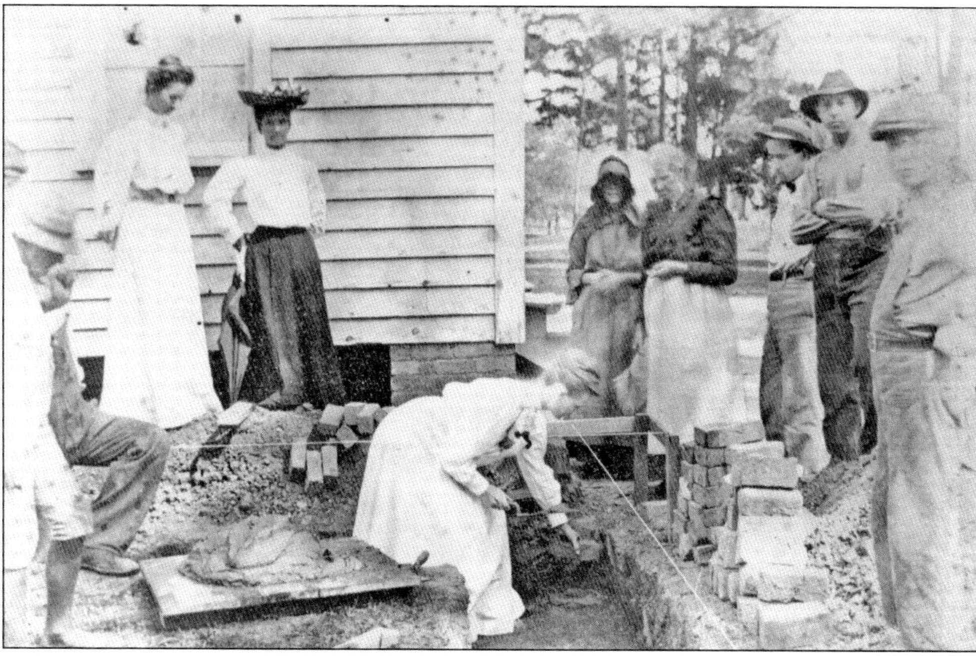

Above, Marie Moss participates in the bricklaying at the new Clemmons Baptist Church in 1905. The old wooden structure is in the background. Moss was the music teacher at Clemmons Moravian School. Nancy Jarvis Cook, whose family donated the land for the church, is fourth from the right. (Courtesy Cookie Snyder Photography.)

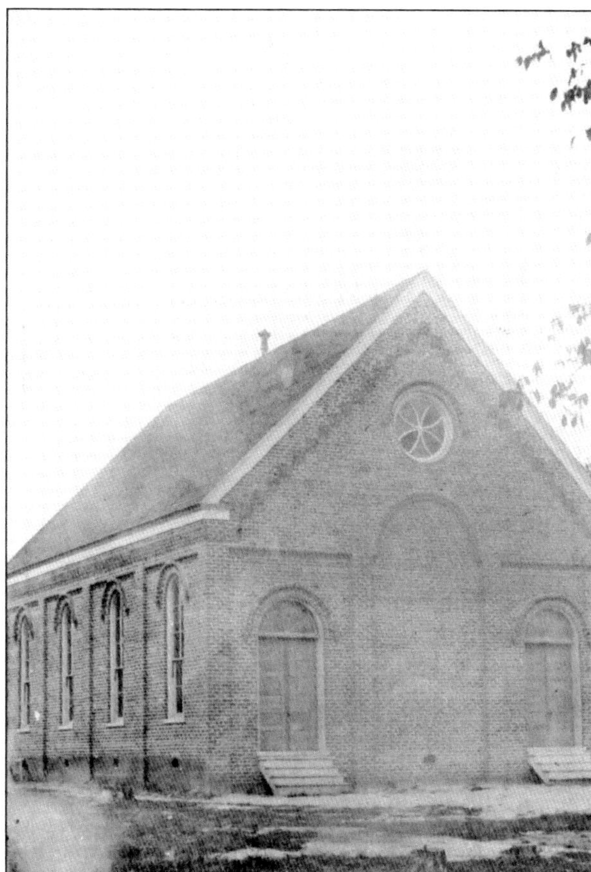

The new Clemmons Baptist Church stands completed in this 1907 photograph. The building was remodeled and expanded several times in the 1950s and 1960s before being replaced in 1994. The church is now known as Clemmons First Baptist Church. (Courtesy Clemmons First Baptist Church.)

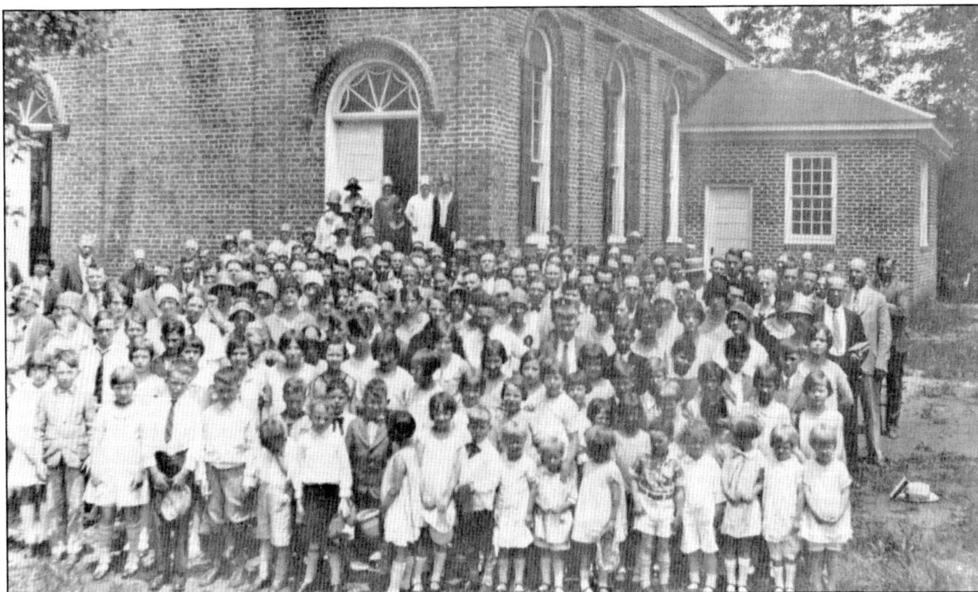

Sunday school was popular at the Clemmons Baptist Church, as seen in this 1933 photograph. Church attendance had grown significantly during the early years of the church after the congregation moved to its current location in Clemmons from Muddy Creek. (Courtesy Clemmons First Baptist Church.)

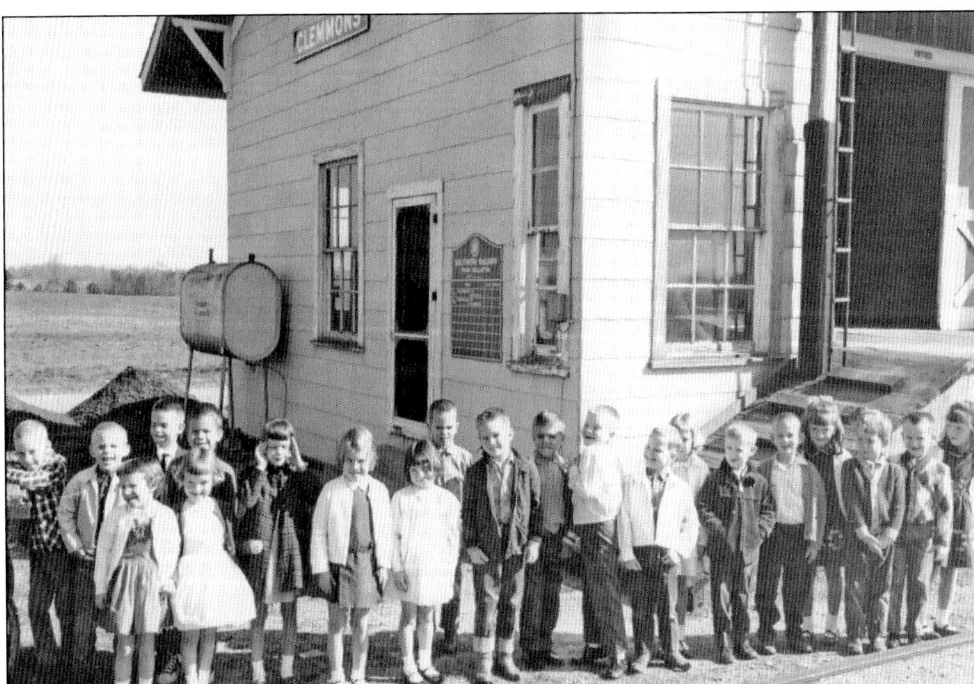

A group of Sunday School children from the Clemmons Baptist Church visit the old train depot off of Idol's Road around 1960. (Courtesy Clemmons First Baptist Church.)

The First Christian Church of Clemmons began as the Muddy Creek Church of Christ in 1882. The congregation was formed in this area after a group of Baptists who had been meeting there moved to Clemmons and became the Clemmons Baptist Church. The Muddy Creek congregation organized in 1882 as the Church of Christ, building the wooden church structure at right. The church, built of wood planks from logs donated by Phillip Hege and Uriah Phelps, was on Frye Bridge Road, across the street from the current structure. The first pastor of the newly formed church was Rev. Richard Poindexter. The next building used by this church was built in 1924 after the first one became unusable due to its age. The First Christian Church, as it came to be known, used the second building until it was replaced in 1983 by the current building. Below, the congregation gathers for a portrait in front of the second building in the late 1940s. Some of the oldest families in Clemmons attend this church. (Both, courtesy First Christian Church.)

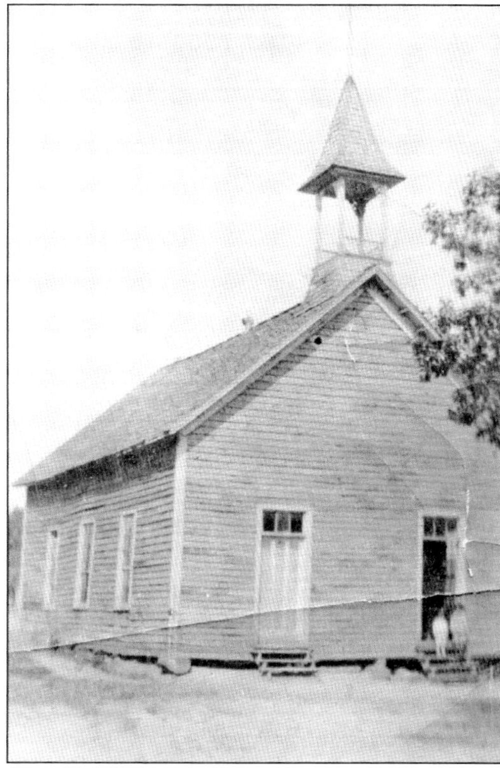

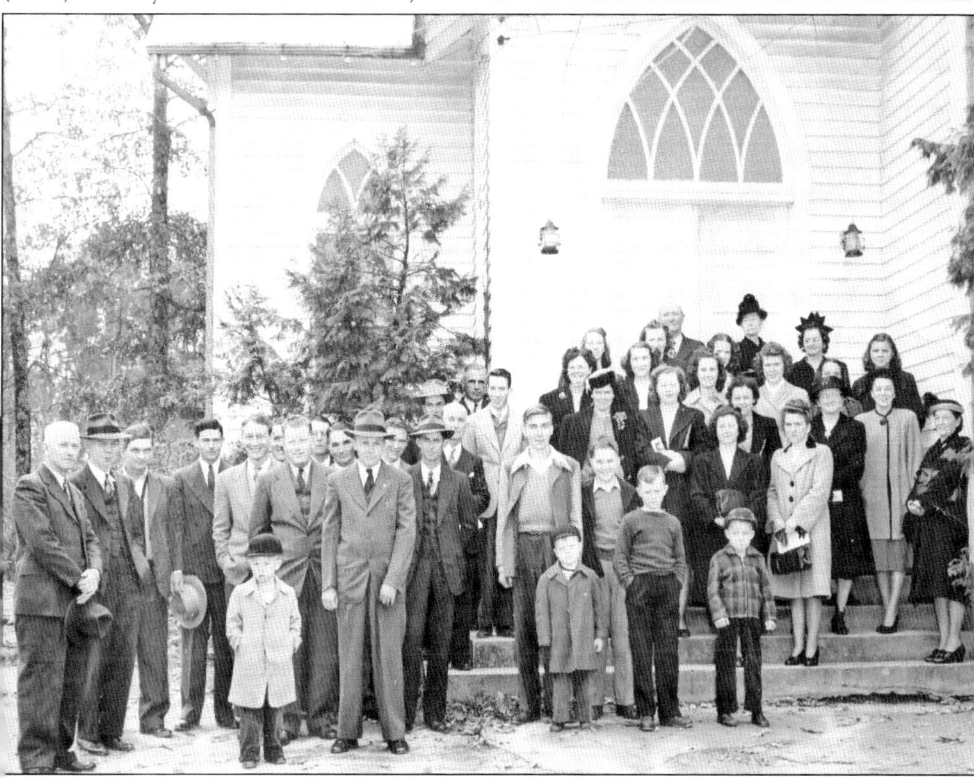

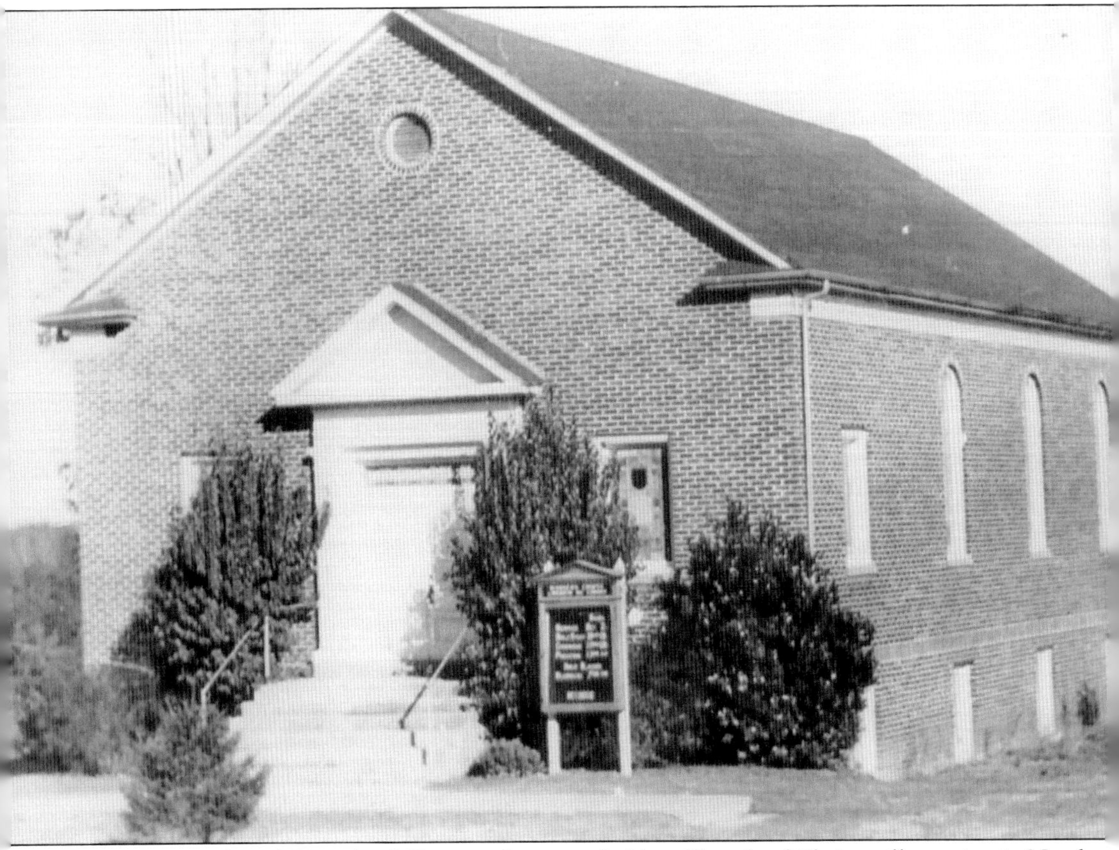

Warner's Chapel Church of Christ is the second-oldest Church of Christ still meeting in North Carolina. In 1880, a small group of individuals in the Warner community, near Clemmons, began meeting at Warner's one-room log schoolhouse on Lasater Road. The small church took the name of the schoolhouse and became known as Warner's Chapel. In 1893, the 12 members of the congregation voted to build their own structure on land donated to them by the Lewis Harper family. Construction on the building above began in 1893, with most of the work done by the church members. The wooden Warner's Chapel building was used until 1937, when it was replaced by a brick structure. Seen here in a photograph from about 1950, the building has since been remodeled and expanded as the church membership has grown. (Courtesy Warner's Chapel Church of Christ.)

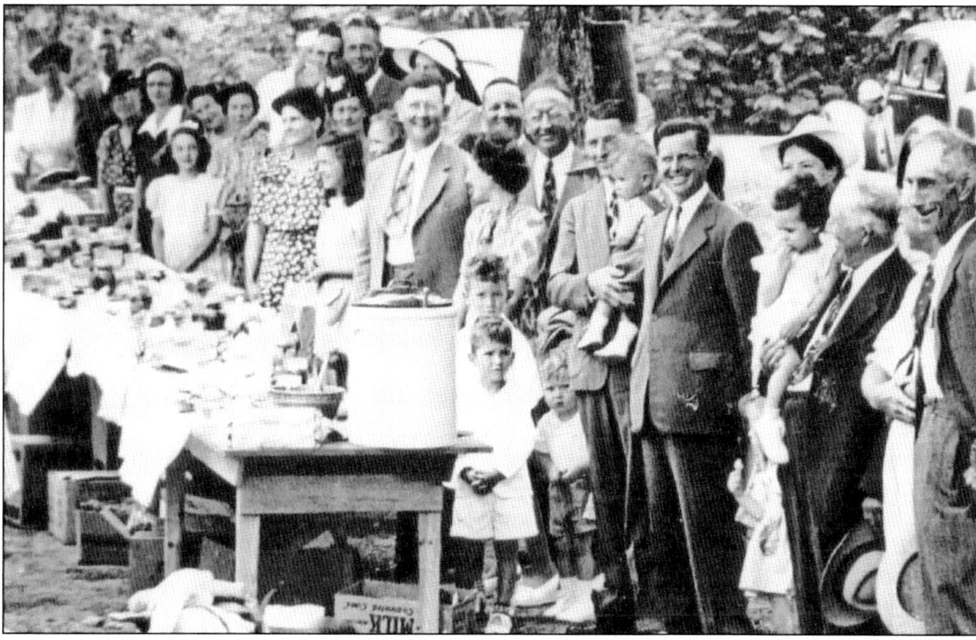

Members of the Warner's Chapel Church of Christ enjoy a congregational meal on the grounds of the church around 1945. Cecil Derryberry is fourth from the left. At this time, the church had no full-time preacher and relied on area preachers to lead worship. Derryberry worked with Warner's Chapel as well as other local churches on a routine basis. He was remembered as one of the most beloved and diligent evangelists to work with the Warner's Chapel congregation. Derryberry moved to Tennessee in 1950, where he died of cancer in 1952 at the age of 40. (Courtesy Warner's Chapel Church of Christ.)

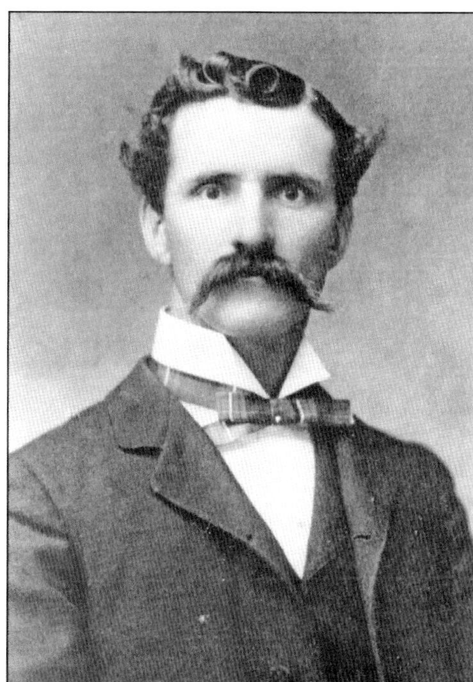

Willis Leander Reeves (1871–1938) was a traveling preacher in Forsyth and Davie Counties in the early 20th century and was the first preacher to preach on a regular basis at the Jericho Church of Christ near Mocksville. He led gospel meetings at Warner's Chapel for several years beginning in 1914. He married Nina Harper of the Warner's Chapel congregation in 1917 and lived beside the church building until his death in 1938. He is buried in the Warner's Chapel cemetery. Reeves was an important early leader in the Churches of Christ in the area. (Courtesy Cannon Harper.)

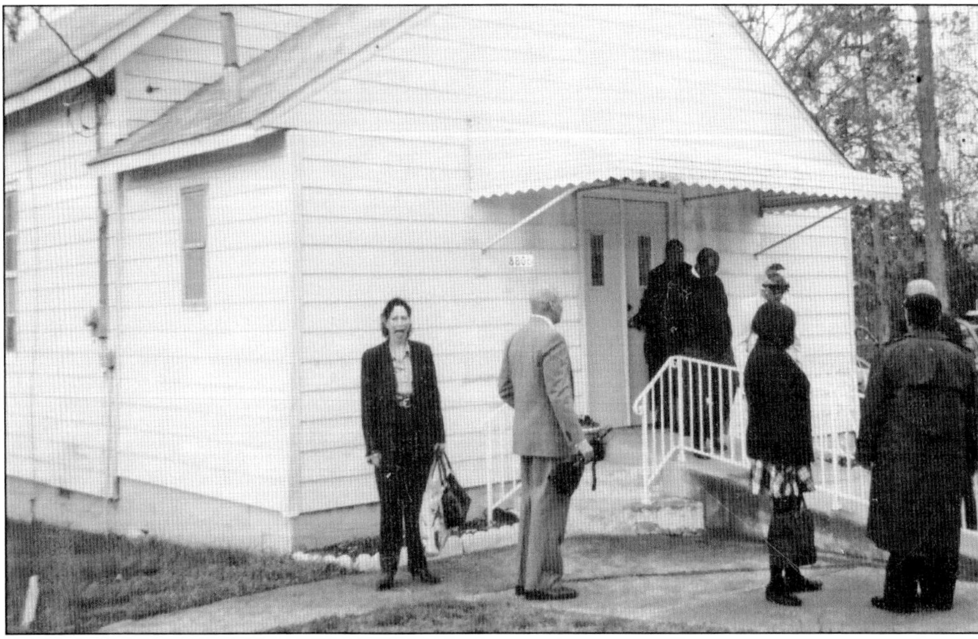

Members of the Capernaum Church of Christ on Lasater Road gather for this photograph before the building was remodeled in 2008. Built in the early 1920s and renovated in 1970, it has served the oldest African American Church of Christ congregation in North Carolina for almost 100 years. The Capernaum congregation had its beginnings at the Warner's Chapel Church of Christ. Warner's Chapel had originally allowed African Americans to attend worship services, and in 1904, the Capernaum congregation decided to formally organize. It continued to meet at Warner's Chapel for a short time before moving permanently to its current location. (Courtesy Capernaum Church of Christ.)

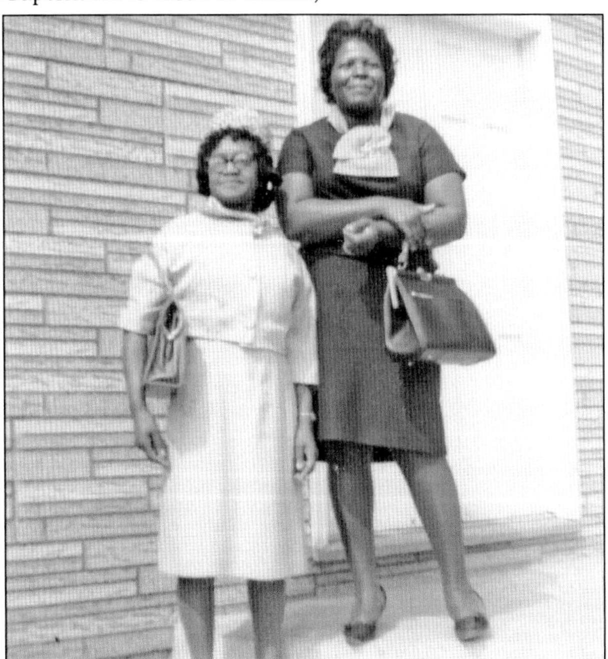

Vivian Evans and Ruby Rucker stand outside the original Capernaum church building in the late 1960s. Evans (1908–2010) was the oldest member of the church for a long time and recalled attending worship services before they were moved from the Warner's Chapel building. A retired cook in the Forsyth County school system, she drove until age 94 and was known for her fried apple pies. Her faithfulness to God and the church was evident; she never missed a service except for once when she was in the hospital. Rucker and her husband, James, are also longtime members of the church. (Courtesy Capernaum Church of Christ.)

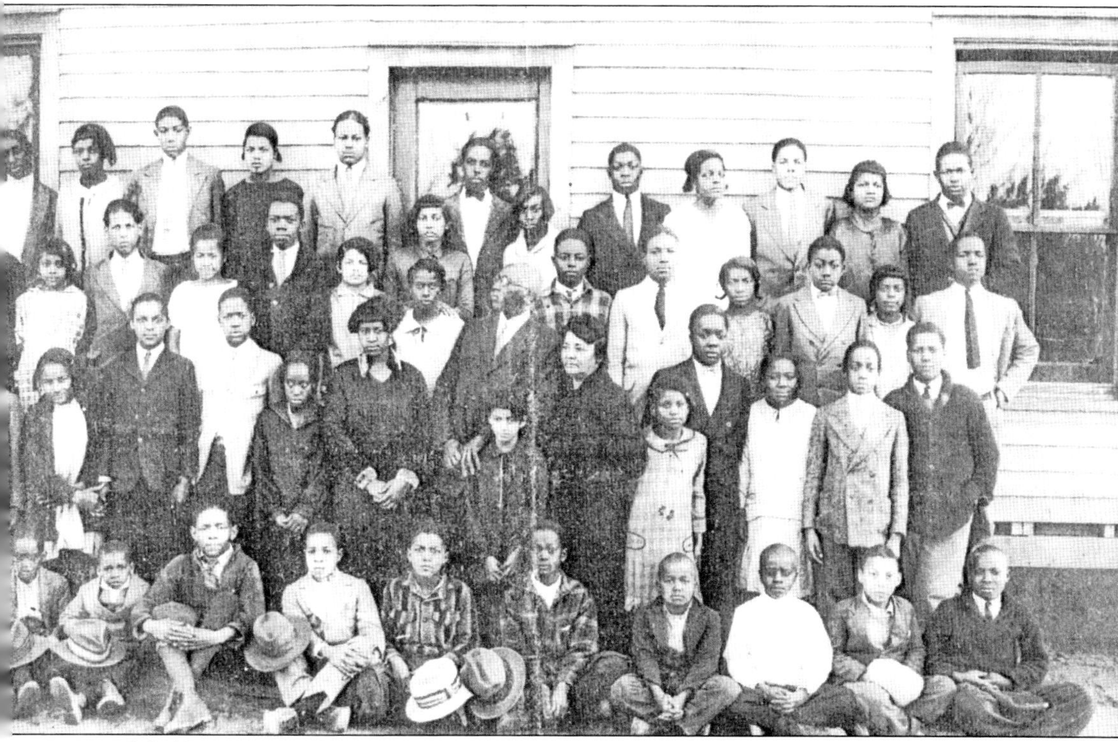

A group of children pose outside the Nelson Preparatory and Industrial School in Clemmons in 1926. The school, founded by Charlie C. Nelson (1873–1940), was south of Clemmons on Hampton Road, where the Winston Salem Shrine Club is today. Built in 1904, the school operated under Nelson's leadership until his death in 1940. Nelson, who was known as a talented musician and singer as well as a strong evangelist, grew up in the fields of Forsyth and Davidson Counties. He was befriended by Sarah Neely, a teacher at the Clemmons Moravian School, who assisted Nelson in his education. As a grown man, Nelson developed a passion for educating and helping the poor and needy, especially young people. His school was both a reform school and an orphanage. Nelson also helped organize several local churches, including Capernaum Church of Christ, of which he was the first minister. He is buried at the Redland Church of Christ in Davie County. Nelson is in the center with his head turned to the side. (Courtesy Capernaum Church of Christ.)

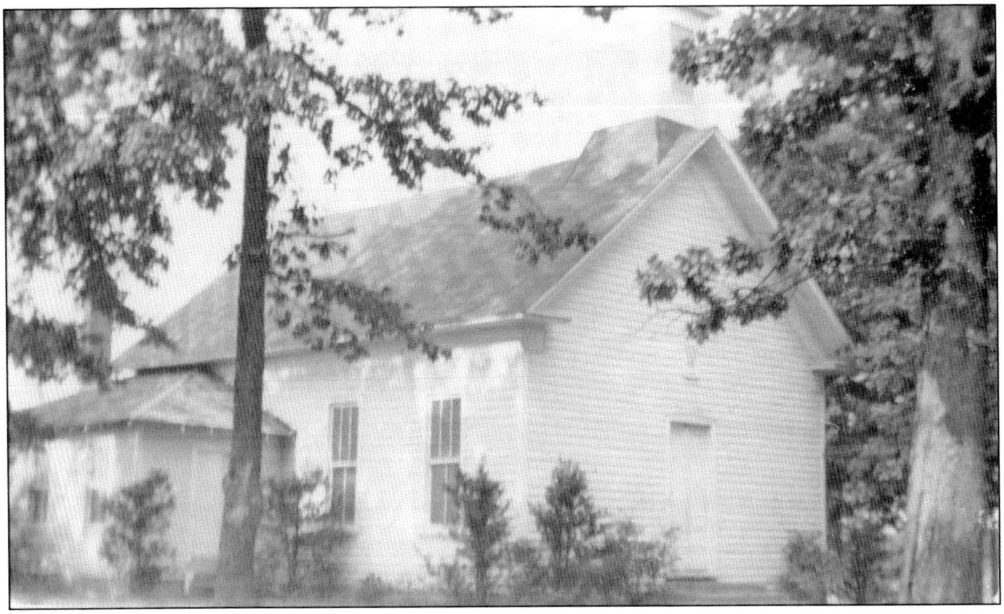

Centenary United Methodist Church is seen here in the late 1940s. The church was organized in 1883 in the Hampton Township south of Clemmons by a traveling preacher named D.S. Earnhardt. The group began meeting in the Hampton School building, and in 1885, they decided to erect their own structure, this time on land just to the north and still on the church property. Local carpenters William Uriah Woosley and W.Z. Hampton were in charge of construction. Membership was transferred from the old school building to the new structure in April 1886. The building was remodeled in 1946 before being replaced by the current structure in the late 1950s. (Courtesy Centenary United Methodist Church.)

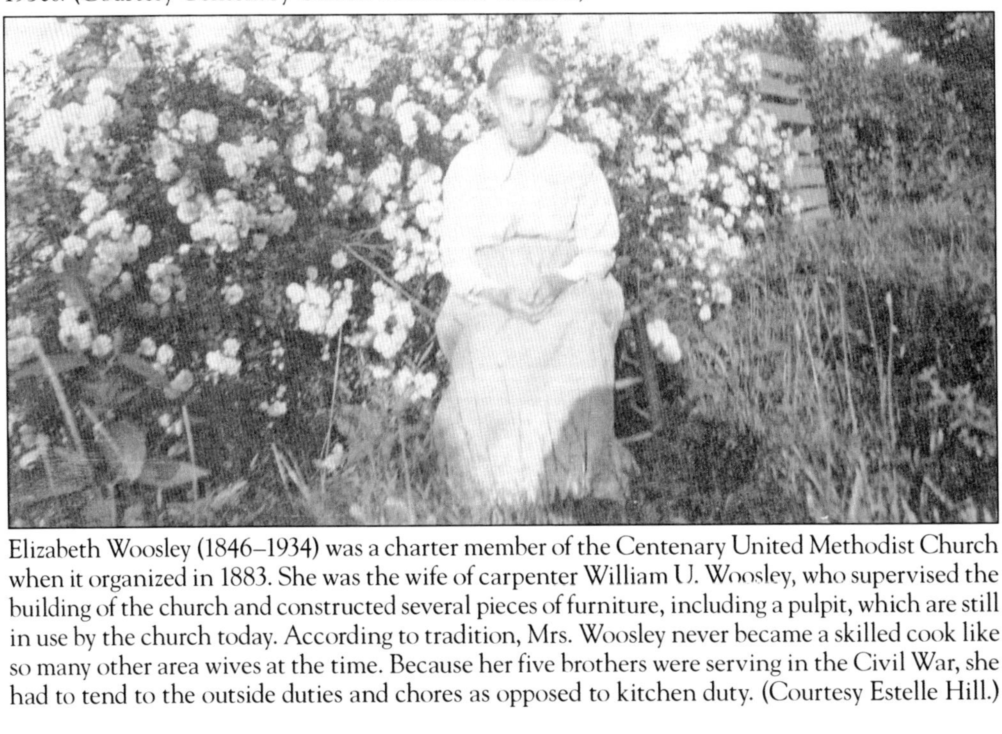

Elizabeth Woosley (1846–1934) was a charter member of the Centenary United Methodist Church when it organized in 1883. She was the wife of carpenter William U. Woosley, who supervised the building of the church and constructed several pieces of furniture, including a pulpit, which are still in use by the church today. According to tradition, Mrs. Woosley never became a skilled cook like so many other area wives at the time. Because her five brothers were serving in the Civil War, she had to tend to the outside duties and chores as opposed to kitchen duty. (Courtesy Estelle Hill.)

Six

TANGLEWOOD

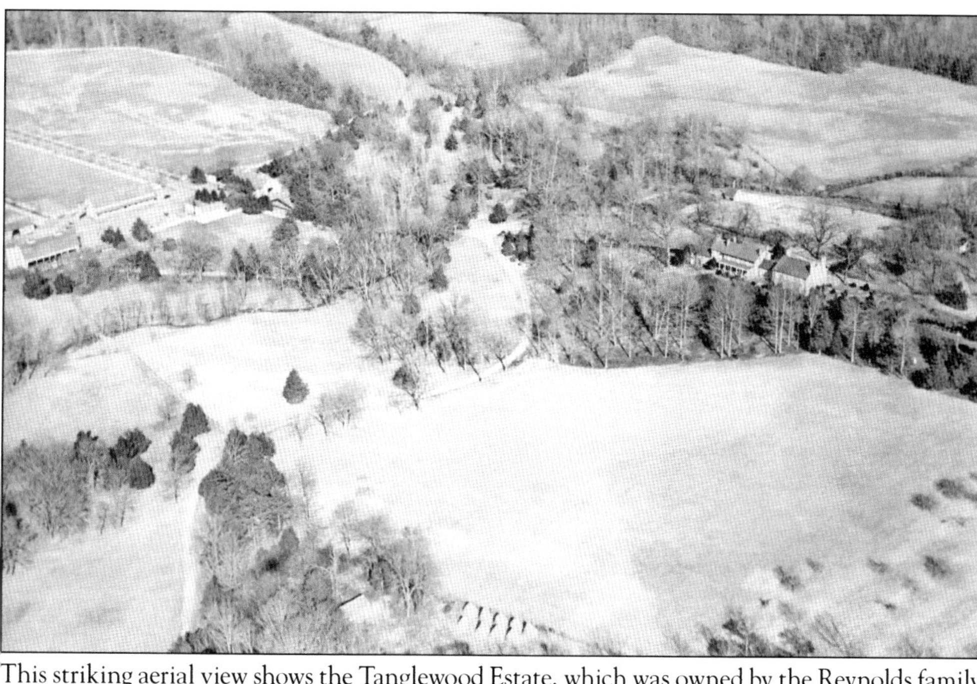

This striking aerial view shows the Tanglewood Estate, which was owned by the Reynolds family from 1921 to 1951 before it was turned into a park. This c. 1950 photograph shows the manor house and the open field in front of the house. The tennis courts and swimming pool now occupy part of this field. (Courtesy Tanglewood Park Photograph Collection.)

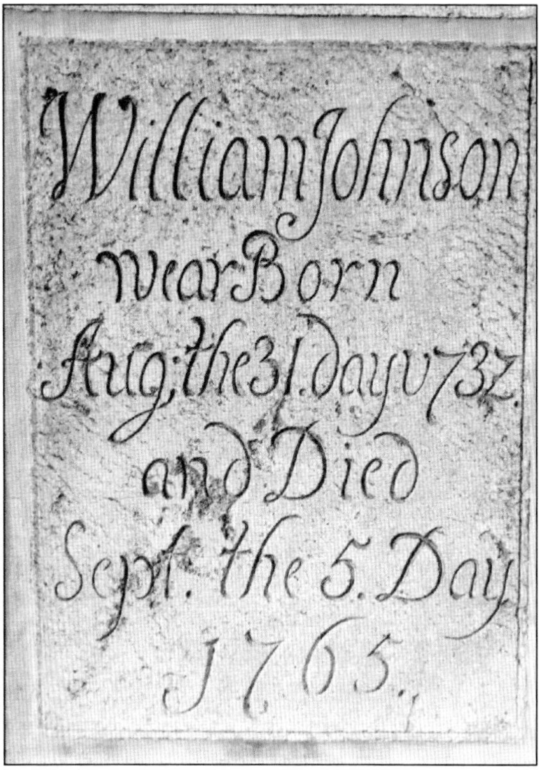

This is the tombstone of William Johnson (1732–1765), the first settler of the area that would eventually become Tanglewood Park. In 1757, he moved to the site with his wife, Elizabeth, and their infant son James after purchasing one square mile of land just east of the Yadkin River from William Linville, another early settler. Johnson's family owned the property until it was sold to the Reynolds family in 1921. This soapstone marker had been lost at one point but was found in 1935. In 1954, it was replaced in the cemetery adjacent to Mount Pleasant Church, where it was encased in a larger granite monument by Johnson's descendants. (Courtesy Tanglewood Photograph Collection.)

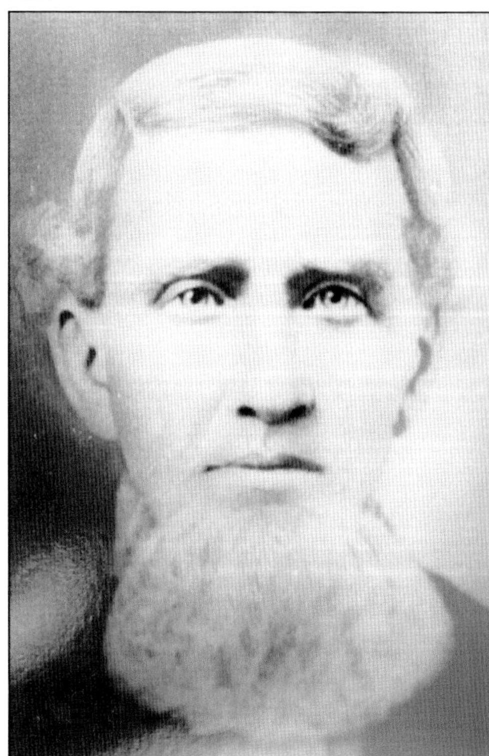

William Coston Johnson (1823–1882) was the great-grandson of William Johnson, who had settled the area that would become Tanglewood. Johnson grew upon the family farmstead before moving to Texas and then coming back to settle in the Winston-Salem area. (Courtesy Jerry Johnson.)

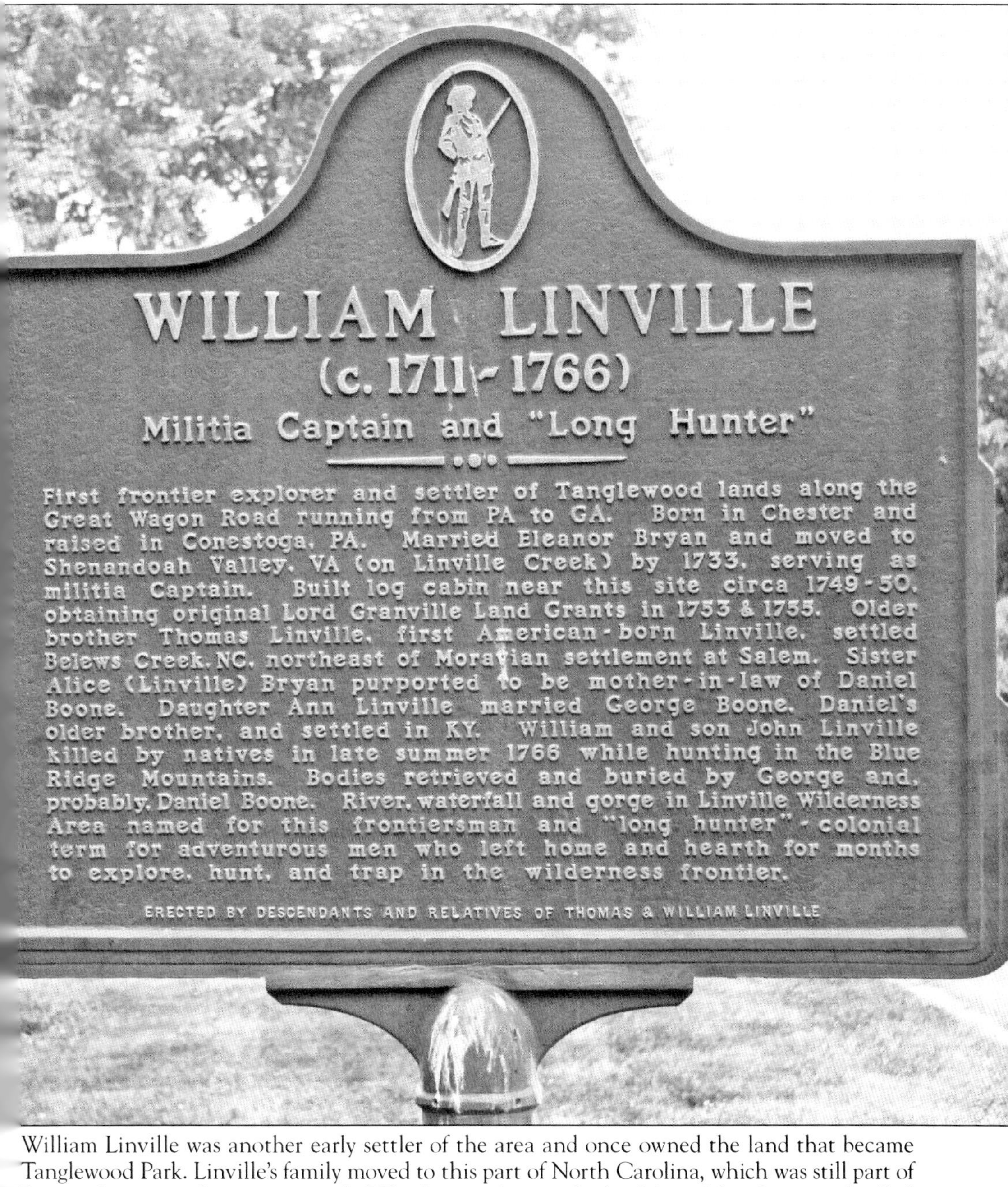

William Linville was another early settler of the area and once owned the land that became Tanglewood Park. Linville's family moved to this part of North Carolina, which was still part of Rowan County at the time, around 1753, after purchasing the land from John Carteret, the Earl of Granville. This early part of the Granville Tract would eventually become the central part of Tanglewood Park. William Linville was killed by Indians while hunting in the mountains of North Carolina in 1766. The area where he was killed was above the waterfalls that soon after came to bear his name. This historical marker was erected by his descendants and is located within Tanglewood Park, near the manor house. (Courtesy Alyson Shulz Photography.)

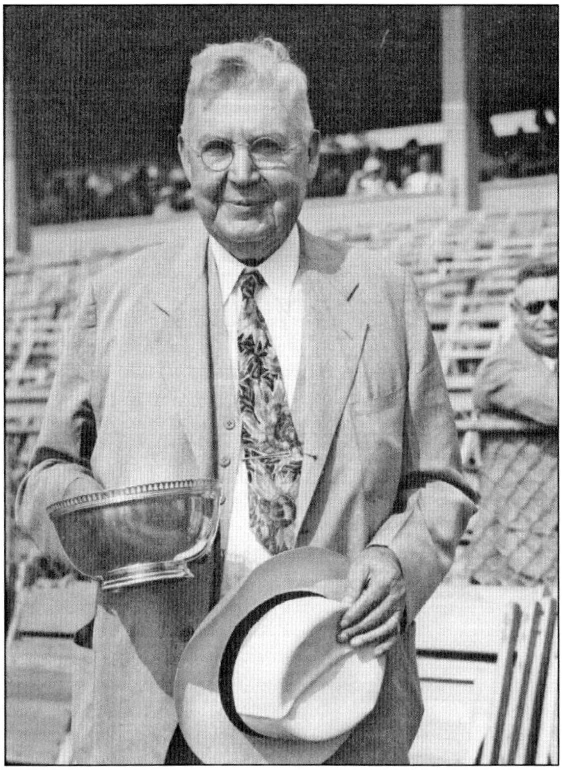

William Neal Reynolds (1863–1951), known simply as "Mr. Will," is seen here in 1947. He was originally from Virginia and settled in the area in 1881 to work with his brother, R.J. Reynolds, the founder of the tobacco company that still bears his name. Mr. Will served in various director roles before moving on to become vice president and then president of the company in 1918, upon the death of his brother. In 1921, Reynolds purchased what would become his Tanglewood estate from the Johnson family. He eventually expanded the property to its current boundaries before donating it to Forsyth County in his will to be used as a park for the enjoyment of the public. Here, Reynolds holds a horseracing trophy. He created a trophy room in the manor house to hold all of his horseracing trophies and memorabilia. (Photograph by Morgan Photograph Service, courtesy Tanglewood Park Photograph Collection.)

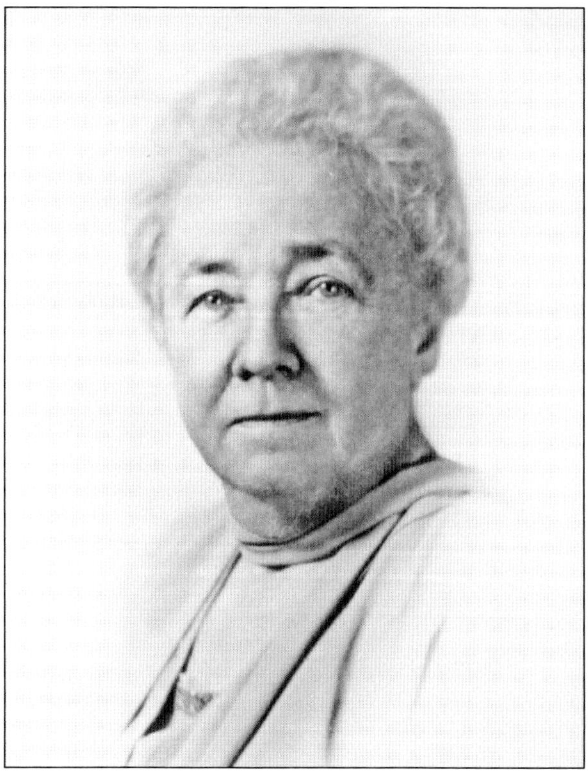

Kate Bitting Reynolds (1867–1947) was raised on a farm near the Yadkin River and married William Reynolds in 1889. Throughout her life, she was interested in addressing issues affecting the quality of health and life for all people. She embarked on various philanthropic endeavors in and around Forsyth County, such as community hospitals for the financially needy. Her will also established the Kate B. Reynolds Charitable Trust, a major trust used to improve the quality of health and life for the poor and needy of North Carolina. Reynolds was also a horticultural enthusiast who sought to beautify the grounds of the Tanglewood Estate with roses, shrubs, trees, and bushes. Today, Tanglewood Park is well known for its arboretum and rose garden. (Courtesy Tanglewood Park Photograph Collection.)

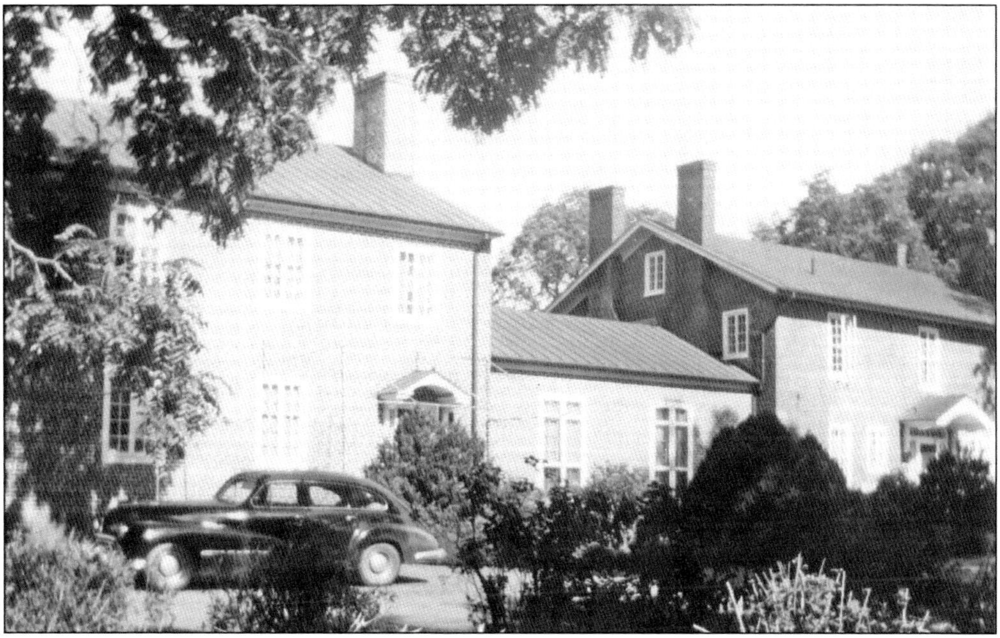

The estate home of the Reynolds family is seen here at Tanglewood in 1947. William and Kate Reynolds lived there from 1921 until their deaths in 1951 and 1947, respectively. Originally a simple two-story structure, Reynolds enlarged it several times, adding two large wings to each side. Today, it is the Manor House Guest Lodge at Tanglewood Park. (Courtesy Tanglewood Park Photograph Collection.)

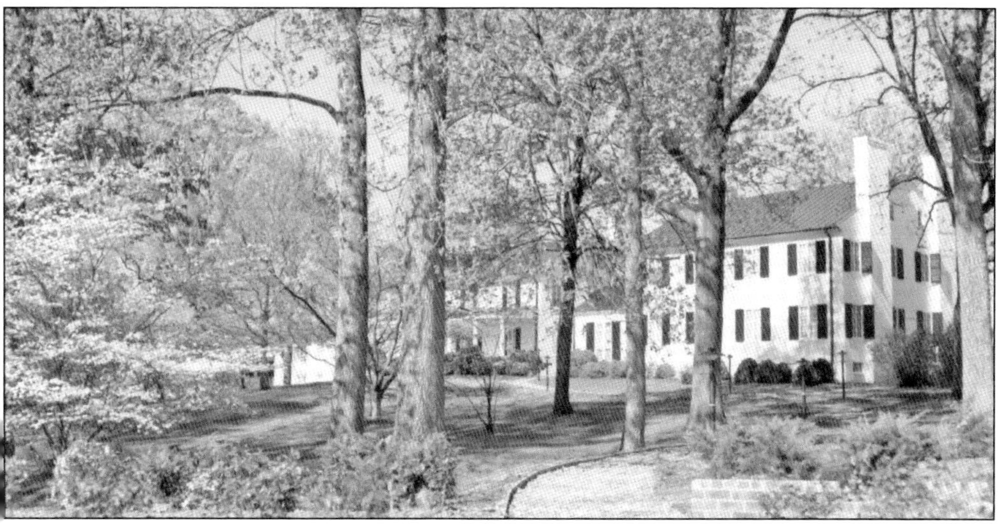

The manor house, formerly the Reynolds home, is seen here after it was renovated into the lodge. The home was built about 1859 as a wedding present from James Johnson Jr. for his daughter, Emily. The central portion of the home is original, with the two large wings added later. After it was sold to the Reynolds family, it was enlarged to 28 rooms. The bricks in the original section of the house are 16 to 18 inches thick and were made on the plantation. Today, the house is operated as a bed and breakfast, offering 10 guest rooms, a restored trophy room, and other theme rooms. The facilities are used for weddings, meetings, and overnight accommodations. (Courtesy Tanglewood Park Photograph Collection.)

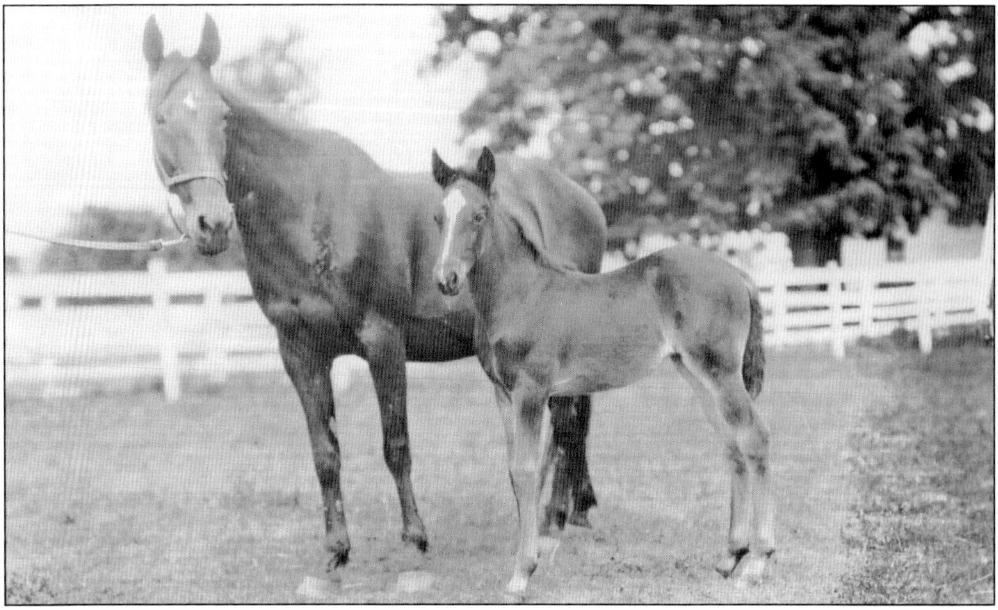

William Reynolds was an avid horseracing enthusiast throughout his life. He owned several farms in North Carolina, Kentucky, and Florida, calling the one in Florida Tanglewood South. The fine standard-bred horses in this 1947 photograph are representative of the horses Reynolds bred and raced. (Courtesy Tanglewood Park Photograph Collection.)

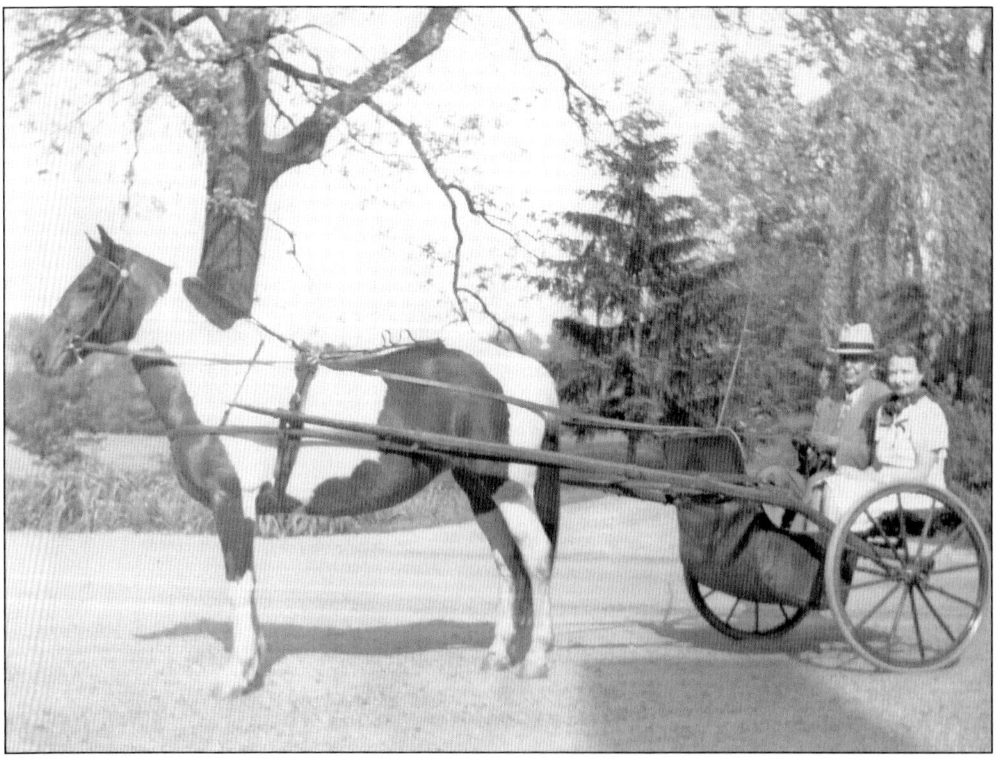

William Reynolds and Nancy Reynolds Bagley enjoy a drive around the Tanglewood estate in 1947. (Courtesy Tanglewood Park Photograph Collection.)

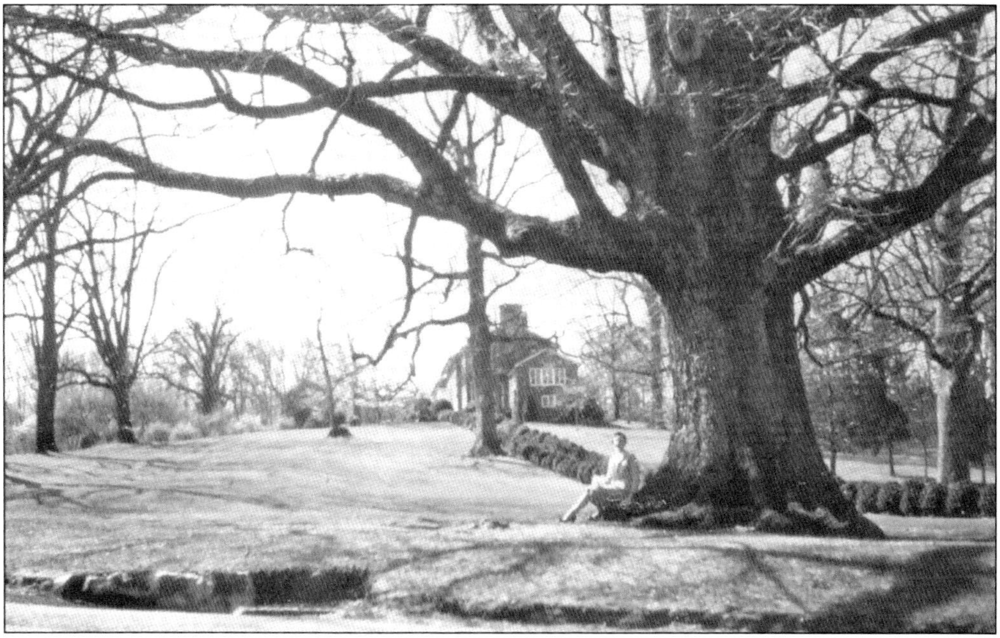

The manor house and grounds are seen here from under the ancient White Oak tree around 1957. The tree, a landmark on the property, is estimated today to be about 400 years old, starting life as a sapling in the early 1600s. In 1987, the tree was designated as a living bicentennial eyewitness to the founding of the United States constitution by the National Arborist Society. (Courtesy Tanglewood Park Photograph Collection.)

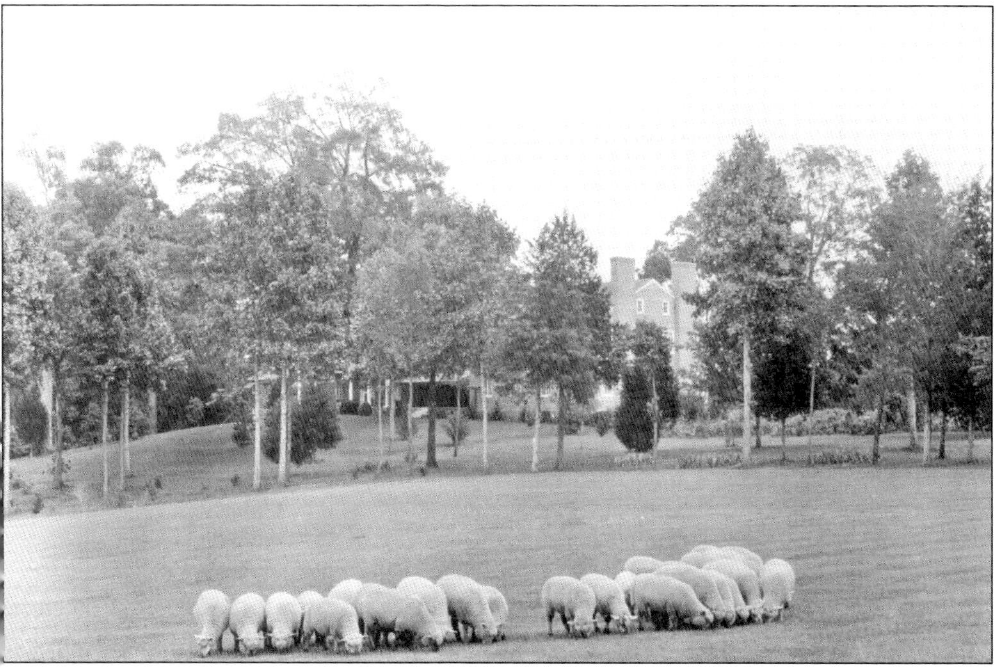

Sheep graze in the pasture that would become the main center of the park in later years, part of it housing the swimming pool and tennis court area. This photograph is from about 1947. (Courtesy Tanglewood Park Photograph Collection.)

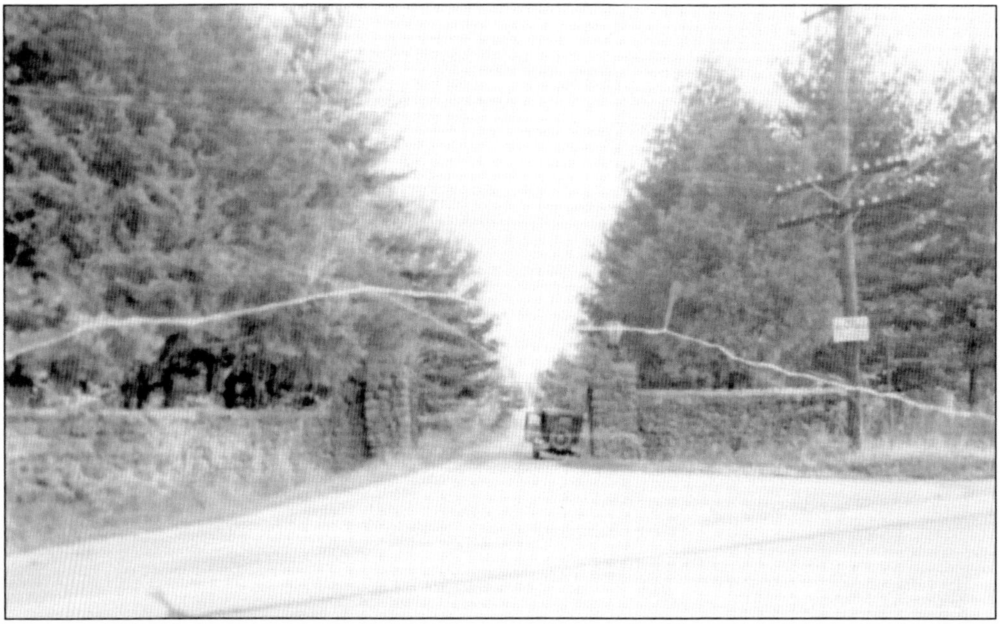

The entrance to Tanglewood Estate off of Highway 158 is seen here in 1951 after the funeral of William Neal Reynolds. The entrance looks similar today, with the exception of the stone walls lining the drive and the new turn lanes off the highway. (Courtesy Forsyth County Public Library.)

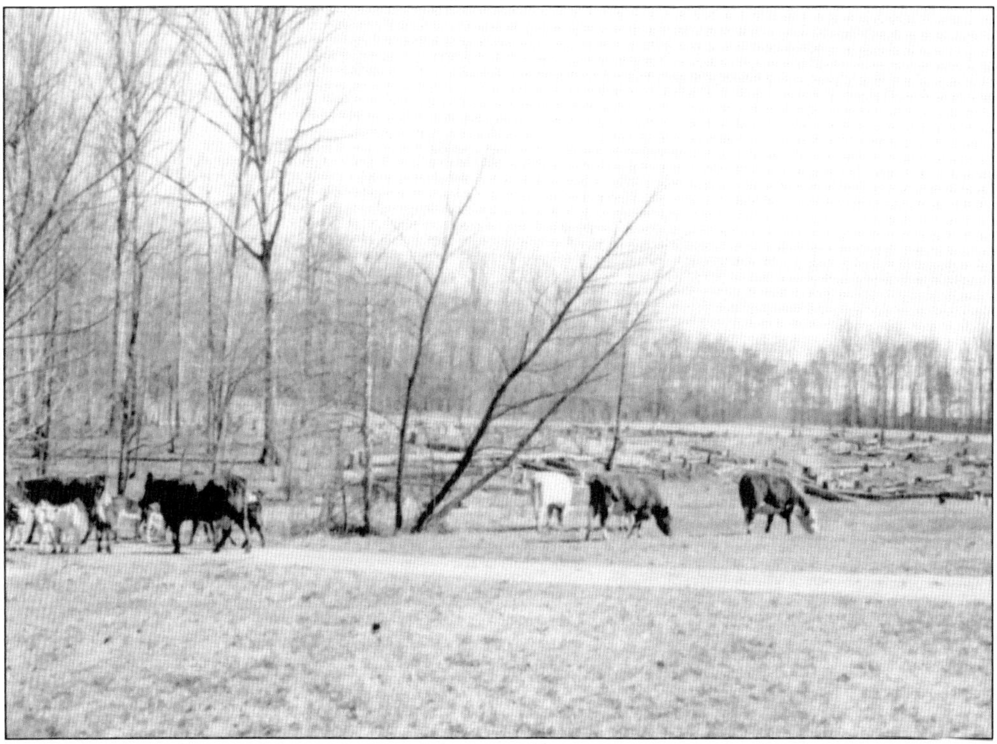

Cows graze on what would soon be the fishing and boating lake, Mallard Lake, in Tanglewood Park in 1953. The land was in the process of being cleared for the lake. (Courtesy Forsyth County Public Library.)

Robert Murray Lybrook (1918–1957) was a farm manager for William Reynolds and became the first park manager of Tanglewood Park. Here, he tests out a mattress in one of the new guest cottages in June 1955. Following his sudden death in 1957 at age 39, he was succeeded by park recreation director Gardner Gidley, who led the development of the park for the next nine years. (Courtesy Tanglewood Park Photograph Collection.)

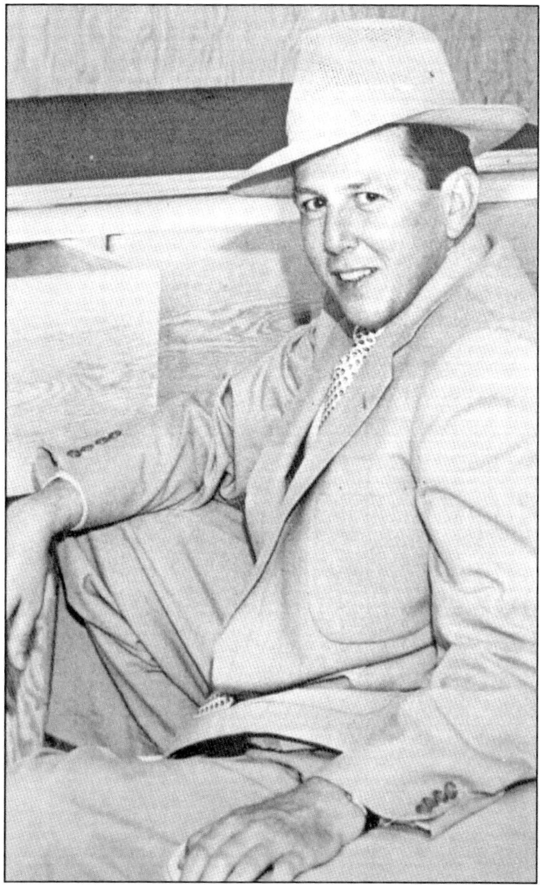

Camp Murray Lybrook Dining Hall is seen below after it opened in 1960. Named in honor of the former park director, the Murray Lybrook Camp provided wholesome and challenging experiences for boys between the ages of 13 and 17. For 11 weeks, these boys lived, ate, worked, and played together. Each boy earned his own tuition by working at various park jobs and by caddying on the golf course. This program provided a worthwhile experience for boys who otherwise could not afford to attend the camp. (Courtesy Tanglewood Park Photograph Collection.)

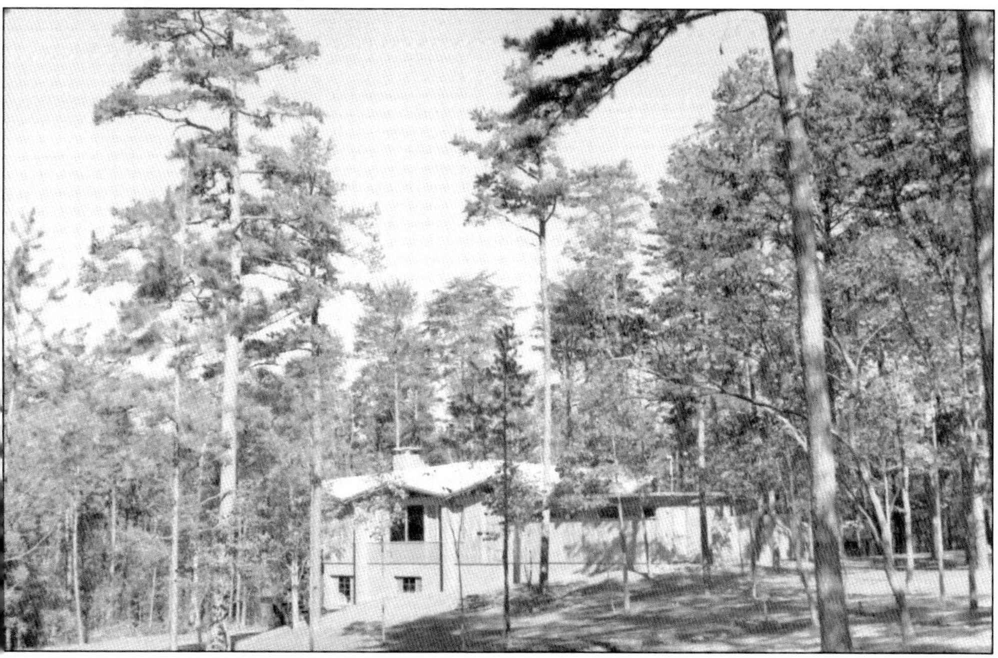

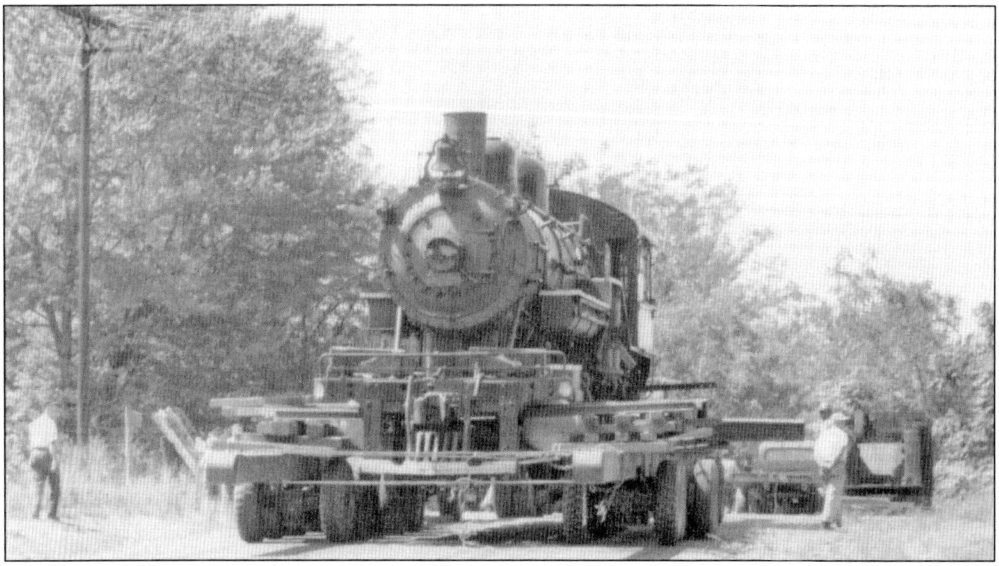

This train locomotive was moved to Tanglewood Park in 1954. Due to its size, the train had to be moved in to the park using the rear entrance from Idol's Road, and was moved by a house-moving company from Mooresville, North Carolina. (Courtesy Forsyth County Public Library.)

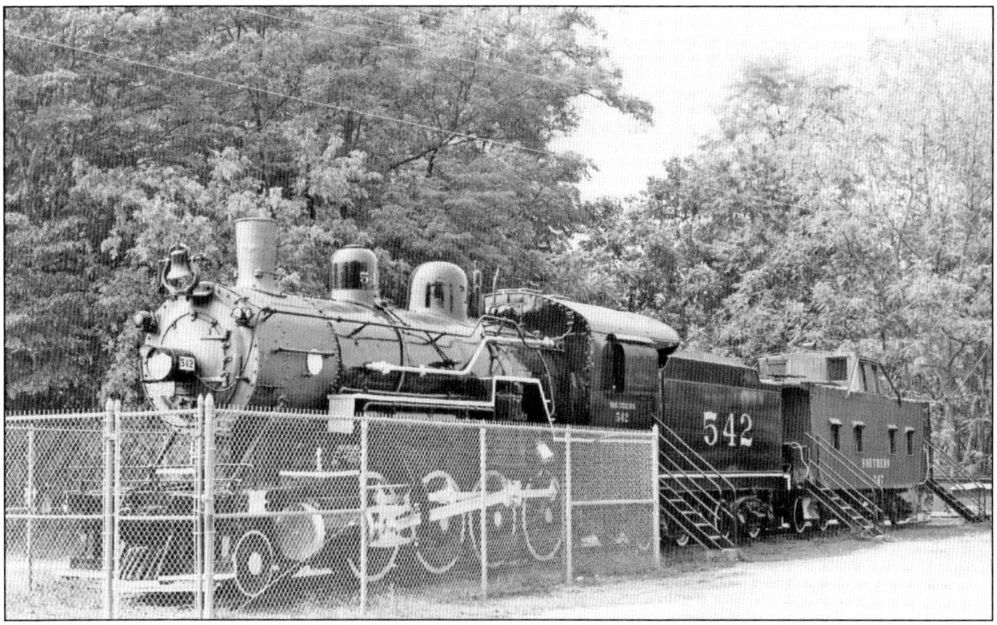

Engine 542 sits at Tanglewood ready for visitors in the 1970s. The locomotive was built by Baldwin Locomotive Works in 1903 and operated on the Southern Railway around Statesville and Winston-Salem. Destined for the scrap pile after retirement, the train was eventually donated to the park in 1954 along with the caboose. After the discovery that this 2-8-0 Consolidation J-class steam locomotive was the last remaining example of its class in 1991, it was moved to the North Carolina Transportation Museum in Spencer, North Carolina. It was replaced by the current Engine 1894, an ex-Illinois Central locomotive. The display is popular, especially for children, and the locomotive even gets a special train-themed treatment at the annual Festival of Lights hosted by Tanglewood Park. (Courtesy Tanglewood Park Photograph Collection.)

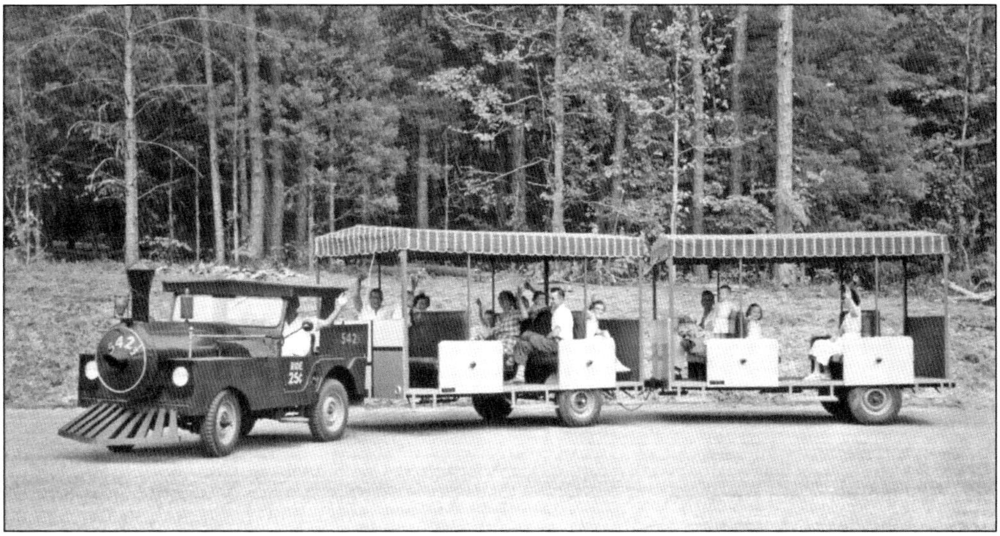

Engine 542 ½, powered by an old Army jeep, takes park visitors on a ride around the picnic area. Engineer Bud Carter is at the controls of the "locomotive" in this late-1950s photograph. (Courtesy Tanglewood Park Photograph Collection.)

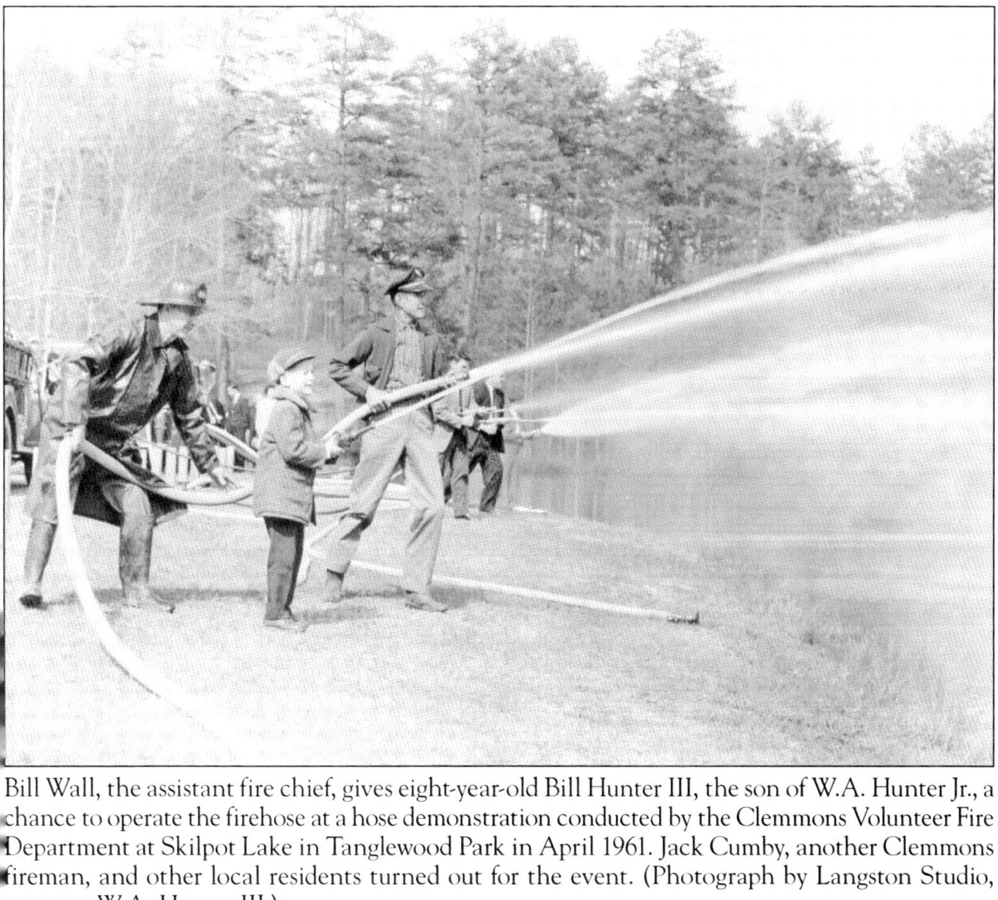

Bill Wall, the assistant fire chief, gives eight-year-old Bill Hunter III, the son of W.A. Hunter Jr., a chance to operate the firehose at a hose demonstration conducted by the Clemmons Volunteer Fire Department at Skilpot Lake in Tanglewood Park in April 1961. Jack Cumby, another Clemmons fireman, and other local residents turned out for the event. (Photograph by Langston Studio, courtesy W.A. Hunter III.)

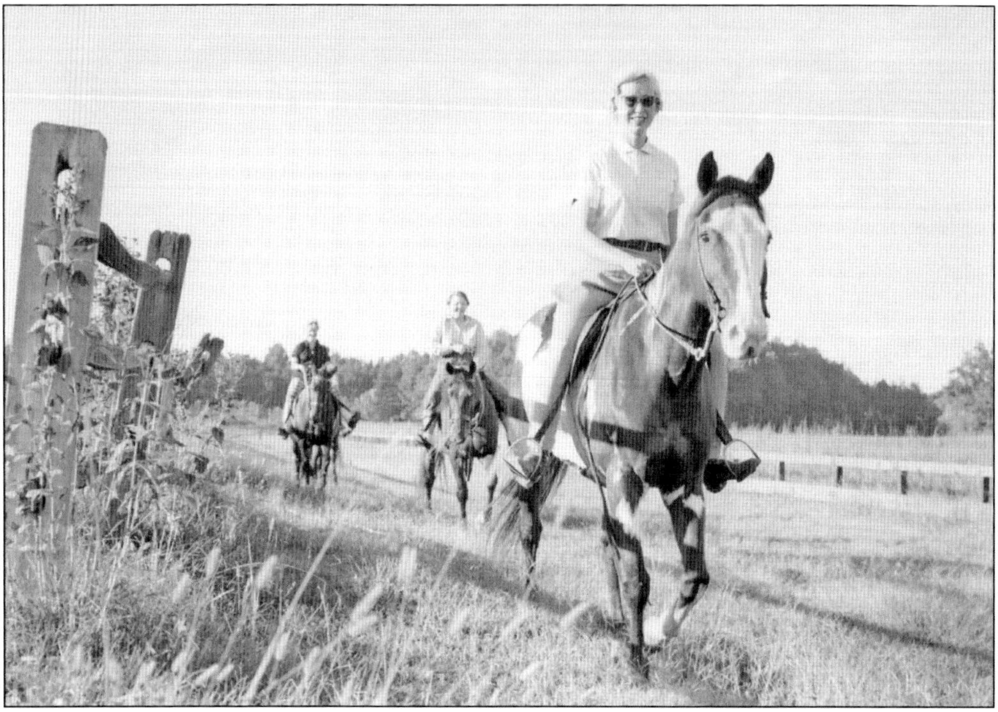

Riding instructor Betty Button leads a group of riders down some of the 10 miles of bridle trails in Tanglewood Park in October 1957. (Courtesy Tanglewood Park Photograph Collection.)

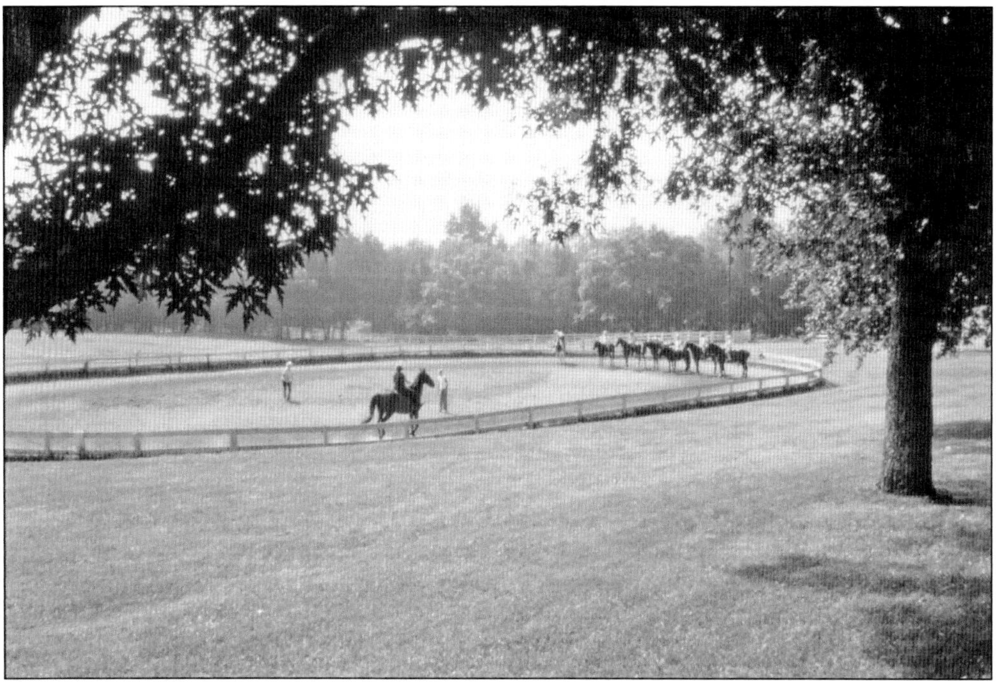

The horse-riding instruction area at Tanglewood is on the left entering the park on the main road. This is a view of the area from about 1969. This service offered by the park remains popular today. (Courtesy Tanglewood Park Photograph Collection.)

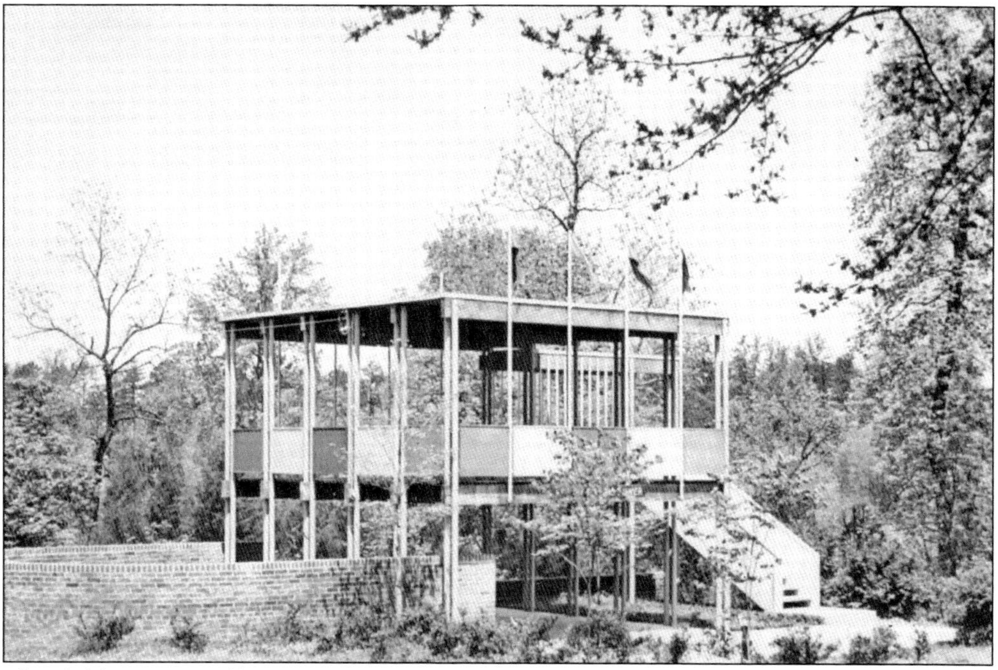

The children's storytelling tower (above) was a feature of Tanglewood Park when it opened to the public in July 1954. It no longer exists, but was in the central part of the park, near where the new shelter number four is today. (Courtesy Tanglewood Park Photograph Collection.)

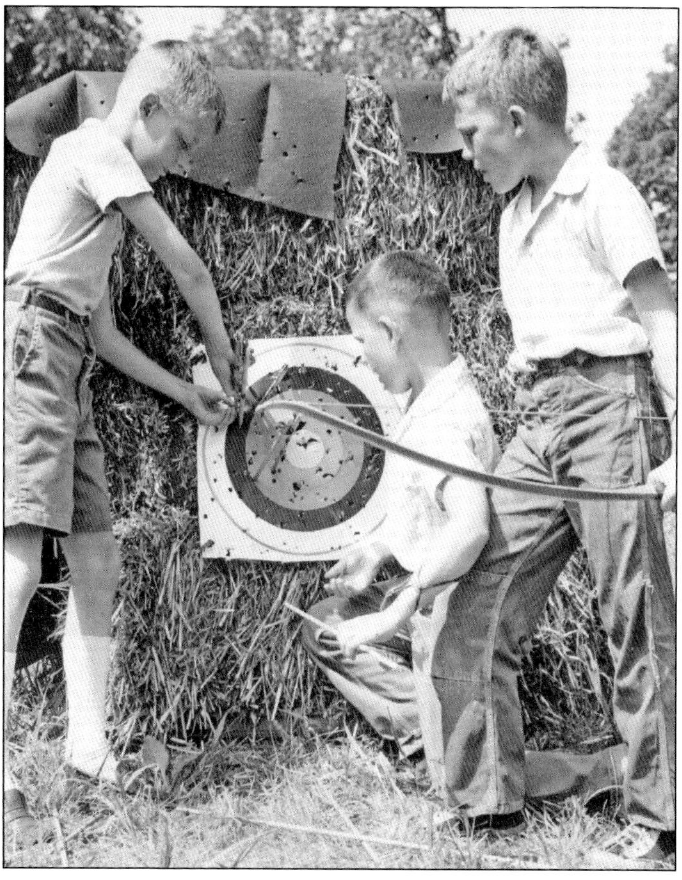

From left to right, Doug Sawyer, Michael Kent, and Gene Swearinger enjoy the archery range, one of many activities offered by the Tanglewood Park camps. As the 1957 photograph shows, the boys' marksmanship was quite good. (Courtesy Tanglewood Park Photograph Collection.)

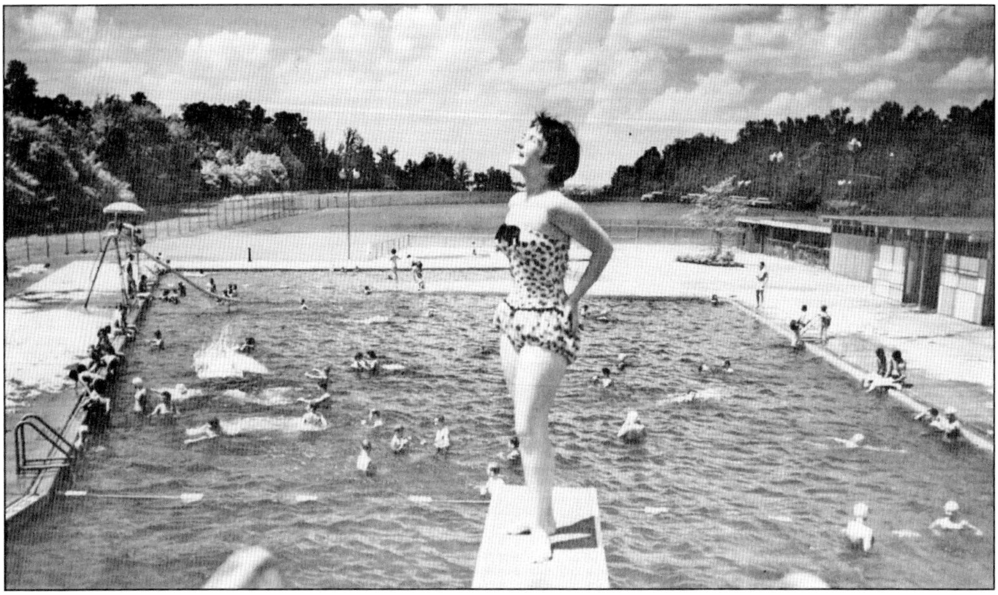

Joyce Carol Hester models for noted *Winston-Salem Journal* photographer Frank Jones on opening day of the new swimming pool at Tanglewood Park in May 1955. The original pool operated until 2000, when it began a series of renovations. (Photograph by Frank Jones, courtesy Tanglewood Park Photograph Collection.)

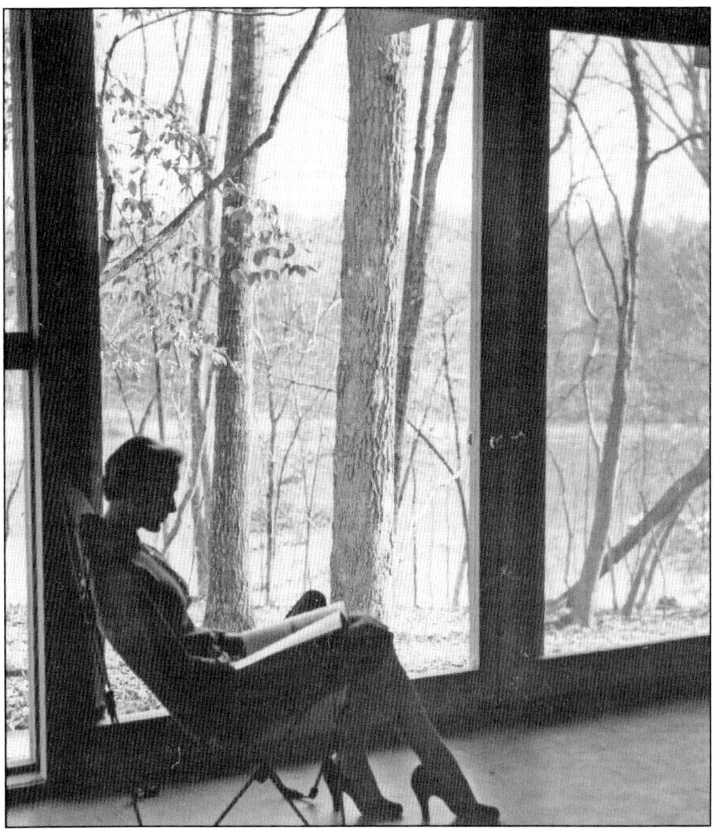

Linda Vogler enjoys a book and a quiet, peaceful setting at Tanglewood Park in the late 1950s. This photograph is from the interior of one of the cottages built for overnight guests of the park. The cottages, adjacent to Mallard Lake, are still enjoyed by visitors. (Courtesy Tanglewood Park Photograph Collection.)

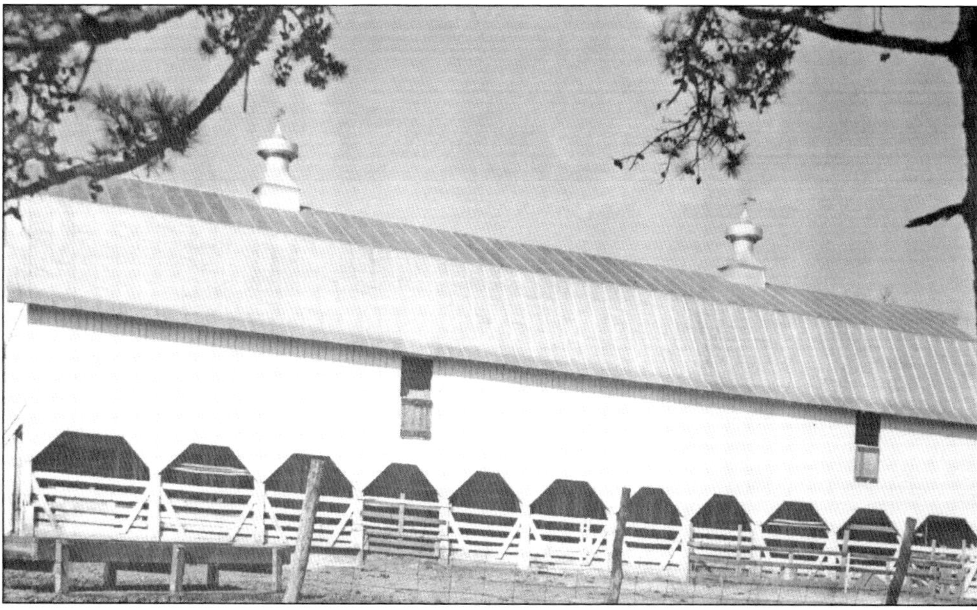

The red barn at Tanglewood Park is seen here before its 1957 renovation, when it had been used as a dairy barn for William Reynolds's dairy cows. (Courtesy Tanglewood Park Photograph Collection.)

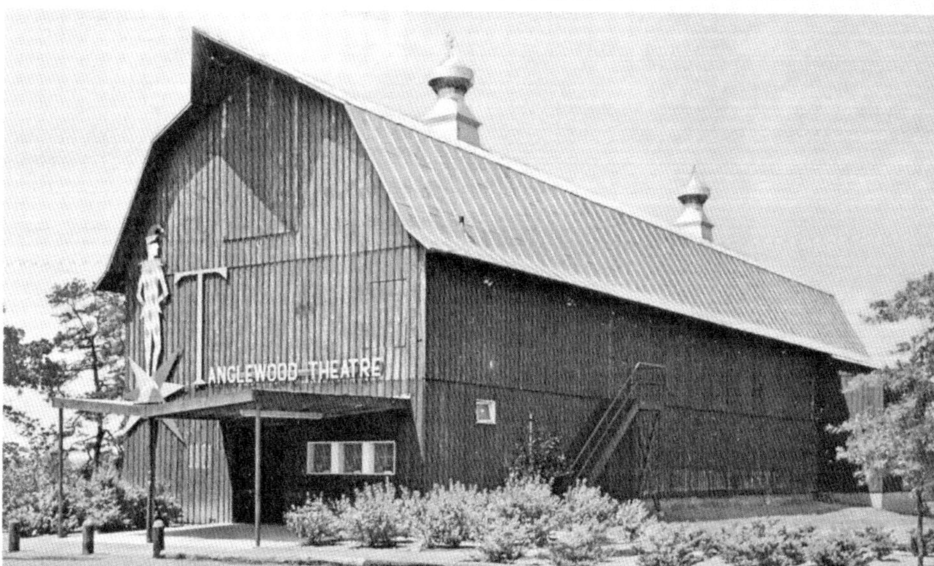

Barn Theatre, Tanglewood Park, Near Winston-Salem

After being renovated, the barn was used as a professional theatre, the first in the area at the time. During production season, people gathered in lines to see the various summer stock theater productions. The productions varied in theme and featured stock actors from all over the country. The barn was used for this purpose until 1965, and today is used for hosting corporate or celebratory activities and meetings. A good year for the Barn Theatre, which usually lasted only 10 weeks during the year, drew more than 15,000 people overall. The harlequin design on the barn was created by artist George Arnold. (Postcard by J.B. Armstrong News Agency, courtesy Tanglewood Park Photograph Collection.)

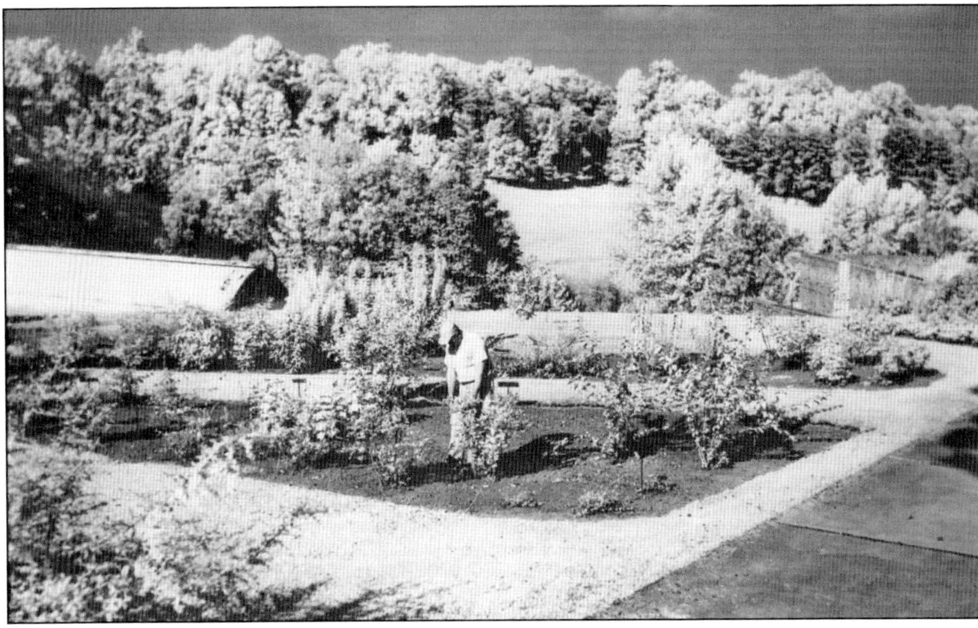

The beginnings of the rose garden and arboretum at Tanglewood Park were the work of Frank Lustig, a native of Germany who worked as a horticulturist for the Reynolds family and then Tanglewood Park for more than 60 years until his death. He is seen here working on the arboretum. Lustig also contributed to the rose garden, which eventually grew to more than 800 bushes. Lustig is buried at Tanglewood Park in the cemetery next to the Mount Pleasant church. (Photograph by Frank Jones, courtesy Tanglewood Park Photograph Collection.)

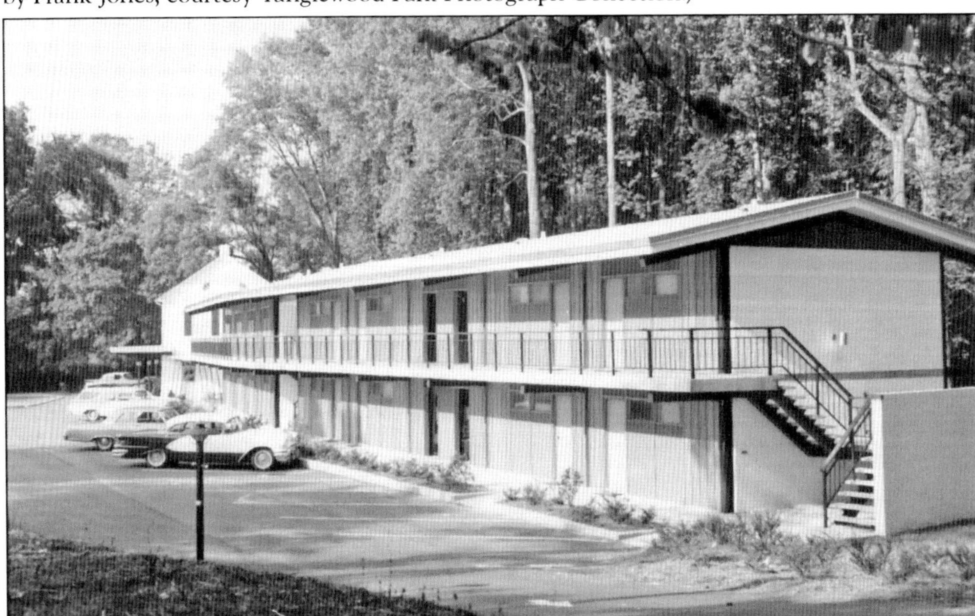

The 18-room lodge at Tanglewood Park was completed in 1961. The units were all well apportioned and even had air conditioning. Along with the manor house and the guest cottages, the lodge brought the available number of guestrooms at Tanglewood to 29. The lodge was adjacent to the manor house but no longer exists. (Courtesy Tanglewood Park Photograph Collection.)

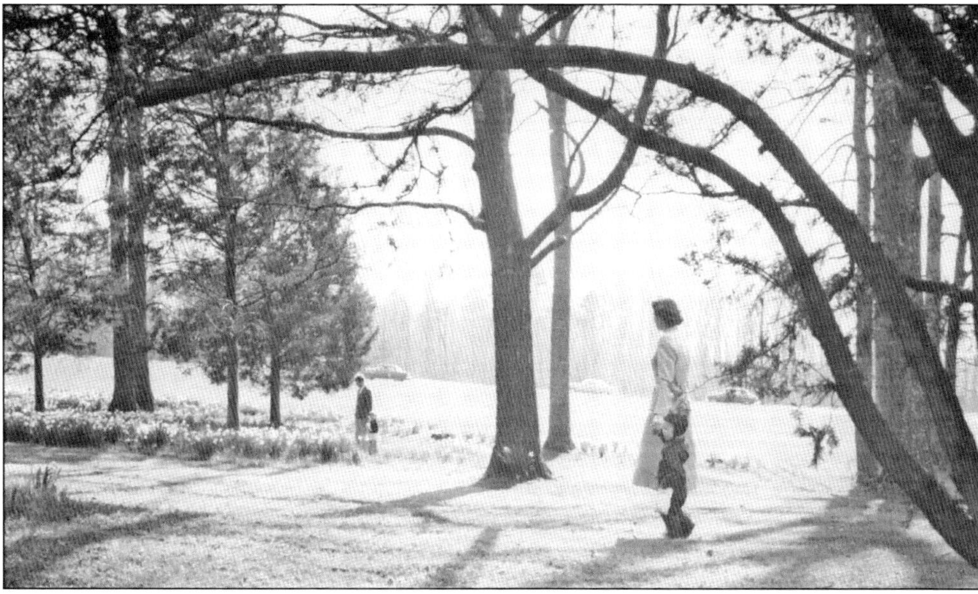

A family enjoys a walk around Tanglewood Park around 1955. When Tanglewood officially opened to the public in July 1954, visitors found horseback riding, a children's visitor center, a family picnic area, lakes, nature trails, an overnight camp for children, the arboretum, and a six-acre deer park. The park was instrumental in driving and helping sustain the local economy. In just 10 years, the park welcomed more than five million visitors. (Courtesy Tanglewood Park Photograph Collection.)

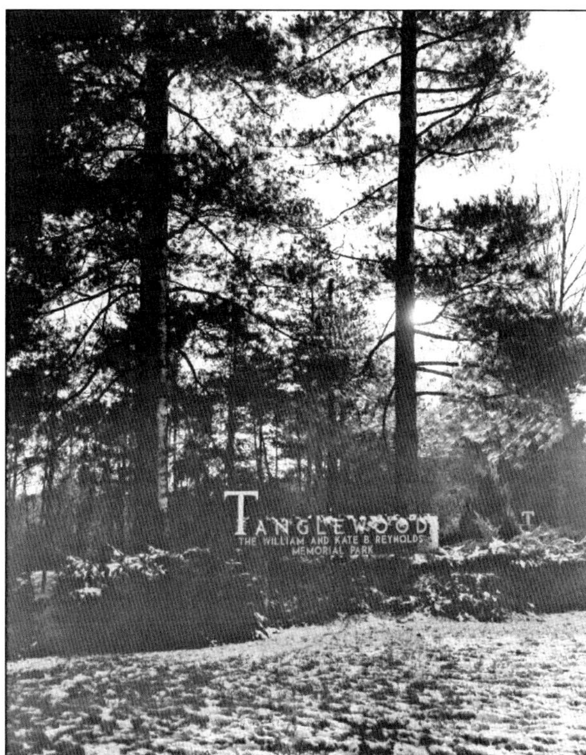

The original Tanglewood Park entrance sign, designed by Gardner Gidley, stands at the front of the park entrance in this mid-1950s photograph. In 1959, a new Y-shaped entrance was designed and installed to break up the traffic that had been bottlenecking on Highway 158 during the park's busy season. This sign has since been replaced by an impressive new stone structure. (Courtesy Tanglewood Park Photograph Collection.)

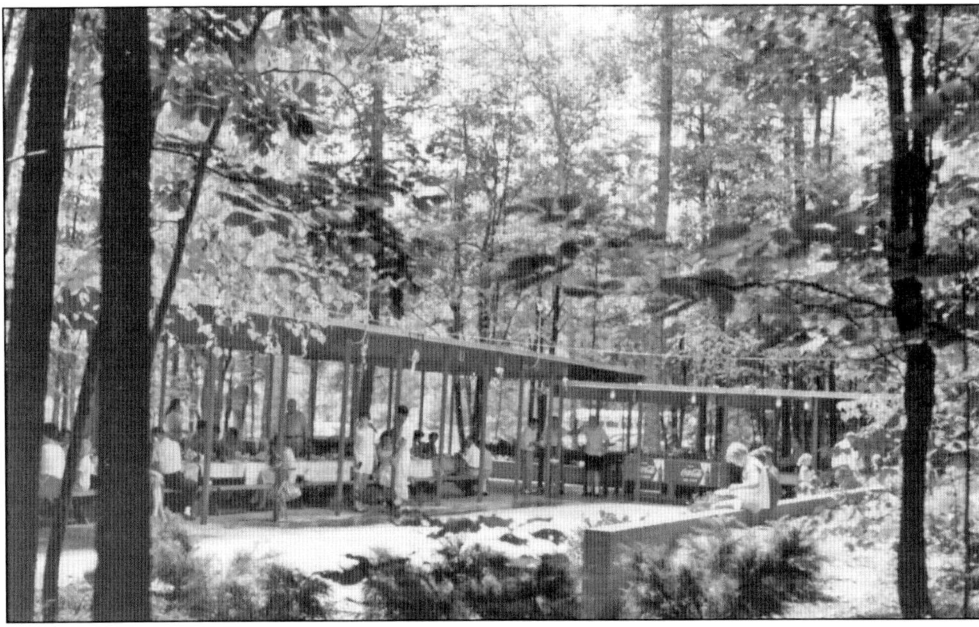

Families enjoy a picnic at Tanglewood Park in this 1959 photograph. This was shelter number two, which was located on the left just at the entrance to the park past the guardhouse. It has recently been renovated into a larger, more substantial shelter. The park had many visitors to the picnic shelters in its early days. In 1959, only five years after the park opened, more than 400 groups and 33,000 individuals had used one of the park's three shelters. The park still provides a nice setting for such activities. (Courtesy Tanglewood Park Photograph Collection.)

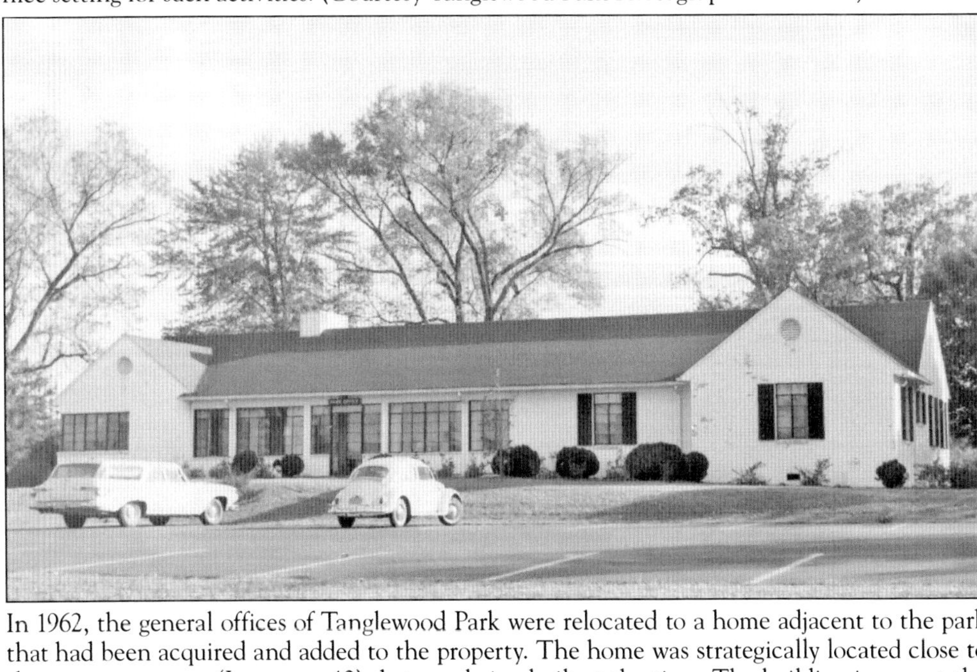

In 1962, the general offices of Tanglewood Park were relocated to a home adjacent to the park that had been acquired and added to the property. The home was strategically located close to the new expressway (Interstate 40) that was being built at the time. The building is now at the end of Nature Trail Drive and, in addition to serving as the main office, it also houses the park's nature and science education materials. (Courtesy Tanglewood Park Photograph Collection.)

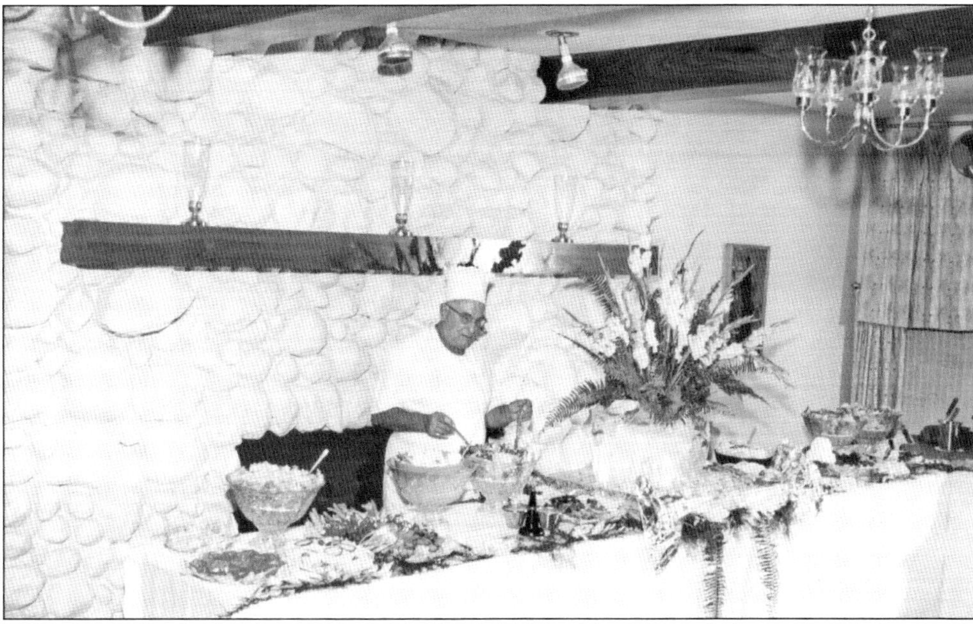

Chef Charles Brodt, who joined Tanglewood as the executive chef at the manor house, is seen here preparing one of his feasts, along with an ice sculpture, which he was also known for. Brodt prepared buffets like this for the Barn Theatre's opening night plays. The former Army cook from Chicago had been the executive chef at the John Sevier Hotel in Johnson City, Tennessee. Brodt, who liked preparing buffets, once met and cooked for Grace Kelly and starred as a chef in her 1956 film *The Swan*. (Courtesy Tanglewood Park Photograph Collection.)

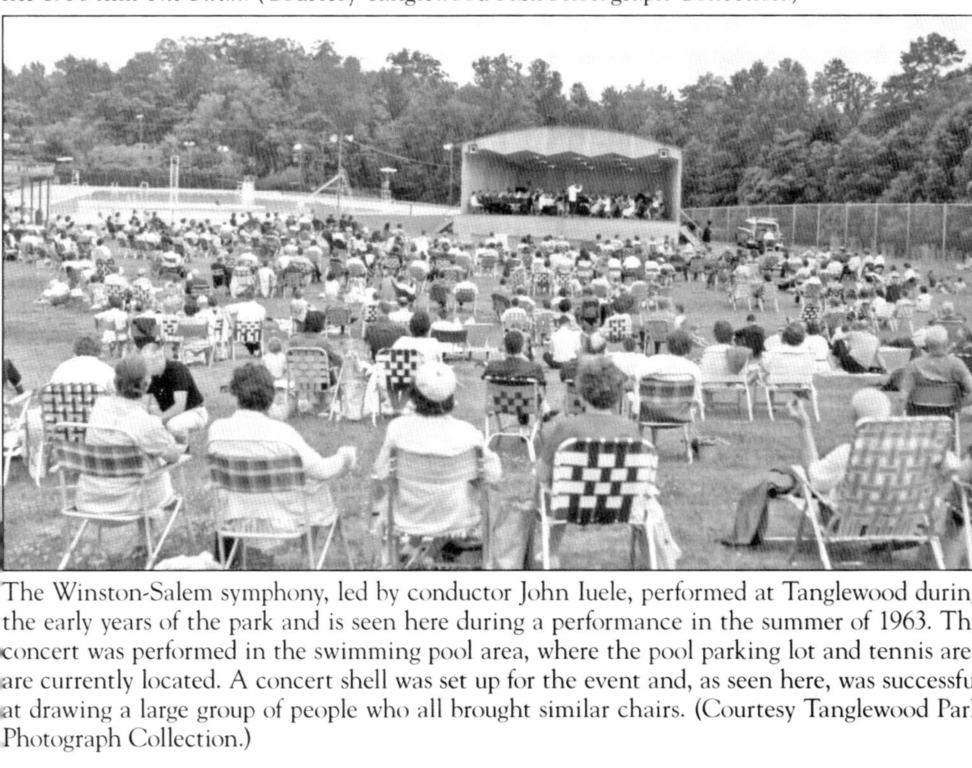

The Winston-Salem symphony, led by conductor John Iuele, performed at Tanglewood during the early years of the park and is seen here during a performance in the summer of 1963. The concert was performed in the swimming pool area, where the pool parking lot and tennis area are currently located. A concert shell was set up for the event and, as seen here, was successful at drawing a large group of people who all brought similar chairs. (Courtesy Tanglewood Park Photograph Collection.)

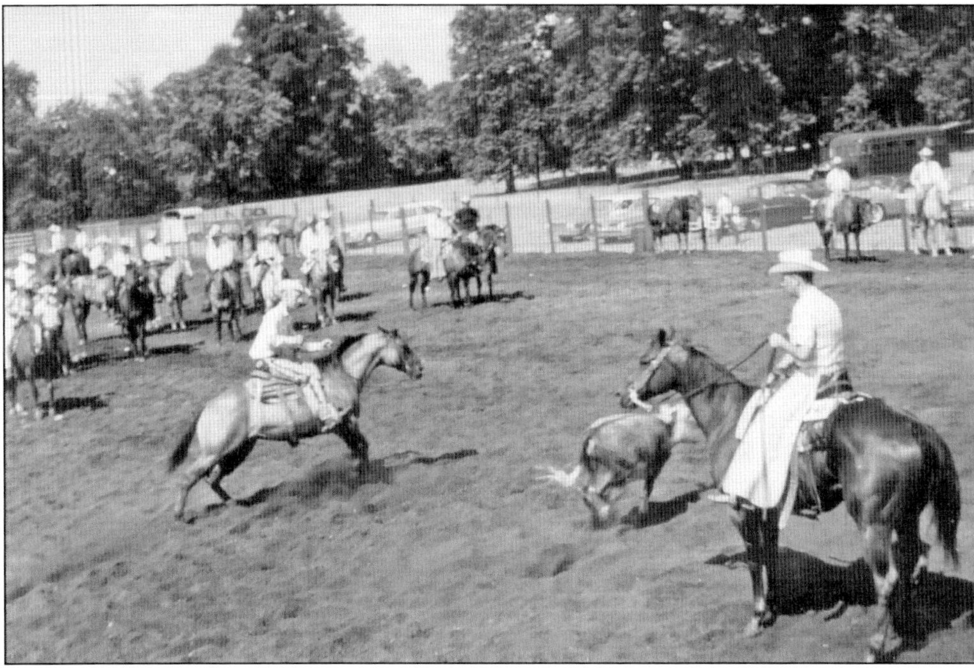

A popular event during the 1964 park season was Remuda Days. Involving wrangling cattle and horses, it is a popular activity with horse and Western enthusiasts. Tanglewood Park was the host of several such events throughout the 1960s. (Courtesy Tanglewood Park Photograph Collection.)

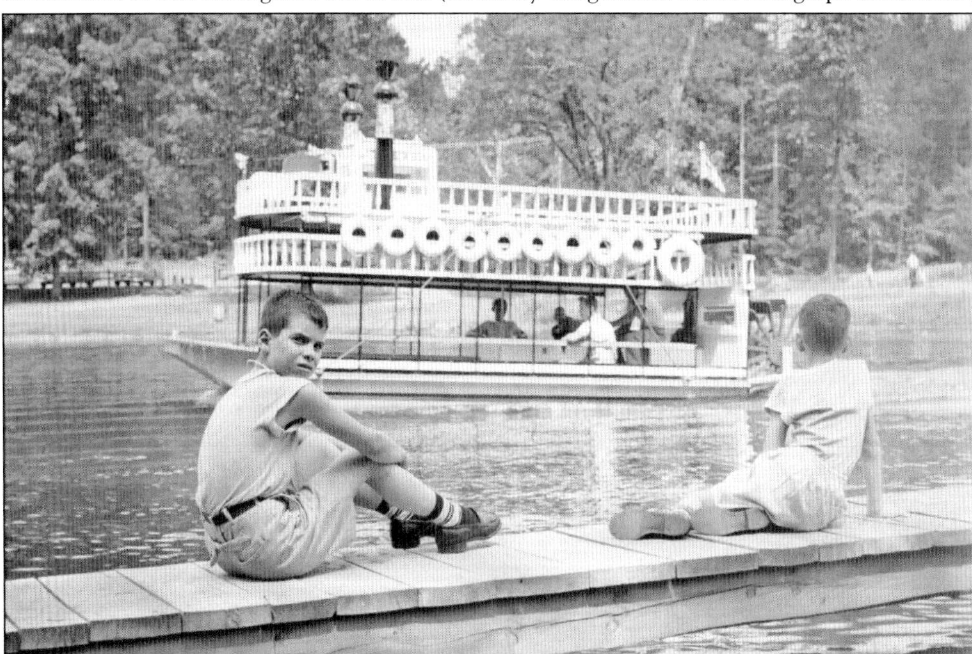

The mini-Mississippi Steamboat, launched in 1958, paddles its way across Mallard Lake while these youngsters await their turn to ride. The steamboat was a popular guest attraction and was used for many years before being retired in the late 1960s. (Courtesy Tanglewood Park Photograph Collection.)

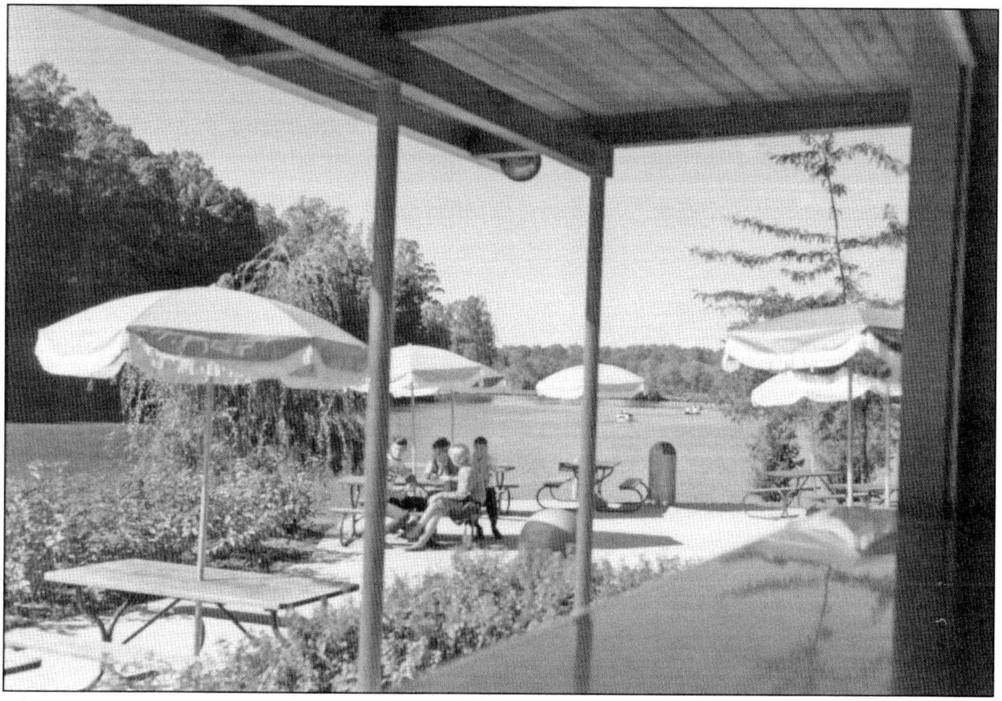

This view from the snack bar at Mallard Lake looks out past park visitors enjoying a quiet lunch on the eating terrace that was added in 1964. The snack bar and terrace still exist and today are used for paddleboat rentals. (Courtesy Tanglewood Park Photograph Collection.)

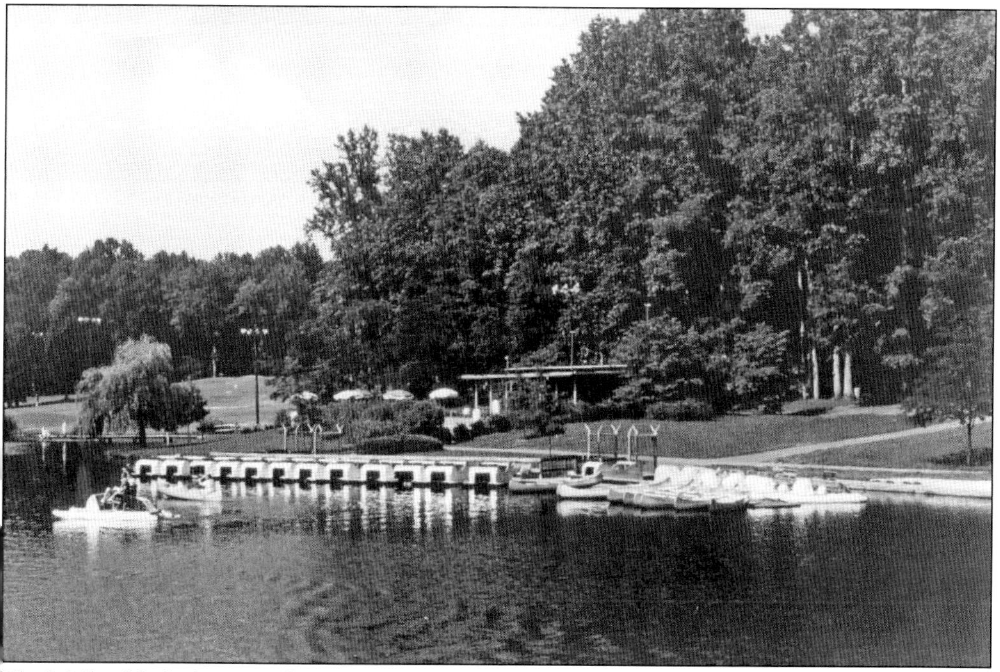

The Mallard Lake boating fleet is seen here in 1967. After the retirement of the mini-Mississippi Steamboat, the fleet consisted of six canoes, six paddleboats, and five bicycle boats. (Courtesy Tanglewood Park Photograph Collection.)

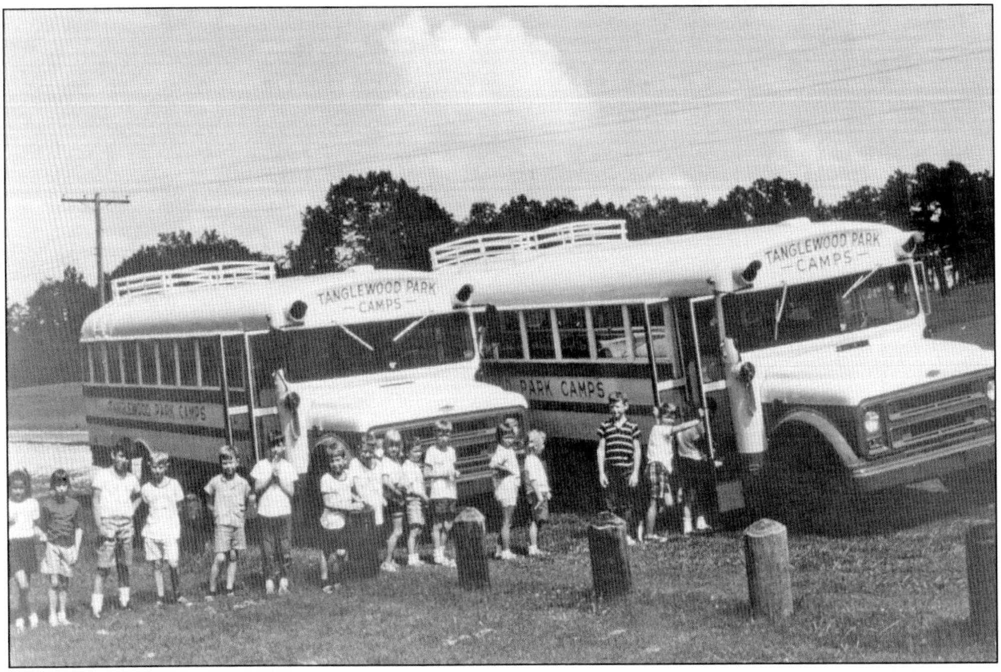

Students line up to board the new 54-passenger buses that Tanglewood acquired in 1967 for use with its youth camps. Tanglewood Park was one of the first parks in the area to begin offering coed camps for boys and girls. (Courtesy Tanglewood Park Photograph Collection.)

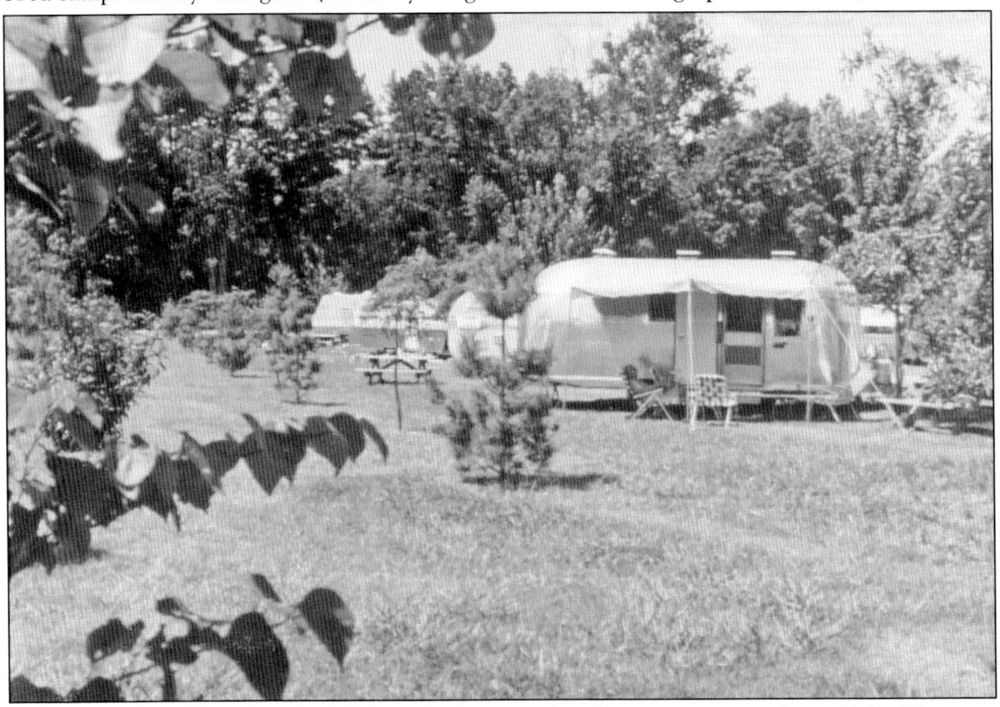

A park visitor enjoys some peace and quiet in the family camping area about 1969. The area remains a popular place for families to camp at Tanglewood. (Courtesy Tanglewood Park Photograph Collection.)

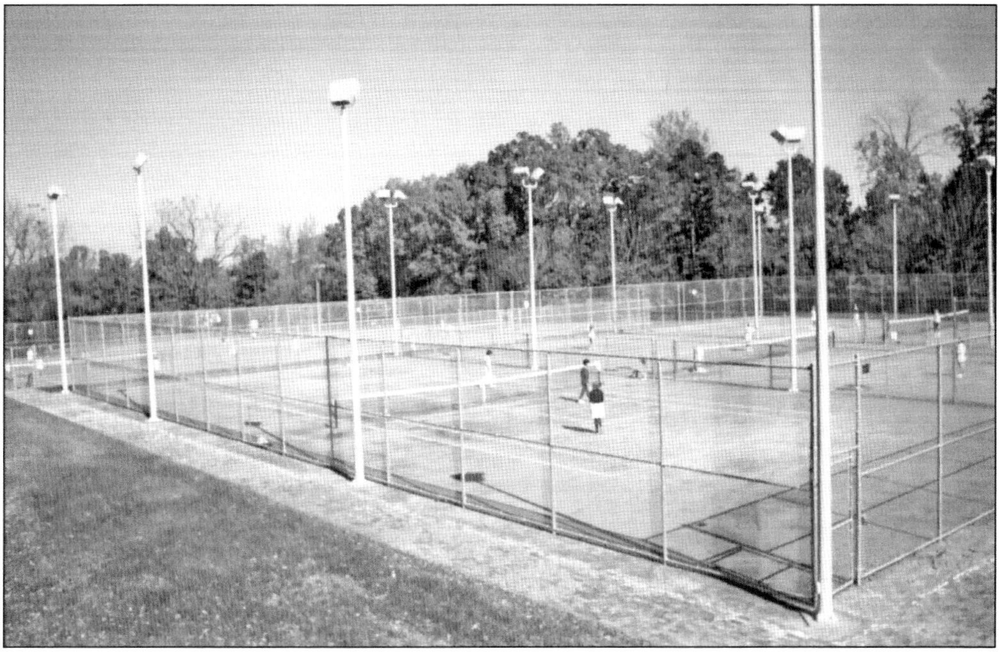

A 1969 gift from the Z. Smith Reynolds Foundation provided for the construction of the tennis courts adjacent to the swimming pool area. Six new professional-size composition courts opened in June of that year, three of which lit for night play. (Courtesy Tanglewood Park Photograph Collection.)

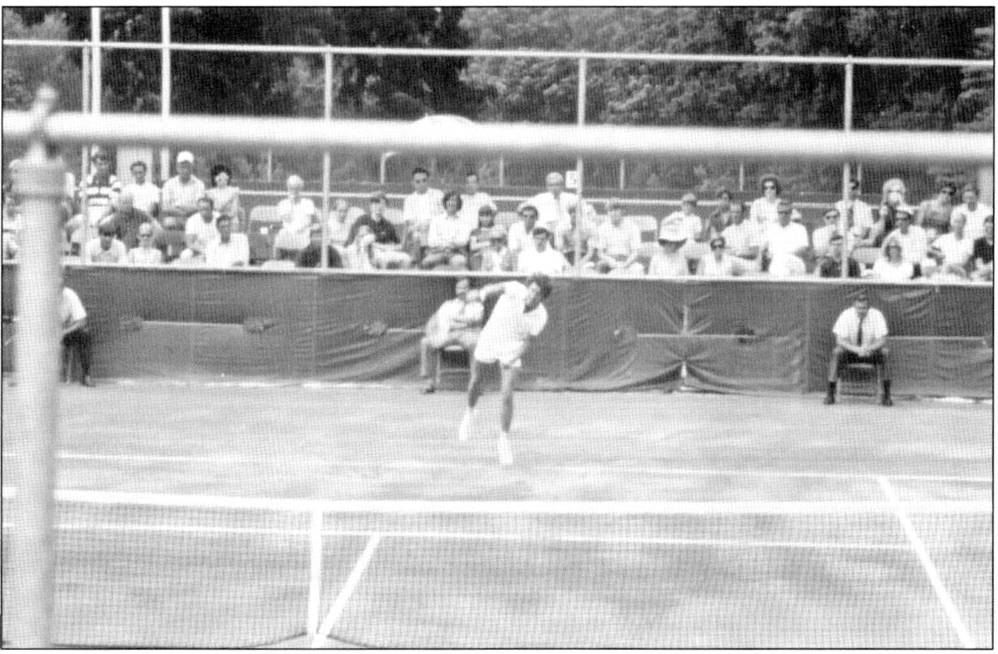

The first Tanglewood International Tennis Classic was held in the summer of 1971 and had a $25,000 purse. More than 2,000 tennis fans looked on as Chile's Jaime Fillol defeated highly regarded Zeljko Franulovic of Yugoslavia. The tennis tournament returned again in 1973, with the tennis courts remaining a popular destination ever since. (Courtesy Tanglewood Park Photograph Collection.)

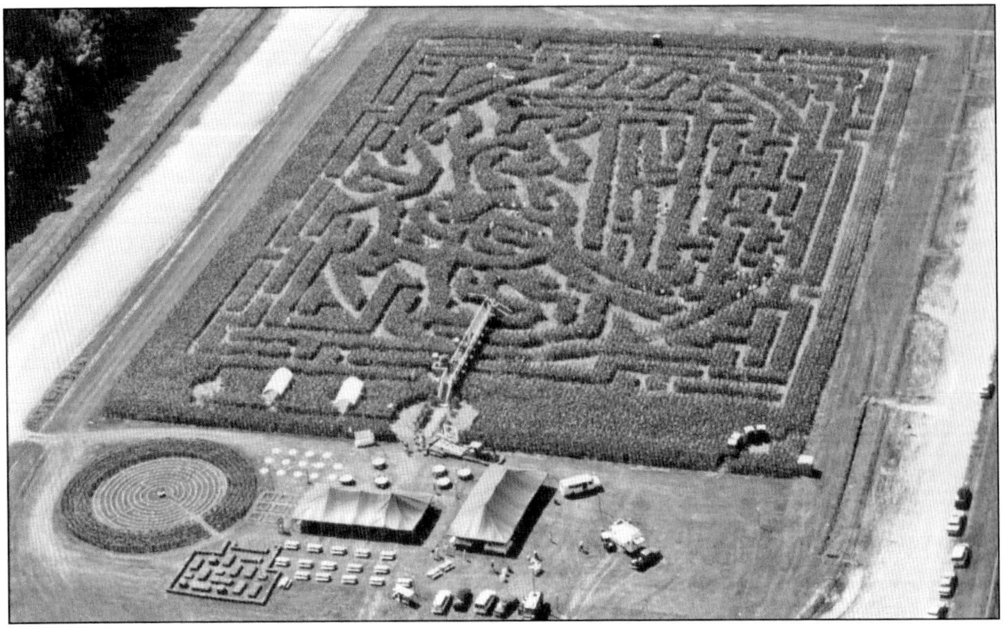

This corn maze was grown over the old steeplechase grounds in 1998 by Cas Booe of Shallowford Farms Popcorn in Yadkinville. The design of the maze shows William Reynolds riding his favorite horse, Tarheel, over a jump at the steeplechase. The maze was designed by Don Frantz, who was an executive with the Walt Disney Company and coproduced Disney's *Beauty and the Beast* on Broadway. The concept was that the maze would attract more visitors to the park. Although it was successful, it was eventually removed. (Courtesy Tanglewood Park Photograph Collection.)

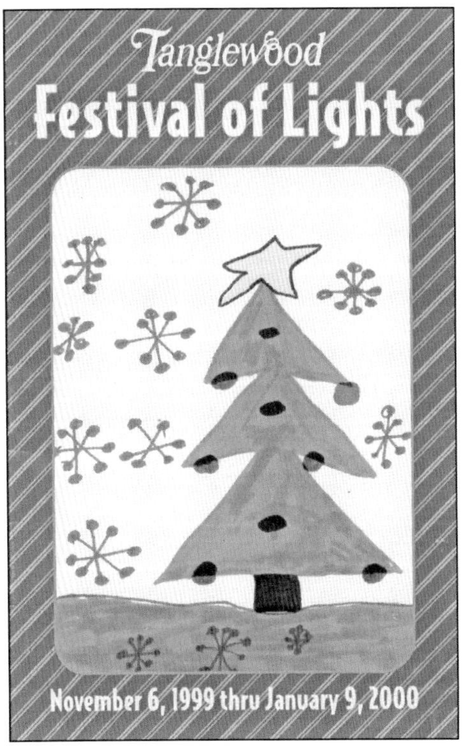

This program is from the Tanglewood Festival of Lights display in the 1999 Christmas season. The festival, which started in 1992, is the region's only large-scale drive-through holiday lights display, boasting more than one million lights. More than 250,000 visitors come to Tanglewood each year to experience the various displays—over 100 in all. During the festival, which runs from November through January each year, the park offers hayrides and horse-drawn carriage rides. A gift village is set up in the barn, where visitors can roast marshmallows and enjoy hot chocolate while shopping local crafts and wares. (Courtesy Tanglewood Park Photograph Collection.)

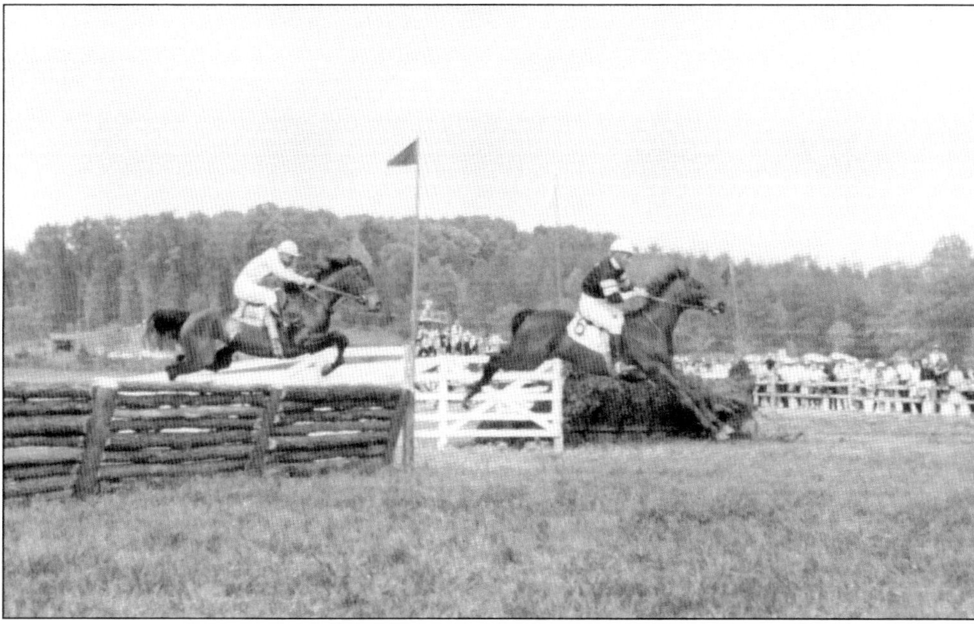

Horses and their riders handle the Timber Jump in this 1963 photograph of the inaugural running of the Tanglewood Steeplechase. The event attracted some of the best horses and jockeys in the region and more than 7,500 spectators. Steeplechase races have their roots in the fox hunt ritual and had been popular in Europe for several centuries. Eventually, match races between horses and their owners became more popular and the most prominent landmarks at the time, church steeples, were used to mark the beginning and end of the races. Steeple chasing in America began around 1900 in New York, quickly spread south to the Carolinas and Tennessee, and remains popular to this day. The track at Tanglewood was used until the late 1990s and then revived in 2010. (Courtesy Tanglewood Park Photograph Collection.)

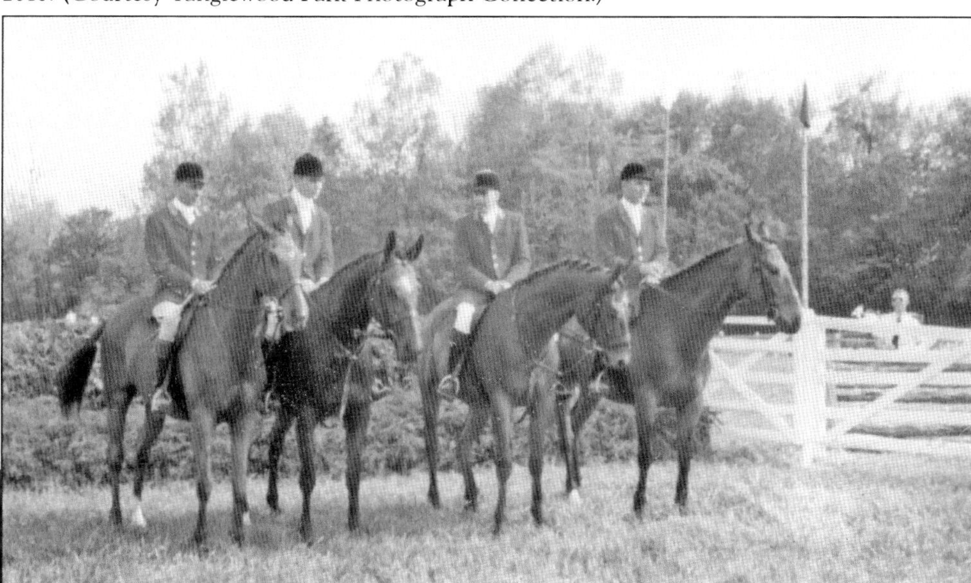

The outriders stand ready and prepared to do their duties at the 1963 steeplechase. The outriders served as crowd control and collected scores. (Courtesy Tanglewood Park Photograph Collection.)

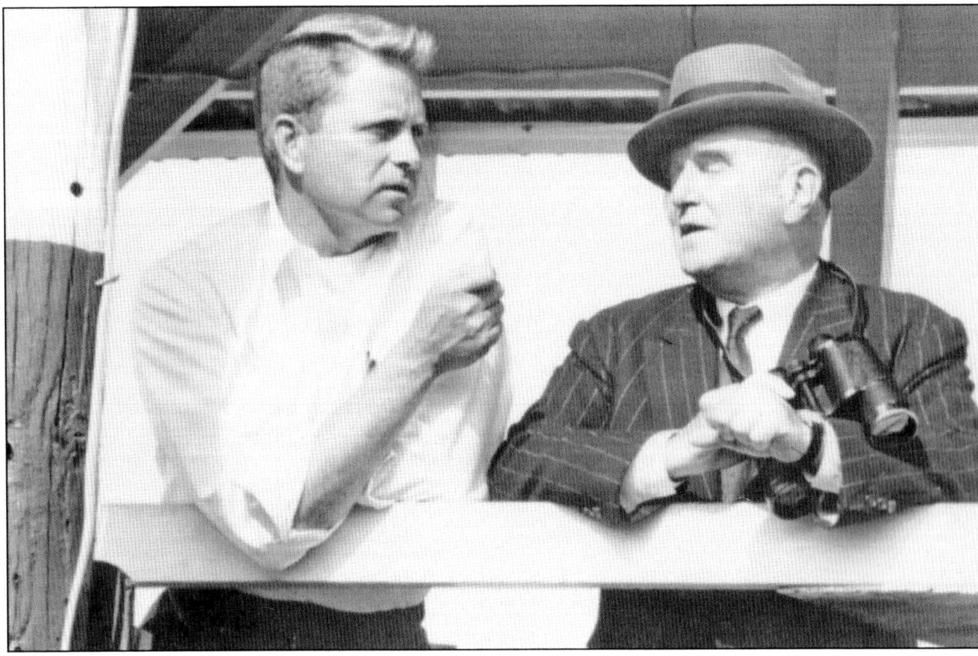

Gardner Gidley and Bryan Field discuss the steeplechase in this 1963 photograph. Gidley was the Tanglewood park director at the time and Bryan Field was the announcer for the steeplechase races at Tanglewood in the 1960s. Field, probably best known as the track announcer for the Kentucky Derby in the 1950s and early 1960s, was brought along with the steeplechase to Tanglewood by National Steeplechase Association member and eventual president John Hanes. (Courtesy Forsyth County Public Library.)

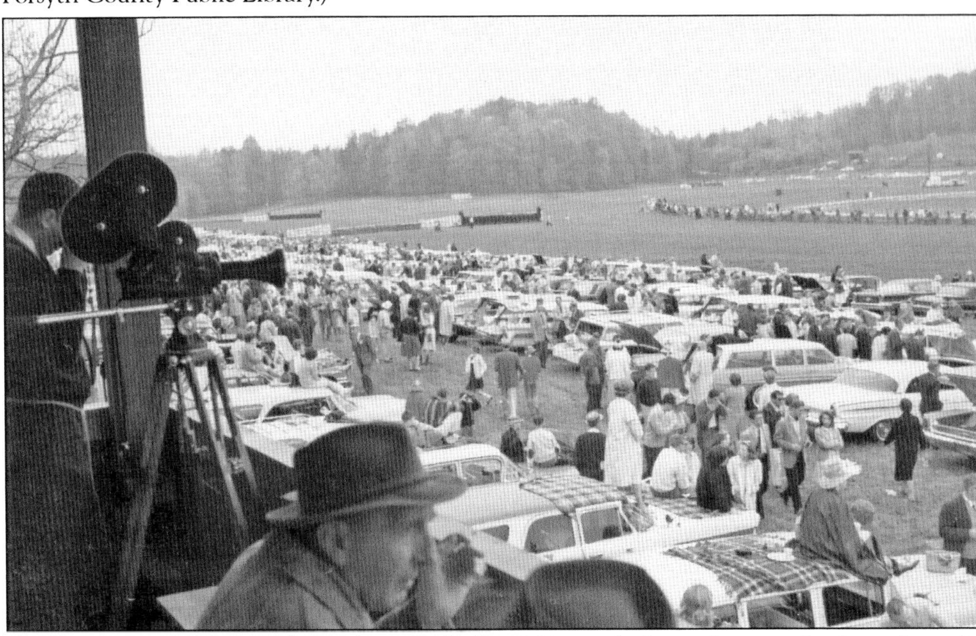

Spectators crowd into Tanglewood to watch the 1964 steeplechase. At its peak, throughout the 1970s and 1980s, the Tanglewood Steeplechase drew 20,000 or more visitors and spectators. (Courtesy Tanglewood Park Photograph Collection.)

Photographer Frank B. Jones (right) and an unidentified person enjoy a moment at the Tanglewood Steeplechase in 1964. Jones (1914–1975) was a noted photographer for the *Winston-Salem Journal* for years and took many photographs of Winston-Salem and the surrounding areas. (Courtesy Forsyth County Public Library.)

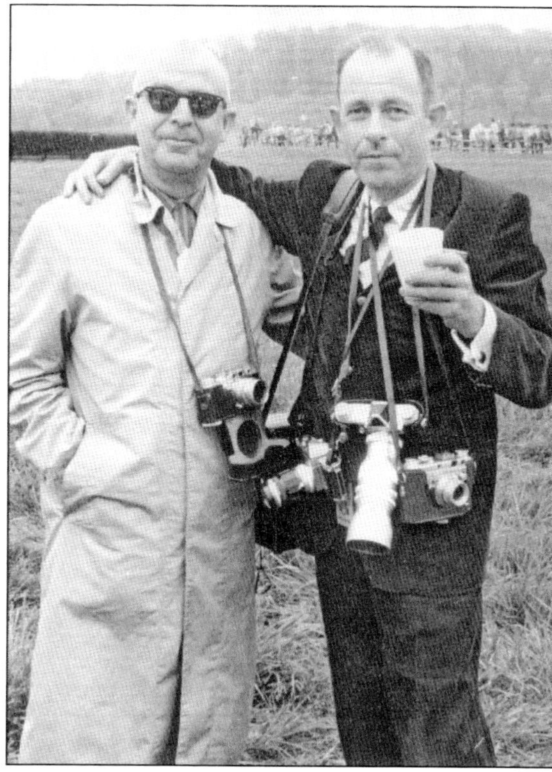

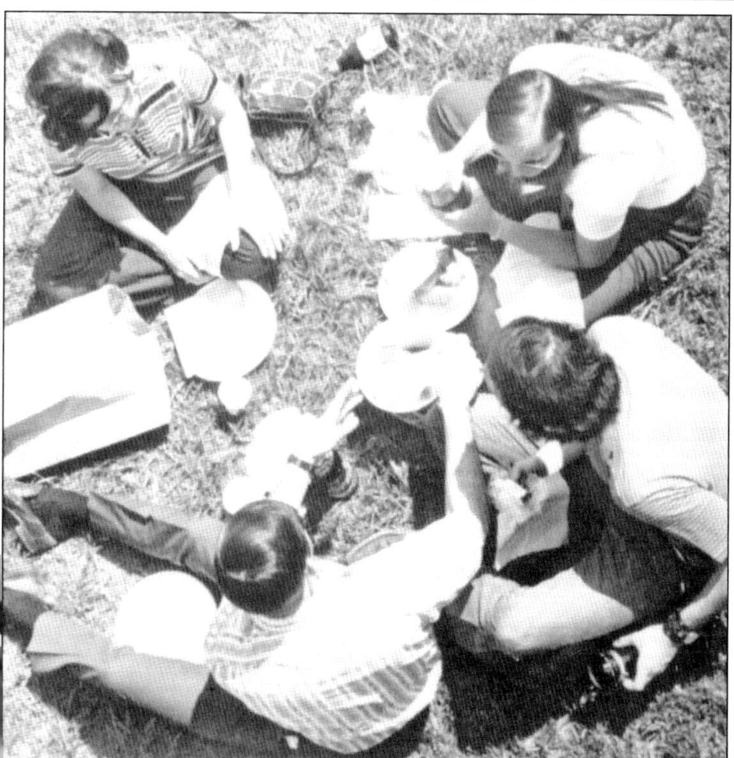

Throughout the years, the Tanglewood Steeplechase gave folks the perfect reason to visit the park and enjoy a day of outside activities. In this 1971 photograph, a group enjoys a picnic. The steeplechase was the only steeplechasing venue in North Carolina for a long time. (Courtesy Forsyth County Public Library.)

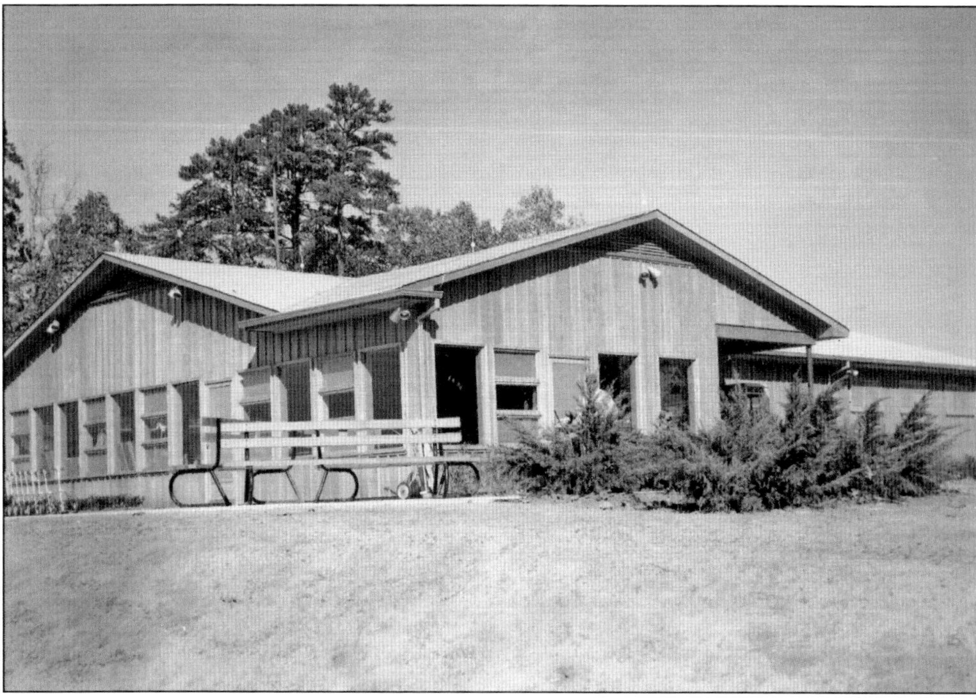

The original Championship Golf Course clubhouse at Tanglewood, along with the course itself, opened to park visitors in 1958. (Courtesy Tanglewood Park Photograph Collection.)

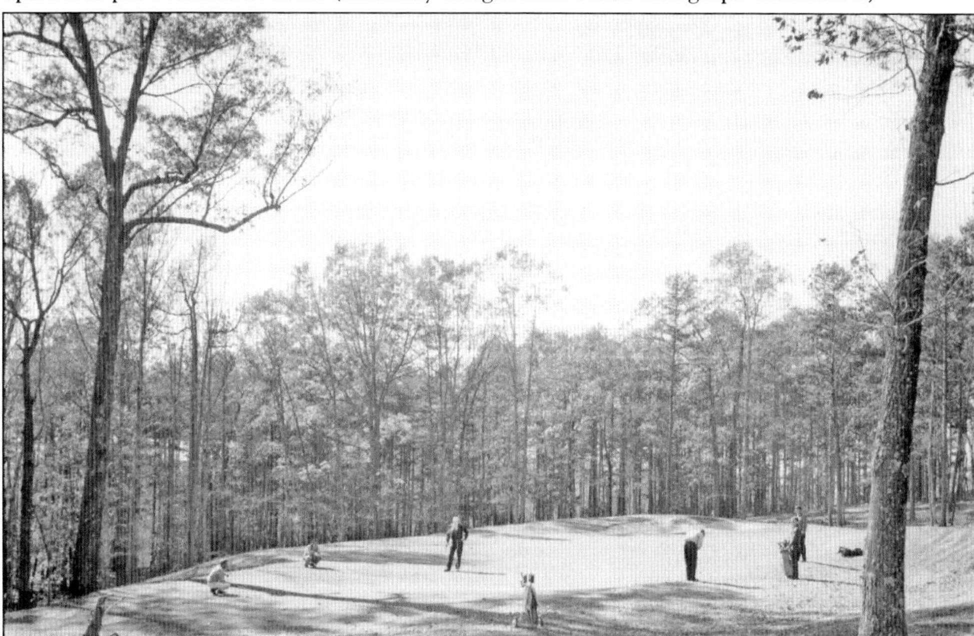

The 18-hole Championship Golf Course at Tanglewood Park was designed by noted golf-course architect Robert Trent Jones. When it opened, it was judged by many to be one of the finest in the country. These golfers enjoy a round in 1959, before the arrival of golf carts. (Courtesy Tanglewood Park Photograph Collection.)

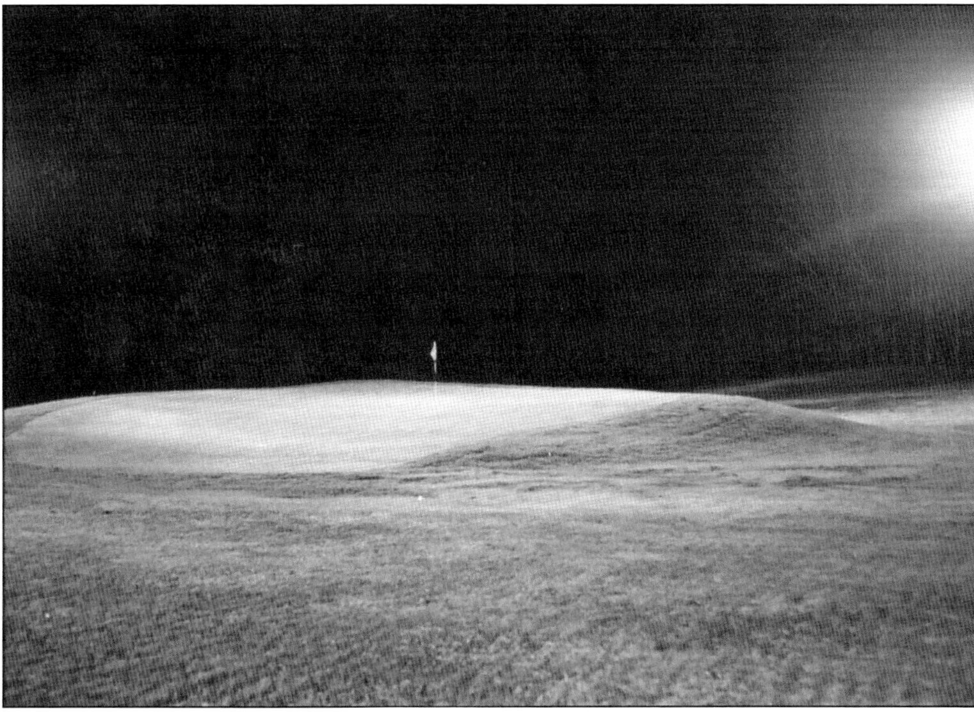

The current par-three course was installed in 1959 and was originally lighted to accommodate night playing. (Courtesy Tanglewood Park Photograph Collection.)

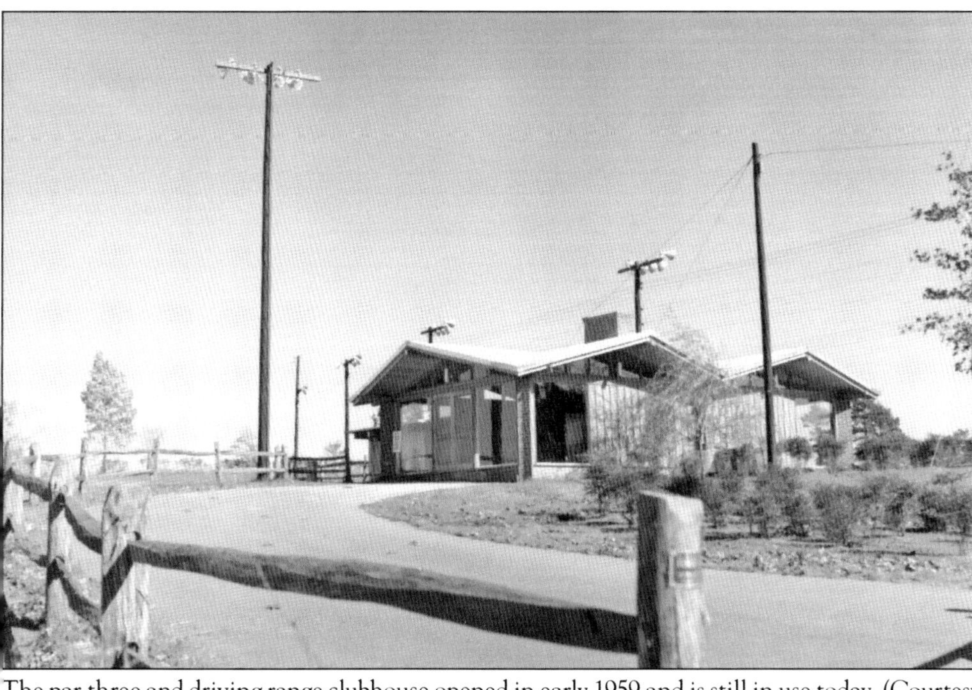

The par-three and driving range clubhouse opened in early 1959 and is still in use today. (Courtesy Tanglewood Park Photograph Collection.)

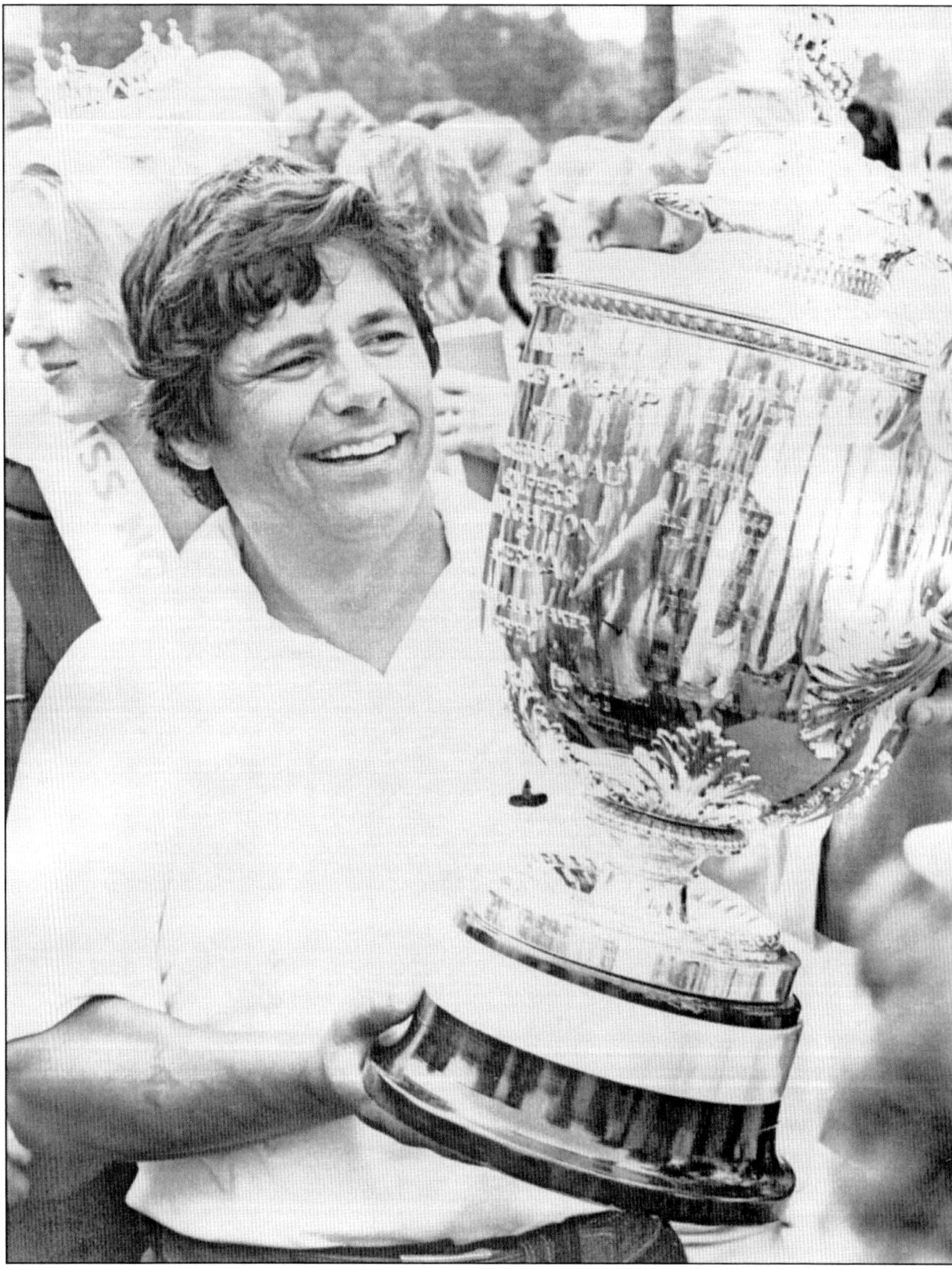

In August 1974, the 56th PGA Championship was held at Tanglewood. On August 11, Lee Trevino overcame a three-over-par opening round to shoot an overall four-under-par total of 276 to win the tournament, edging Jack Nicklaus by one stroke to take the $45,000 grand prize. (Courtesy David H. Hauser.)

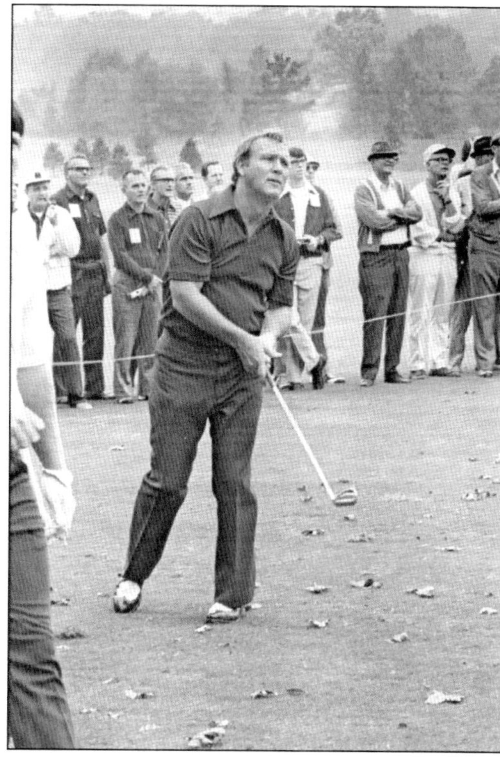

Arnold Palmer (right) and Jack Nicklaus (below) are seen here competing at the 56th PGA at Tanglewood. Palmer struggled with a five-over-par second round, finishing tied for twelfth place. Nicklaus fared a little better, putting on an impressive performance throughout the tournament but ultimately finishing in second place, one stroke behind Trevino. Hosting one of the largest tournaments of the golf season is one of the brightest highlights of the park's history. While already having an admirable reputation in the golf world, the event solidified Tanglewood's ranking among the great golf courses in the United States. (Courtesy David H. Hauser.)

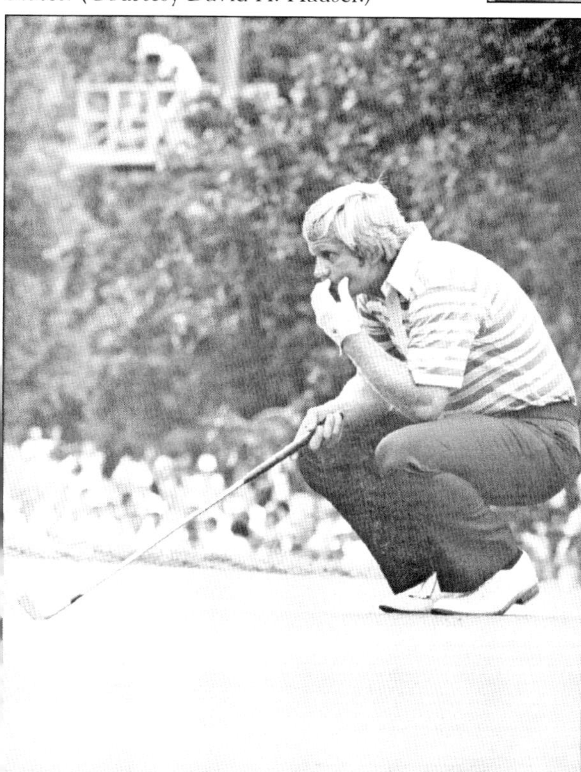